Library of Exact Philosophy 8

Joseph Horovitz

Law and Logic

A Critical Account of Legal Argument

Springer-Verlag New York Wien 1972

Printing type: Sabon Roman
Composed and printed by Herbert Hiessberger, Pottenstein
Binding work: Karl Scheibe, Wien
Design: Hans Joachim Böning, Wien

K

1468

ISBN 0-387-81066-8   Springer-Verlag New York - Wien
ISBN 3-211-81066-8   Springer-Verlag Wien - New York

To Sara

General Preface to the LEP

The aim of the Library of Exact Philosophy is to keep alive the spirit, if not the letter, of the Vienna Circle. It will consequently adopt high standards of rigor: it will demand the clear statement of problems, their careful handling with the relevant logical or mathematical tools, and a critical analysis of the assumptions and results of every piece of philosophical research.

Like the Vienna Circle, the Library of Exact Philosophy sees in mathematics and science the wellsprings of contemporary intellectual culture as well as sources of inspiration for some of the problems and methods of philosophy. The Library of Exact Philosophy will also stress the desirability of regarding philosophical research as a cooperative enterprise carried out with exact tools and with the purpose of extending, deepening, and systematizing our knowledge about human knowledge.

But, unlike the Vienna Circle, the Library of Exact Philosophy will not adopt a school attitude. It will encourage constructive work done across school frontiers and it will attempt to minimize sterile quarrels. And it will not restrict the kinds of philosophical problem: the Library of Exact Philosophy will welcome not only logic, semantics and epistemology, but also metaphysics, value theory and ethics as long as they are conceived in a clear and cogent way, and are in agreement with contemporary science.

Montreal, January 1970

Mario Bunge

Acknowledgments

This book originated from my doctoral thesis, prepared at the Hebrew University in Jerusalem under the supervision of Professor YEHOSHUA BAR-HILLEL[1]. I am deeply grateful to him for his inspiration and guidance.

The following persons, either by their support of my requests for leave and funds or by their encouragement, advice, and constructive comments, helped me substantially in the preparation of the present version of my work: Professor YEHOSHUA BAR-HILLEL, Jerusalem; Professor BEN-AMI SCHARFSTEIN, Tel-Aviv; Professors Sir ISAIAH BERLIN, HERBERT HART, and GILBERT RYLE and Mr. ALAN MONTEFIORE, Oxford; Professor CHAÏM PERELMAN, Brussels; and Professor MARIO BUNGE, Montreal. I extend my gratitude to them all. Grateful acknowledgments are due to Tel-Aviv University for financial aid and a leave of absence, to the Hebrew University, Jerusalem, for a supplementary grant, and to Linacre College, Oxford, for a research fellowship.

I wish to thank all those, too numerous to be named, who contributed to the stylistic aspects of the book.

Last but not least, I acknowledge my indebtedness beyond repayment to my wife SARA for her unfailing supply of encouragement and comfort throughout my work, as well as for her expert and indefatigable typing of the several drafts of the manuscript.

I need hardly declare that responsibility for any shortcomings this study may have is entirely mine.

New York, May 1972   Joseph Horovitz

---

1 *The Problem of the Logical Specificity of Legal Argument,* in Hebrew, submitted in 1965, unpublished.

Contents

Errata

(1) p. 20, line 5, instead of: ordinary calculus; read: ordinary functional calculus.

(2) p. 41, line 3, instead of: circle; read: circle of similarity.

(3) p. 44, line 17 from bottom, instead of: Metalogical; read: Metalegal.

(4) p. 62, line 23, instead of: simili; read: simile.

(5) p. 82, line 3, instead of: recource; read: recourse.

(6) p. 100, line 7 from bottom, instead of: relates the; read: relates to.

(7) p. 107, line 8 from bottom, instead of: fromal; read: formal.

(8) p. 109, line 15 from bottom, instead of: Georges; read: Jan.

General Introduction

This book has two related aims: to investigate the frequently voiced claim that legal argument is nonformal in nature and, within the limits of such an investigation, to ascertain the most general properties of law as a rational system. Examination of a number of views of legal argument, selected from recent discussions in Germany, Belgium, and the English-speaking countries, will lead to the following main conclusions. The nonformalistic conceptions of the logic of legal argument are ambiguous and unclear. Moreover, insofar as these conceptions are capable of clarification in the light of recent analytical methodology, they can be seen to be either mistaken or else compatible with the formalistic position. Because law is socially directive and coordinative, it is dependent upon theoretical psychosociology and calls, in principle, for a deontic and inductive logic. The primary function of legal argument is to provide continuing reinterpretation and confirmation of legal rules, conceived as theoretical prescriptions. On the basis of this conception, the old jurisprudential conflict between formalism and rule-scepticism appears substantially resolved.

Aristotle, the founder of the theory of argument, conceived it as "the science of establishing conclusions" (ἐπιστήμη ἀποδεικτική), designed to guide people in rational argumentation. In time, however, logic forsook its practical function and developed as a highly abstract and disinterested study, today called "formal logic"; and the theory of practical argument was either neglected or relegated to an appendix to rhetoric. Can this neglect be regarded as transient, or is it due to an essential unsuitability of the formal means of modern logic to the rational assessment and guidance of reason-

ing in various fields? At any rate, is there a nonformal logic capable
of assuming these tasks effectively?

A thorough elucidation of these questions, on which scholars
are widely divided, must involve the confrontation of the formalistic standpoint with the positions of its opponents. In recent years,
nonformalistic views of argument — in rational fields such as
philosophy, science, law, or ordinary business — have indeed been
repeatedly set forth and defended with more or less insistence, or
else have been implied more or less clearly, by many influential
authors. Among professional philosophers, Chaïm Perelman and
Stephen E. Toulmin have been particularly emphatic in alleging the
existence of essentially nonformal and yet rational modes of argument. Toulmin goes as far as to maintain that only in the field
of mathematics are arguments to be found that fall within the
scope of formal logic. Perelman admits that formal argument may
be found in science as well as in mathematics.

It is no accident that both these philosophers are concerned,
though in different ways, with legal argument. Perelman, the leader
of a group of Belgian lawyers and logicians who have been engaged
in the study of legal reasoning since the early fifties, firmly opposes
legal logic to formal logic. Toulmin, though not a student of law,
considers legal argument to be the archetype of all nonmathematical
argument; accordingly, he countenances the replacement, outside
mathematics, of the old "geometrical" model of logical form by
a "procedural" pattern. Apparently nonformalistic implications with
respect to legal reasoning are found in the writings of such other
noted analytical philosophers as John Wisdom and Herbert L. A.
Hart. Legal argument thus appears as a proper test case of logical
nonformalism. Accordingly, this book should be read not only as
a discussion of legal argument, but also in the light of these larger
issues in the philosophy of logic in general.

In view of the insistent claim that legal argument is logically
peculiar, it is particularly interesting to compare the general logical
and methodological aspects of law with those of science. Prima
facie, it would seem that a considerable part of the methodological
analysis of empirical science may be found to apply to law, insofar
as the latter is rationally brought to bear upon empirical social
realities. Among the relevant principles, the formalistic conception
of logic and the logicoempiricist conception of empirical science are

basic[1]. As these conceptions form the background of the present inquiry, I shall now proceed to sketch them, bearing in mind the needs of subsequent exposition[2].

Logic may be viewed as being primarily the theory of the *rational force* of inference or argument. As such, it consists of deductive logic and inductive logic, according to the kind of argument dealt with[3]. A *deductive argument* is either *valid* — i. e. its premises entail its

---

1 In fact, the formalistic conception of logic is a tenet of logical empiricism; however, the former can also be adhered to independently of the latter.

Since the appellation "logical empiricism" is apt to confound and mislead, an explanatory comment is in place. The main point is that the philosophical movement in question has changed considerably since it originated in the Vienna Circle in the mid-twenties. Initially, its adherents were strictly "positivistic" in alleging the reducibility of scientific knowledge to observation. Gradually, however, they came to recognize the presence of and the essential role played by nonobservational elements in scientific theory. Consequently, logical empiricism may be thought of at present as a combination of empiricism and rationalism rather than as plain empiricism. This evolution assimilated logical empiricism considerably to other major trends in the contemporary analysis of science.

In the elaboration of the principles of logical empiricism, the contribution of Rudolf Carnap has been particularly outstanding. The interested reader may consult LOTHAR KRAUTH's work [48] and the collective volume [67].

(A numeral between square brackets is a direction to the List of References.)

2 The reader not sufficiently acquainted with recent analyses of science is likely to find the following outline far too condensed to be comprehensible, especially when read before the rest of the book. As a remedy, the following works may be consulted. The books by WESLEY C. SALMON [66], CARL G. HEMPEL [30], and RICHARD S. RUDNER [65] are excellent general introductions; they include indications for further reading. For a more detailed study, MARIO BUNGE's two-volume treatise [07] will be found most useful; in this work, rich material is thoroughly treated from a progressive, avowedly nonpositivistic point of view, and stimulating problem exercises as well as ample, specialized bibliographies are included. Topical bibliographies are also provided by HENRY E. KYBURG, JR. [49] whose approach is markedly formalistic. PETER ACHINSTEIN [01] offers a critical analysis of current positions.

3 In the present book, the division of logic into deductive and inductive is taken to be a dichotomy; accordingly, all recognized types of nondeductive argument — analogical, statistical, reductive, and so on — are regarded as falling within the scope of inductive logic. This use, however, though more and more current, has not been generally adopted: induc-

conclusion — or else fallacious; the rational force of a deductive argument resides in its validity. In an *inductive argument,* the premises do not entail the conclusion but lend it more or less strong *inductive support;* accordingly, the rational force of an inductive argument is, in principle, a matter of degree[4]. The rational force of an argument is relevant to the methodological question of how well the argument establishes its conclusion. The question primarily concerns *sound arguments,* i. e. nonfallacious arguments in which all the premises are sound, i. e. well established and hence acceptable. A sound deductive argument is *conclusive:* it establishes its conclusion as acceptable. Deductive validity can therefore be said to be "acceptability-preserving". Induction, on the other hand, is doubly limited. Firstly, a sound inductive argument is *nonconclusive:* it is only capable of establishing its conclusion more or less firmly, according to the strength of the inductive support involved. Secondly, since the addition of a premise to an inductive argument may strengthen or weaken the overall inductive support, such an argument cannot be regarded as establishing its conclusion to whatever degree of firmness unless it includes all the available relevant data among its premises. This limitation is known as *the requirement of total evidence.*

Thus conceived, logic involves a suitable inferential apparatus, consisting, in principle, of *rules of inference* and *inductive procedures:* the former determine deductive validity, whereas the latter serve the purpose of assessing (comparing, estimating, or precisely evaluating) inductive support. An exact theory of the rational force that arguments have in a given field necessitates an appropriate reconstruction of the field's language. This is required in order to make the language fulfill certain conditions of adequacy, especially that of unambiguousness. Logic can thus be seen to require a rigor-

---

tion is often thought of as involving generalization, and hence inductive argument is considered to be only one type of nondeductive argument. It will appear presently that inductive logic (in the nonrestrictive sense) presents serious difficulties.

4 The syllogistic inference *barbara* — "all M are P; all S are M; so, all S are P" — is a classic paradigm of deductive argument. An elementary, nonproblematic (and hence nontypical) example of inductive argument is provided by the so-called *statistical syllogism* — "p percent of S are P; x is S; so, more or less likely or unlikely (according to the strength of the inductive support, which is here adequately measured by the value of p), x is P".

ous development of field *systems*. The vocabulary of a reconstructed language consists of *logical* and *nonlogical expressions*, except in purely logical systems, which contain no nonlogical expressions. The logical expressions include variables, connectives, quantifiers, and other kinds of operators. Mathematical expressions, when employed in an empirical system, should also be classed with its logical vocabulary. In addition, inductive procedures in principle involve mathematical tools[5].

The idea of *logical form* is essential to the conception under consideration. The logical form of an expression, in particular of a sentence or of an argument, is obtained by its *formalization*, i. e. its formulation in the reconstructed language and the replacement of its nonlogical components by suitable variables. The basic formalistic tenet is this: *the rational force of an argument resides in its logical form;* more generally: *inferential properties and relations are determined by the logical forms of the expressions concerned and are, in this sense, essentially formal.* The designation "formal logic" is construed accordingly but is regarded as redundant.

Relevant to the characterization of logic is the well-known tripartition of semiotics (the science of language) into syntax, semantics, and pragmatics. *Syntax* is the study of linguistic expressions of various kinds in their interrelations within a system, in abstraction from their meanings and users. *Semantics* is the study of the meanings of expressions and their applicability. *Pragmatics* is an empirical investigation of the human use of language. A system's logic can be construed either narrowly or widely. In the narrower sense, it coincides with the syntax and semantics of the system's logical expressions alone; this is what is commonly known as *pure* or *general logic*. In the wider sense, a system's logic is conceived as the syntax and semantics of the entire system, including its nonlogical expressions; this is what is commonly known as *applied* or *special logic*. The nonlogical vocabulary and the syntactic and

---

5 Under the nonrestrictive construal of logical induction adopted in this book, numerous mathematical methods current in scientific research and in other fields of empirically controlled action — e. g. calculations of probabilities and of margins of error — as well as methods tentatively advanced in various theories of confirmation, verisimilitude, and so on, either constitute or else are directly relevant to assessments of inductive support. In particular, mathematical statistics should be thought of as importantly involved in inductive procedures.

semantic rules relative to it are described specifically as "special", and so is the field of application. Applied logic comprises the detailed study of the sentences capable of serving as premises and conclusions in arguments in the special field. The determinant conditions of logical properties and relations in general — whether pure or applied and whether inferential or not — are semiotic (and not, say, ontological or psychological); moreover, they are syntactic and semantic, not pragmatic. Logic is not concerned with the argumentative processes or acts and their psychosociological or historical aspects, but with their linguistic products as subject to syntactic and semantic rules. It is not concerned, that is to say, with the *context of discovery* of either conclusions or premises, but with the *context of justification* of the conclusions by the premises. Then again, the determinant conditions of the rational force of argument are purely formal. To be sure, the inferential apparatus in special logic should be suitably adapted to the special field; but it is nevertheless inherited, as it were, from general logic: rules of inference and inductive procedures relate only to logical forms. However, special *inductive* logic constitutes a difficult problem, as will be pointed out further on in this introduction.

A system, ideally conceived as couched in an adequately reconstructed language, is conveniently considered as a set of interrelated sentences, subject to logical (i. e. syntactic and semantic) rules. An *empirical system* is a system applied to an empirical (or "real") domain; the vocabulary of such a system contains terms that possess empirical meaning. The terms and sentences of a *nonempirical* or *pure system,* on the other hand, have no empirical meanings assigned to them by the semantic rules and are, moreover, considered in abstraction from all possible empirical interpretation. A pure system may, however, be given application to some special domain, either empirical or pure. Many scientific systems are thus erected as systems of applied mathematics, and every applied system is "embedded" in a system of special logic. Pure systems, in particular those of logic and mathematics, are usually developed by the *axiomatic-deductive method.* In this method, the system's sentences are deduced, as *theorems,* from some of them that are accepted as primitive sentences, or *axioms.*

Systems of empirical science are generally spoken of as "theories". A theory, or *theoretical system,* is characterized by the presence of *theoretical terms* in its nonlogical vocabulary. *Theoretical* can, in this context, be conveniently contrasted with *observational*. An observational term (concept) denotes (is the concept of) a directly observable object, property, relation, state, event, or process; e. g., "cat", "hot", and "contiguous", as used in ordinary language, are observational in the aforesaid sense. Accordingly, a theoretical term (concept) is a nonlogical term (concept) the denotatum of which is not directly observable; e. g., "electron", "intelligent", and "competitor", as terms or concepts of physics, psychology, and economics, respectively, are theoretical. To be sure, direct observability is found to be a relative characteristic, capable of degrees, rather than an absolute one. It is proper, therefore, to construe "observational" and "theoretical" too as relative and to say, e. g., that the concept of being ten inches apart is more observational, or less theoretical, than that of being a millionth of an inch apart or that the concept of famine is more observational, or less theoretical, than that of inflation.

However, the two terms also have an important quasi-absolute and, as it were, elliptical use. Namely, "theoretical" is used to describe terms and concepts which are theoretical (in the preceding sense) to such a degree that they are not clearly understood unless they are *explicated*, i. e. unless their meanings are specified (in a manner that will be explained presently) within the framework of a theoretical system. Explication thus amounts to the replacement of a confused theoretical concept, the *explicandum*, by a precise one which is intelligible to experts, the *explicatum*. "Observational" is used accordingly to describe terms and concepts sufficiently observational (in the preceding sense) to be intelligible apart from all theory of learned formation. The corresponding distinction is made between nonobservable and observable denotata. Henceforth, "theoretical" and "observational" will be used in this quasi-absolute way, except in some rare cases in which the relative sense will be clearly implied by the context.

An observable *domain of application* is naturally presupposed by an empirical system. Indeed, a scientific theory with no observational concepts would have no genuine *empirical import* and hence no genuine descriptive, explanatory, or predictive power. However, the *observational applicability* of an empirical system need not be direct: the direct domain of application of a theory may be a nonobservable domain postulated by another theory. A classic example is that of the kinetic theory of heat as applied to the nonobservable domain

postulated by the kinetic theory of gases. What is required, methodologists point out, is only that the direct domain of application of
a theory be *antecedently available* and *antecedently understood;* but
the understanding in question may be theoretical. Still, indirectly at
least, an empirical system must have observational applicability. The
remaining part of this introductory account will be limited to empirical systems with a *direct* observational applicability. That this is
not a serious restriction is made clear by the following consideration.
If *A* is an empirical system with direct observational applicability,
and *B* is a system applicable to the nonobservable domain postulated
by *A*, then *A* and *B* can be fused so as to form a single system with
direct observational applicability; e. g., the combined kinetic theory
of gases and of heat. It follows that any empirical system either has
or else can be supplemented so as to acquire direct observational
applicability.

If, then, an empirical theoretical system fulfills the said proviso[6],
its nonlogical vocabulary contains both theoretical and observational
terms. Some of them are *primitive*, i. e. undefined, while the remaining ones are *defined* as logical compounds of the primitives. Considered as a set of interrelated sentences, such a system consists of
three kinds of sentences (besides the rules of logic): they are distinguished according to whether the nonlogical terms of a sentence are
all observational, all theoretical, or partly observational and partly
theoretical. They can be conveniently designated as "(purely) observational", "purely theoretical", and "mixed" sentences, respectively.
Sentences of the second and third kind are usually called "postulates" or "principles"; they constitute an essential part of the theory;
without mixed sentences, in particular, a theory would have no
empirical import. The purely theoretical sentences are also designated as *internal postulates (principles)*, the mixed ones as *bridge
postulates (principles)* or *rules of correspondence.* The less central
and hence more easily modifiable bridge postulates are sometimes
referred to as *rules of interpretation, interpretative sentences,* or
the like. The sentences in a system of empirical science, as a whole,
have an analytic and a synthetic aspect: they can be construed
either as conventional *meaning rules* or as *factual statements* subject
to empirical *confirmation.*

---

6 The restriction in question can be removed by substituting "antecedently understood" for "observational", and "intratheoretical" for "theoretical", in what follows.

The theoretical terms of an empirical system get their *observational interpretation* from the observational terms with which they are connected in the bridge postulates. The observational meaning of a theoretical term is, however, never completely determined; if it were, the term would be observational rather than theoretical. Accordingly, a bridge postulate is never an equivalential definition of a theoretical term as a logical compound of observational terms alone. In fact, the bridge postulates are more or less complex conditionals, with theoretical and observational terms variously distributed in the antecedents and the consequents. Moreover, a conditional implication in an empirical system must often be construed as a weakened probabilistic implication rather than the ordinary if-then connective. Furthermore, some theoretical terms may not occur in any bridge postulate at all. Such terms get their observational meaning through the mediation of the internal postulates in which they occur. Their observational interpretation is thus not only partial but indirect. Empirical research renders the observational interpretation of theoretical terms gradually more articulated and more precise.

Observational terms are vague. But the applicability of an observational term, though indeterminate in the term's margin of vagueness, is nevertheless definitely determined outside of that margin. On the other hand, the observational applicability of a theoretical term cannot be definitely determined even in part. This characteristic of theoretical terms is called their "open texture". Friedrich Waismann, who introduced the concept of open texture and the very term (a translation of the German "Porosität"), explains: "*Vagueness* should be distinguished from *open texture*. A word which is actually used in a fluctuating way (such as 'heap' or 'pink') is said to be vague; a term like 'gold', though its actual use may not be vague, is nonexhaustive or of an open texture in that we can never fill up all the possible gaps through which a doubt may seep in. Open texture, then, is something like *possibility of vagueness*. Vagueness can be remedied by giving more accurate rules, open texture cannot. An alternative way of stating this would be to say that definitions of open terms are *always* corrigible or emendable" ([77], p. 120). Open texture thus is that radical "nonexhaustiveness" of the observational interpretation of theoretcial terms owing to which a theoretical statement is never, in principle, strictly equivalent to any finite logical compound of observational statements.

The internal (i. e. purely theoretical) postulates of a theory have no observational meaning whatsoever in isolation from the bridge postulates. But also the entire theoretical system, including the bridge postulates, can, at a definite stage in its development, be *considered as purely theoretical* — that is to say, in abstraction from the meanings of the observational terms. It can, in particular, be reconstructed as an axiomatic-deductive system, similar to the axiomatic-deductive systems of pure mathematics. The axioms of such a "congealed" and "purified" system will normally be chosen from among those of its postulates that contain primitive (undefined) terms alone. This is done so as to ensure that the remaining postulates of the system can be derived from the axioms according to the rules of the system. To the extent that, alongside deductive rules of inference, inductive procedures are also employed within a system, the current designation of the system and method as "axiomatic-*deductive*" becomes improper. In point of fact, many purely theoretical *inductive systems* have been set forth in recent years.

However, *special* inductive logic, as already noted, remains problematic. Disappointingly, none of the aforementioned inductive systems has turned out to be applicable to the existing empirical fields, except in a tentative and fragmentary way[7]. In other words, the prima facie inductive nature of nonconclusive argument, whether in science, in law, or in various other domains of empirically controlled reasoning, has so far not been satisfactorily explicated. Moreover, though research with a view to the construction of comprehensive systems of inductive logic for empirical fields proceeds actively, there is no unanimity among scholars as to the prospects of positive achievements. A wide range of fluctuating opinions separates those who firmly believe that inductive support can be uniformly explicated as an effectively applicable quantitative concept from those who altogether discard the very idea of applied inductive logic.

---

7 To be sure, a variety of *specific* inductive procedures, i. e. such as concern certain partial aspects of inductive support, have been long since in constant employment in scientific research. What is lacking is a *comprehensive and united* inductive logic for empirical fields.

An original inductive procedure, involved in a theory of "inductive support from variety of circumstance", has been recently outlined by L. JONATHAN COHEN [08]; in a section dealing with "inductive support for legal hypotheses", he shows that the procedure in question, designed primarily for scientific hypotheses, is applicable to "legal arguments from judicial precedents" as well.

In view of this situation, claims to the effect that certain types of nonconclusive argument in empirical fields are inductive in nature seem to require qualification. Obviously, "inductive nature" in such claims cannot be taken to mean conformity to some existing system of inductive logic. What may be implied is rather that the types of argument in question belong prima facie to the *open scope* of inductive logic, conceived as the theory of the rational force of nonconclusive argument. The underlying assumption is that the types of argument in question are types of *rational* argument, as opposed to uncontrollable inference by hunches and to merely heuristic processes. I admit, however reluctantly, that this assumption may be mistaken, with respect to law as well as with respect to science. Properly construed, my claim concerning the domain of law is therefore guarded: typical legal argument, *to the extent that it is rational*, is in principle formalizable within the framework of some appropriate, so far nonexistent, theory of inductive support.

This position of *qualified legal inductivism* does not depend on any particular doctrine of or approach to formal induction. It does, however, presuppose that the rationality of argument involves, among other things, amenability to formal-logical analysis and appraisal. Although this presupposition has long since seemed to me most natural and plausible, I was nonetheless prepared, when undertaking the present inquiry, to relinquish it for a yet more cogent conception of the rationality of argument. However, in the light of the accumulated findings, the presupposition in question, far from being refuted by the nonformalistic claims, emerges reinforced by the exposure of their untenability.

Since logic and system are interdependent, the eventual application of inductive logic to law must involve a proper development and adaptation of the legal system. This rather complex undertaking is all the more called for inasmuch as the requirement of total evidence, already mentioned, necessitates appeal to copious data. In addition to the linguistic prerequisite of a suitably unified formulation of the premises, the effective inductivization of legal argument will depend on an adequately elaborated body of law proper and on a sufficiently articulated and well-established body of relevant scientific knowledge. The acquisition of this latter requires appropriate mathematical, especially statistical methods. The four interrelated activities involved in the undertaking — viz., formally adequate reconstruction of legal language, elaboration of specifically legal principles and rules, promotion of scientific research relevant to law, and progressive introduction of inductive procedures — are in this book conjointly referred to as *rationalization* — of the legal system, of legal argument, or, briefly, of law. Accordingly, the thesis of qualified legal inductivism may be construed as a basic principle guiding the rationalization of law.

A system, whether pure or empirical, can of course become the object of investigation. Thus, as explained before, logic is the syntactic and semantic study of systems. *Methodology* — or, more precisely, *analytical methodology* — investigates the theoretical aspects of the construction and readjustment of systems. It is concerned both with systems in their actual condition and with their rationally reconstructed counterparts and is thus capable of guiding the development of the former through an analysis of the latter. In particular, the analytical methodology of empirical systems involves both the study of the existing canons of application and confirmation and their establishment as rational. The ideal system as a guiding idea or *regulative principle* thus constitutes the basis for a distinction between the rational *nature* of entities, properties, relations, rules, and procedures and their realization in actual fact — i. e., a distinction between what they are ideally or *in principle* and what they are *in practice*.

It should be noted that the investigation and inventory of the practical methods, techniques, and devices is also usually called "methodology". Whenever there is risk of misunderstanding, this latter field may be conveniently designated as *practical methodology*. It is closely related to *pragmatics*, which is the empirical investigation of the psychological, sociological, and historical aspects of the use of systems, and it comprises *heuristics*, which is the art of discovery.

The language of logic and methodology, inasmuch as it is used to describe and to analyze an *object language*, i. e. the language of a system under investigation, is a *metalanguage;* the logical and methodological study of a theory can be said to be *metatheoretical*. But the principles and findings of that study, especially those concerning empirical systems, are usually set out in an informal way rather than built up into rigorous *metasystems*.

The foregoing characterization of methodology concludes the outline of the general principles of the methodology of science that form the background of the present inquiry.

The prima facie expectation of a considerable methodological similarity between law and empirical science should not cause us to disregard their patent dissimilarity. Science is *descriptive:* scientific laws describe regularities of nature or of society; a well-developed and well-established scientific theory has explanatory and predictive power. Law, on the other hand, is *prescriptive:* legal rules prescribe norms of action; a well-developed and well-established legal system has justificatory and coordinative power. A nonlogical scientific term is naturally considered descriptive, but it seems prima facie improper to regard all the special terms of law as descriptive. More fundamentally, the prescriptive nature of law points clearly to the dependence of legal systems on *deontic logic,* the vocabulary of which includes the operators of obligation, prohibition, and permission.

The present study of law and logic is metalegal in a very general way. This is reflected in the use of language: whenever, in what follows, a word is used that belongs both to the terminology of general methodology and to that of law or jurisprudence (e. g., "sentence", "formal", "theory"), it is intended in the general sense unless the special sense is clearly implied by the context. The present study is, at the same time, philosophical in motive and character, in that it is concerned with what things are in principle rather than with what they are in actual fact and practice. More precisely, it is philosophical in that it aims at the elucidation of the ideal, rational nature of legal argument, legal logic, and legal systems rather than at the faithful description of their existing embodiments. Accordingly, the results of the present study, whatever their purely philosophical interest, cannot be expected to be of any appreciable practical significance for the legal profession, except perhaps in the diffuse way in which understanding may, in general, affect routine, and possibly also in the remote perspective of the guided development of the legal system. In particular, the conclusion that legal argument, insofar as it is rational, must be considered formal in nature, i. e. formalizable at least in principle, does not appear to be likely to have any direct bearing today on the texts elaborated by legislatures nor on the utterances of the courts. As a philosophical conclusion, on the other hand, it seems capable of generalization, inasmuch as nonformalists generally regard legal argument as the paradigm of nonformal argument. The conclusion itself will certainly not be much of a revelation to the formalistically minded reader.

He may, however, find some interest in the account of the several formalistic and nonformalistic conceptions discussed, as well as in the emerging positive suggestions concerning the general ideal structure of the legal system.

The texts to be dealt with in the present book, although a small sample of the vast literature relevant to the subject[8], represent three largely independent lines of study and discussion. Professor Klug's *Juristische Logik* was, to the best of my knowledge, the first book-size attempt to apply modern symbolic logic to modes of reasoning employed in the courts. In arousing a number of nonformalistic reactions, it became a major focus of discussion in Germany. In Belgium, research has been promoted by the group headed by Professor Perelman. Their organ Logique et Analyse is an important forum of discussion on legal logic. In the English-speaking countries, the tenor of discussion is largely influenced by the case-law method and by English analytical philosophy, whose most prominent representative among jurists is Professor Hart. I have selected the texts so as to avoid leaving out any important version, or mode of defense, of the nonformalistic position. I have not shunned overlap between the texts selected: in view of both the insistence with which nonformalistic claims are advanced and the caliber of the claimants selected, a certain amount of repetition seems fitting, especially since it may be found useful as a device of exposition. Attempts to apply formalized logic to law (e. g., studies by logicians concerned with law, as Professor Georg Henrik von Wright, or by lawyers concerned with logic, as Professor Ilmar Tammelo) do not, as such, fall within the scope of the present study. Those few that are dealt with have an intrinsic bearing on its aims.

My method is critical in two ways, in that it involves not only a sustained scrutiny of ideas and views in conformity with my initial

---

8 Bibliographical lists or ample references are given in the textbooks by ULRICH KLUG [46], GEORGES KALINOWSKI [42], and ILMAR TAMMELO [72] and in the works by SPIROS SIMITIS [69], THEODOR HELLER [29], JULIUS STONE [71], HERBERT L. A. HART [28], and GIDON GOTTLIEB [23]. The following periodicals include articles (and, occasionally, bibliographical information) concerning legal logic and methodology: Logique et Analyse [54], especially volumes published also as Etudes de Logique Juridique [17]; Jurimetrics Journal [39], formerly M. U. L. L. [57] (see [09]); Law and Computer Technology [51]; and, less frequently, Ethics [16] and ARSP [04], among others. The three Indexes [34], [35], and [36] are, under the heading "Philosophy", useful guides to legal periodicals.

design, but also a supervening attempt at their refutation out of genuine disagreement. I shall dwell upon considerations apparently basic to each particular position and shall have frequent recourse to quoting the author either literally, whenever the original is in English[9], or in a literal translation into English[10].

---

9 The original spelling, writing of compounds, and punctuation have occasionally been modified in these quotations for the sake of uniformity.

10 As a rule, titles of non-English works and of their component parts are quoted in the main text in English translation. The original titles of the works referred to (but not of their component parts other than individual contributions to a collective study or volume) are given in the List of References. Since most sections of this book are devoted each to a single text, reiterated reference to the same source has been largely avoided; as a rule, direction to the List of References is made in the main text, by means of a numeral between square brackets, whereas a page reference is given between parentheses, immediately after the quotation.

Part I

The German Discussion

Introduction

Part I is devoted to some of the most significant writings on legal argument and legal logic that have appeared in Germany since the early fifties. Klug, in *Legal Logic* which has become a major focus of discussion, attempted to couch types of legal argument in formulae of modern symbolic logic, making use of some rudiments of the functional calculus and the theory of classes. Although his symbolic transcription is open to criticism, I shall not discuss it, since my concern is only with Klug's conception of legal logic and of the types of argument with which he deals. In my exposition of his analyses I shall utilize a simple modified symbolism and shall have recourse to a fairly free, though sufficiently faithful paraphrase of his explanations. My account of Klug's book in ch. 1 is not exhaustive: the arguments *a simile* and *e contrario* are included, but not the other "special arguments of legal logic"; however, the most important of these remaining types of argument will be dealt with later on[1]. Engisch, who is well known in Germany for his work in legal logic and methodology, opposes Klug, declaring: "Legal logic is material logic whose task is to draw attention to what should be done to achieve — as far as possible — true legal cognition. This is philosophical logic, not technique" ([12], p. 5; see also [11]). Engisch's position is well represented in his two articles discussed

---

1 Several omitted passages of Klug's work are discussed in detail in my article [31], of which the following ch. 1 is a shortened and otherwise modified version.

in ch. 2. Simitis's article, discussed in the last section of ch. 2, is marked by a vehemently expressed antiformalistic trend, suggestive of Perelman and Toulmin. Heller's book, to which ch. 3 is devoted, likewise argues for the exclusion of legal argument from the scope of formal logic[2].

Two influences of unequal scope and vigor can be distinguished in the German line of discussion. The less pervasive influence is that of recent analytical philosophy and methodology, transmitted chiefly through writings in German, including those inspired by the neo-positivistic Vienna Circle and its heirs. Among the four authors discussed in pt. I, Klug and Heller display familiarity with a background of this kind. Klug, in particular, is favorably disposed towards modern formalistic logic. However, the dominant influence is that of the idealistic tradition of German philosophy. That it is deep-rooted in each of the four authors selected can be seen in more than one way. Their tendency to confound logical with pragmatic matters is conspicuous, and is the more significant since it was no other than the German Hans Reichenbach who introduced and insisted upon the distinction between the contexts of discovery and of justification. Also reminiscent of idealism are the mutually related views that the application of logic is in principle restricted to science and that law is a branch of science. The decisive factor in the adherence to these views is no doubt the traditional usage of the German word "Wissenschaft", which includes, besides the formal and empirical sciences, such other alleged spheres of "cognition" as ethics and law.

An explanatory remark seems in place here. In discarding the view that law is a branch of science, I do not wish to imply that law does not depend on science. On the contrary, the intimate connection between law and psychosociology is a basic tenet of this book. The point is as simple as it is fundamental: prescribing modes of action is radically different from describing aspects of reality, and law is irreducibly prescriptive; but it is nonetheless an empirical field and requires empirical confirmation. The topic of *legal confirmation* will be dealt with in a very general though adequate way in what follows. The detailed investigation of the problem must, of course, be consigned to a specialized psychosociological level. It should

---

2 The quotations in pt. I have been specially translated from the German, excepting those in ch. 2, sect. 4, which have been taken from the published English translation of Simitis's article.

be noted that the expression "legal confirmation" in this book means confirmation *of* legal rules and utterances, not confirmation *through* them. The scientific, primarily psychosociological domain basic to law and relevant to legal confirmation will be referred to as "the *paralegal* domain" or as "legal psychosociology".

The following final remarks may be found useful. *Analogical argument* (or *argument by analogy* or, simply, *analogy*), as usually presented in textbooks of logic, is of the form:

> (The object) *x* is (has the properties) *A*, *B*, . . . , *F*, and *G*; (the object) *y* is *A*, *B*, . . . , *F*; therefore, presumably, *y* is *G*.

This is a kind of inductive argument. It is important to note that, as it stands, its rational force (i. e. the inductive support that the two premises lend to the conclusion) must be reckoned very weak. The impression of cogency given by certain analogies is due to a background of relevant knowledge which, though not explicitly stated in the argument, is psychologically effective. Accordingly, a substitution instance of the logicians' foregoing form cannot be properly deemed a strong argument unless it is viewed as an *enthymeme,* i. e. an incompletely formulated argument with *implicit premises.* Another noteworthy kind of enthymeme is the so-called *informal* or *analytical inference;* for example: "The new teacher is a devoted father; therefore, the new teacher is male". Here the meaning rule to the effect that whoever is a father is male is an essential implicit premise.

Chapter 1

A Pseudoformalistic Position: Klug

1. *The Concept of Legal Logic*

In the introductory section of his *Legal Logic* [45][3], Klug declares that by "logic" he means formal logic. He seems to believe that his conception of logic closely follows that of Carnap. Yet, in his Introduction he characterizes logic in general as part of

---

3 The discussion of legal logic in Germany, as represented in pt. I by Klug, Engisch, Simitis, and Heller, was stimulated by the first two editions of Klug's book. My account is based on and refers to the *second*

the theory of science, viz. that part of it which provides the technique of scientific proof. This conception of logic is not quite consistent with Carnap's views. In the first place, for Carnap only predicative logic, i. e. the logic of indicative sentences suitable for the formulation of factual statements, is a part of the theory of science. But he also recognizes the logic of "optatives", i. e. sentences suitable to express a wish, a command, a decision, an assent, etc.[4] Moreover, while Carnap identifies the logic of science with the *syntax and semantics* of the language of science, Klug confines formal logic to scientific *proof*. Finally, in identifying logic with syntax and semantics, Carnap excludes from its sphere all pragmatic investigation. On the other hand, Klug's reference to the *technique* of proof seems to suggest that he conceives of logic as having a pragmatic dimension.

Klug maintains that the differences between the various spheres of science are not due to the logic applied to them but rather are due to the diversity of the subject matter contained in the premises of the arguments. "Therefore, when *legal logic* is spoken of, this is a designation not of a logic for which special laws are valid, but rather of that part of logic which finds application in the science of law" (5). Klug's point is not clear. Indeed, how can we reconcile an unqualified claim of the existence of one logic of general validity with the multiplicity of existing and possible logics — many-valued, intuitionistic, modal, deontic, and inductive? The claim of the intuitionists regarding mathematics is well known, as is the claim that certain branches of modern physics should be based on a special kind of logic. To the extent that these claims are justified, the opinion that the differences between the spheres of science lie only in the contents of the premises and not in the logic applied calls for qualification. However, the view is often adhered to that for the needs of empirical science ordinary extensional logic, i. e. the standard functional calculus of suitable order, is sufficient. Klug pre-

---

edition, which differs very little from the first. Since a few significant changes were made by Klug in the third edition, my account fails occasionally to apply to it or calls for qualification. This divergence is specified in the Appendix, which will be most fittingly read after pt. II, sect. 7.

4 See [67], pp. 999—1013. It is doubtful if Carnap *ever* intended to identify logic in general with the logic of science. The impression that he did may have seemed borne out by the fact that for many years he dealt almost exclusively with predicative logic and used the term "logic" elliptically for "logic of science".

sumably intends to represent such a position, even though he does not clearly state this. In any event, he does not recognize the clear-cut distinction between law and the applied sciences: he takes law to be a branch of science, and his legal logic does not stray, in the main, from the framework of the ordinary calculus of first order.

The use of the term "science" according to which law is a branch of science is misleading and pointless. For Klug a sphere is scientific insofar as it depends on logic. "Science" in this sense is virtually synonymous with "sphere of rational argument". The use in question conceals fundamental differences between spheres as dissimilar as pure mathematics, empirical sciences (conceived as domains of descriptive knowledge), ethical systems, law, or games with rules. Klug assumes, as if this were self-evident, that ordinary predicative logic is adequate for law. He cannot altogether avoid the use of deontic expressions, and indeed the deontic expression "are to" occurs in the general premise and in the conclusion of his sub-sumptive syllogisms; for example: "All professional fences are to be punished by a term of imprisonment of up to ten years" (50). This expression, however, is construed by Klug as a component of the predicate ("are-to-be-punished-by-imprisonment-of-up-to-ten-years"), not as a logical operator or constant in itself. Only when he is discussing legal "teleologics" (see below, sect. 5), does he dis-join the deontic element from the expression descriptive of a human action (153), and it is only then that he casually mentions G. H. von Wright's deontic logic (154). Since he regards law itself as a descriptive field, he speaks without any hesitation of "legal cogni-tion".

To the extent that law requires deontic logic, legal logic cannot be unreservedly considered part and parcel of the general logic of the sciences. It should be noted in this connection that applications of intuitionistic logic to law have been suggested. Consequently, much weight cannot be given to allegations of "general validity" of certain laws and rules. Among the three principles mentioned by Klug as examples, only one — the law of contradiction — is indeed a regular feature of rational systems that involve negation; the other two, viz. the law of double negation and the principle of *reductio ad absurdum,* are invalid in intuitionistic logic. In general, there is the danger of confusion and fallacy in any unqualified reference to logi-cal laws and modes of inference in abstraction from definite logical systems.

Regarding the alleged "part of logic" relevant to law, Klug puts the point somewhat more precisely when he says that legal logic "is not the entire logic with all its laws, but is only part, very essentially more elementary than, for example, the part of logic required for the construction of mathematics" (5). Presumably, he intends to state here, among other things, that the functional calculus of first order is sufficient for law, while the various branches of mathematics require functional calculi of higher orders. But he does not explain this. It may be argued that law requires at least simple arithmetic and thus the functional calculus of second order. However, it is impossible to deal with such questions fruitfully without first analyzing, in outline at least, the special structure and characteristics of the legal system as a whole.

Klug does not even attempt an analysis of sufficiently large portions of legal language. He asserts, nevertheless, that it is the link with logic in all the branches of legal research and legal practice that transforms law into a science. Logic, he claims, plays a decisive role in the systematic development of law, since the concept of a system is clearly a logical one; the historical investigation of law also requires logic insofar as it involves proving and drawing conclusions; the question of the a priori foundation of law is likewise a logical question. However, he points out, it is not customary to view legal logic as encompassing all these spheres; it is customary to limit its scope solely to adjudication, i. e. to the application of law to concrete cases for the purpose of reaching a verdict and passing a sentence. Klug states: *Legal logic is the theory of the rules of formal logic applied within the framework of adjudication*" (6). As he sees it, legal logic is "an instance of *practical* logic", as opposed to general logic — "pure or theoretical" (6). For the purposes of adjudication "arguments are always presented — that is, conclusions are drawn" (7). What, then, are the forms of argument peculiar to legal logic? The previous characterization in itself does not provide an answer to this question: "It should be added, of course, that the previous definition of the concept of legal logic does not permit the unequivocal delimitation of the sphere of investigation. Nevertheless, it is convenient to follow the linguistic usage in the stated manner. If an exact delimitation is desired, one should define as follows: legal logic is the theory of the forms of inference mentioned in §§ 9—16 of this investigation (*argumenta a simile, e contrario, a maiori ad minus,* etc.)" (7).

Thus Klug simply adopts, together with their Latin names, a list of "arguments" as singled out by his predecessors within the framework of traditional logic. They constitute legal logic according to his conception, and the principal part of his book is devoted to them. The result is, therefore, that the aforementioned "part" of general logic by which legal logic is defined is not one or another system of logic at all, but rather a set of a few "forms of inference". These are not primitive rules of inference, such as *modus ponens* or the basic rules of substitution. What, then, singles them out from among the derivative rules of inference? Moreover, what justifies the underlying assumption that the given list indeed includes all the important modes of argument likely to be of use in legal reasoning? Klug avoids all clarification of these questions. Further on it will become clear that the traditional "forms of inference" studied in his book are not primarily logical but heuristic in nature.

However, a certain confusion of the logical context with the pragmatic is in fact already evident in his Introduction. This finds expression in the limitation of the scope of legal logic to the actual framework of adjudication. Logic, Klug admits, is needed by anyone who argues, i. e. anyone who proves something and draws conclusions, whether in the systematic study of law, its historical investigation, the philosophical study of its foundation, or in its practical application by the judges; but it is only the last-mentioned function, he maintains, that constitutes the special sphere of legal logic. Klug's reason for this limitation, viz. that it is generally accepted, paradoxically disregards the fact that those who engage in legal argument make frequent use of systematic, historical, and philosophical considerations. It may be granted that the descriptive history of law logically constitutes a field distinct from law itself (although the possibility of logical relationships between the two fields, especially in the context of the confirmation of laws by historical considerations, should not be discarded in advance). On the other hand, there seems to be no adequate justification for excluding the systematic study of law or the study of its foundation from the scope of legal logic.

Klug's assertion that the concept of a system is logical in nature can be regarded as lip service to the conception of legal logic, in principle, as an extensive syntactic and semantic theory of the legal system. In his Introduction he briefly explains the nature of the applied axiomatic-deductive system, and at the end of the book he even points out the need for the axiomatization and formalization of law (see below, sect. 5). Yet these remarks remain vague and unconnected with the body of the work. As we have seen, Klug in fact limits legal logic to the study of certain modes of reasoning customary in courts of law; consequently, he regards himself as absolved from making any contribution whatsoever to the clarification of the systematic nature of law. In particular, we should search in vain in his book for even the beginning of a discussion of such basic methodological questions as the distinction, within a legal system, between descriptive and prescriptive elements, between analytic and synthetic elements, between axioms, correspondence rules, and so on, or an analysis of the logical aspects of justification and confirmation in law and of central concepts in jurisprudential theory, such as those of a duty, a right, and a corporation.

Klug holds that the foundation of law is "suprapositive" in nature. As indicated, he excludes its study from the scope of legal logic, despite the fact that he takes it to be a "logical question". He qualifies the alleged foundation as "teleological" and as involving a priori "judgments of obligation", whose study he relegates to the philosophy of law. Without embarking now upon a criticism of this conception, which is nurtured by the tradition of German philosophy, I wish only to suggest an interpretation of its role in Klug's position: the a priori principles of law absorb, as it were, his distortions of legal logic; in particular, they represent the price that he pays for the conception of legal logic as part of the logic of science. Exact legal philosophy, I shall maintain, has no need to assume a nonempirical foundation for law.

In the cited characterization of legal logic as "an instance of practical logic" as opposed to "pure or theoretical" general logic (6), there is an implicit confusion between two different distinctions, viz. the distinction between pure and applied systems and the distinction between theoretical and technical (practical-methodological) fields. Legal logic is actually applied logic (or "special" logic, in the sense that specific nonlogical constants occur in its formulae). However, this circumstance does not deprive it of its theoretical nature, as Klug, who apparently identifies the applied with the practical or the technical, seems to believe. On the contrary, a rational conception of field logic does in fact require a clear-cut distinction between logic and the methodology and technique of reasoning. Logic itself, in principle, concerns the formalized system: it determines the system's syntactic and semantic characteristics, and thus also the rational force of the arguments formulated within its framework. The conception of legal logic as a pragmatic and practical investigation of the processes or acts of legal reasoning should, I suggest, be replaced by the conception of legal logic as the syntax and semantics of legal language, parallel to the corresponding conception of the logic of science.

Klug rightly agrees with Leibniz and Carnap who claim that it is easy to err about matters of form. Yet, by divorcing legal logic from the study of the legal system as a whole, he ignores the most common and serious of such errors: viewing matters of form as if they were matters of substance. The elucidation of alleged "material relations" as formal relation is possible only within the framework of the entire system. The dissociated, enthymematic argument appears at first glance to involve a "substantive" or "material" inference. In fact, it cannot be adequately developed and completed unless it is viewed against the background of the entire language of law. It is true that Klug is not prepared to recognize the existence of "material" legal logic. On the contrary, he emphasizes that logic is formal by its very nature. However, this progressive outlook is unfortunately not accompanied by an adequate conception of the field. Within the narrow and confining framework allotted by Klug to legal logic, his attempts to represent the modes of legal reasoning as purely formal inferences appear (as will become evident later) as manifest distortions of the objects of the study.

Beyond the analysis of several syllogistic forms which attracted attention in traditional logic, there is a wide field of study that the logician must not neglect. Claims as to the absence of opposition between logic and life and assertions to the effect that logic is the "sole forum considered absolutely binding" (8) appear somewhat paradoxical and futile as long as there is no assurance that the "logical forum" is conceived in its proper extension, as the sphere of rigorous language erected into comprehensive systems.

2. Discussion of Antilogical Doctrines.
Legal Confirmation. The Background of Legal Logic

Before turning to the Special Part of Klug's book, I shall examine the defense of legal logic he holds up against the objections of its alleged opponents, viz. the supporters of the doctrine of free judgment *(Freiheitsschule)* and of the doctrine of interests *(Interessen-jurisprudenz)*.

Klug does not develop his debate on the proper plane and thus, to a great extent, it becomes pointless. To begin with, his characterization of the positions of the two doctrines is too simple and vague, since he attributes to them the "paradoxical claim that adjudication is possible without the aid of logic" (9). One cannot be sure of the exact meaning of this phrase, in which pragmatic and logical elements are intermingled. Should it be understood as affirming (*a*) that adjudication is possible without any reasoning whatsoever, in the psychological sense; (*b*) that the judge does not always complete his enthymematic considerations and formulate them as formalized arguments; (*c*) that such formalization is not always required for ensuring good adjudication; or (*d*) that such formalization is not always possible? It is very doubtful if anyone ever seriously opposed claims (*b*) or (*c*) or if anyone ever seriously defended claim (*a*). In any event, none of these four contentions can be seen as implicit in the considerations of the two doctrines under criticism, as they are presented by Klug himself.

The major genuine question whose clarification is required in this context seems to be the following: What relative role do the general premises drawn from the legal system itself, on the one hand, and those which the judge must supply, on the other, play in good adjudicative arguments? There is also a preliminary question: What is the difference between good and bad adjudication? These two questions should be clarified as referring (*i*) to a legal system in existence today and (*ii*) to a perfect legal system that could be constructed in the future or ideally conceived as a regulative principle. The "opponents of logic", in defending their criteria for good adjudication, argue mainly along the lines of (*i*): they point out that in the framework of actual adjudication the possibilities of deduction are limited, so that verdicts and sentences are only rarely deduced unequivocally from the factual data with the aid of the existing legal system. Consequently, nondeductive operations that lean heavily on intuition — and, in this sense, are nonlogical — have an important role to play in actual legal reasoning. However, it is also possible to interpret part of the considerations under discussion as an attack along the lines of (*ii*). Klug does not disagree with the criteria suggested for good adjudication. He too avoids the proper development of the second path of argument, despite the fact that his struggle along the first path may be regarded as an attempted defense of a lost cause. Indeed, he is unable to deny the main point of the genuine "antilogical" contention. On the contrary, he admits that the judge is often compelled to supplement the law and amend it. He naturally does not find it difficult to refute what he construes as a "paradoxical claim". He explains that the substitution of premises in legal arguments does not require relinquishing the use of rules of inference. But in this he is obviously tilting at windmills, since it should not be assumed that the adherents of the doctrines under criticism would deny the existence of those "operations of legal logic" which "begin only when the premises are already present" (12). Their only comment would be that the operations in question are rather unimportant as compared with the acts of subjective decision upon which the supplementation or amendment of the law depends. In short, the discussion, as Klug presents it, misses the central point. It is necessary to develop it and to elucidate its implicit aspects.

Today, the importance of nonlogical operations (in the aforesaid sense) in adjudication is great. This contention itself cannot be opposed: it is correct both with respect to good critical adjudication and with respect to bad routine adjudication. Many authors, in fact, do emphasize the role of these operations in adjudication. In view of the prevalence of this emphasis, it is worth examining the problem from time to time in its various aspects. Such an examination necessitates a clear distinction between the factual affirmation of the state of contemporary law and the question concerning the possibilities of its development and formalization. It also necessitates a distinction between obstacles in practice and obstacles in principle that stand in the way of the rationalization of adjudication.

A legal system is constructed in order to allow adjudication by logical means. As long as the system is not sufficiently developed, such possibilities are in themselves limited. Reasoning without a system is obviously impossible: it is not enough to have factual data in order to draw legal conclusions in a formal argument. In law as in science, the construction of a theoretical system precedes the setting out of arguments; in law as in science, the operations of the construction of the theory are, in the initial stage, more numerous than the operations of its employment. In the perfect state of law (and I am disregarding social change for the moment), the judge only puts the system of laws to use; in fact, however, he must also

take part in its construction. It is impossible to derive a new law
from the system to which it is being added; it is precisely this feature
that makes it a *new* law. To be sure, here the question concerns not
so much the legislation of entirely new laws as the "substitution of
premises", i. e. the modification of existing laws. But even in this
case the modes of change obviously cannot be derived from the
system itself. Thus arises the question of the criteria for the distinction between a good legal system and a bad one. A scientific system
is tested, first and foremost, by empirical confirmation. In what
sense is it possible to speak of the confirmation of a legal system?

The adherents of the doctrine of free judgment emphasize the
need for adapting law, firstly, to the "intentions" of the governing
authority and, secondly, to the current intuitions of equity and
justice. The doctrine of interests demands the consideration of the
respective interests represented in court by the parties. But, in fact,
what are the functions of law? Science describes phenomena, makes
it possible to explain them and to predict them. Law, which is
applied to society, does not have a cognitive function as does
science: it is not meant to describe society but to direct it. While
science describes regularity, law establishes regularity by determining rules of action; while science formulates statements of fact, law
commands and warns; while a scientific theory provides explanations for the phenomena to which it applies, a legal system provides
justification and sanction for the decisions of the judge. Just as the
soundness of a scientific theory is tested by the correspondence of
its predictions to observations, so is the soundness of a legal system
tested by the correspondence of its consequences to human volitions.
However, this analogy is deficient in an important respect: while
scientific observations are intersubjective and fairly stable (though
dependent on methods of observation and measurement which
develop with the passage of time), substantial differences exist between the volitions of the members of a society, and these volitions
are greatly affected by social change. The problem of the criteria for
adequate confirmation, thus, is far more complex in law than in
science. One cannot escape serious consideration of the question of
whose volitions are decisive in legal confirmation.

The adherents of the doctrine of free judgment reply as follows.
In principle, the soundness of a legal decision is tested by its correspondence to the volitions of those who hold the reins of power
at the time of adjudication, since they, in a sense, are the masters

of the legal system which serves them as an instrument of government. Just as the noncorrespondence of scientific predictions to observations requires changes in a scientific theory, so the noncorrespondence of legal conclusions to the volitions of those in power requires a change in the law by virtue of which the conclusions were derived. When the volitions of those in power are not clear to the judge, he must make use of the criterion of the simple intuition of justice which represents the general will of society, whose components are weighted, as it were, in accordance with the social balance of forces. The reply of those who adhere to the doctrine of interests is not essentially different: the judge must evaluate the tangible interests involved in the case under consideration. The social factors whose balance controls the authorities in power are here explicitly mentioned. It is convenient in this context to use the term "general will" or "effective will" as a theoretical term of legal psychosociology.

The "antilogical" position common to both doctrines can be interpreted in the following manner. Even in cases where the judge is in possession of explicit and clear laws, he cannot be satisfied with drawing conclusions automatically, but must subject them to the criteria of legal confirmation. He must reject any conclusion which does not appear sufficiently sound, and he must amend the law accordingly. Like the scientist, the judge should ensure the appropriateness of the theoretical system to its basic functions. However, since confirmation in law is not intersubjective and stable to the same degree as is confirmation in science, in law the use of theory is disturbed by its construction to a far greater extent than in science. Furthermore, the obstacle in the path of the systematization of law is not the result of special circumstances limited in time, since the subordination of logical operations to nonlogical ones constitutes a permanent feature of law.

Klug does not even commence such a discussion. He explains that logical operations are not affected by the fact that judges provide their arguments with new premises. He adds that the new premises themselves are derived from principles, "the governing principles of the state" or "simple teleological principles" (10). But what is the status of these principles? Is it possible to formulate them in advance and incorporate them in the legal system? Klug does not claim that this is possible; but it is clear that such a claim would be ineffective against doctrines emphasizing the dynamism of law. Only an analysis based on the concepts of empirical confirmation, as indicated above, properly reflects their position. Only such an analysis will be acceptable to anyone unwilling to adopt an aprioristic viewpoint. Like science, law is in need of confirmation "from below" in the absence of any possibility of deducing it from "superior" principles. To the extent that the two doctrines represent such an empiricist trend, they seem to merit serious consideration.

However, it also seems that there is room to blunt the edge of the "antilogical" criticism. Law, as an instrument of power, serves not only to impose will in general but, primarily, to organize life in society and to coordinate opposing volitions. This function, based on the social nature of man, strengthens law in its actual application. Organization and coordination require theory and consistency to a greater extent than does the imposition of will in general. The desire for organization and coordination, when guiding private isolated volitions, limits the opposition between them and in this way lessens the tension between law and the effective will. Accordingly, differences between individual volitions do not make law as different from science, where the intersubjective nature of confirmation is concerned, as it perhaps appears at first sight. Furthermore, the function of law as a factor of organization and coordination increases its stability. It is possible to analyze this phenomenon as a process of progressive consolidation. As law becomes more stable, it succeeds in coordinating volitions more efficiently, and as the volitions are more efficiently coordinated, they grant a greater degree of stability to the system of law which they confirm. This tendency is related to the indefiniteness of legal confirmation. The question of the correspondence or noncorrespondence of a legal rule or decision to the effective will cannot be resolved as sharply as can the question of the correspondence or noncorrespondence of a scientific law or prediction to an observation; nor does the former question require as sharp a resolution as the latter. This indefiniteness and flexibility of the effective will serves as a safety valve for law in its directive and coordinative social function.

It is true that law is greatly influenced by changes in the material aspects of society — that is to say, by technical and economic development — through the mediation of changes in the balance of the social forces which determine the general will. With respect to these phenomena, the distinction between a pure theory and the interpretation connecting it with the antecedently available domain is relevant. Owing to the indefiniteness of those psychosociological factors which underly law, there is much latitude in providing an interpretation for the theoretical legal system. Consequently, material changes have less influence on the pure theory than on the rules of interpretation. Moreover, it is in the power of a sagacious legislation, directed towards increasing the stability of law, to limit in advance the influence of economic and social changes on the internal postulates of the legal system and to increase the degree of absorption of this influence by the rules of interpretation. Finally, it is worth pointing out in this context the relative independence that usually exists between the numerous parts of a legal system. As a result of this, a change made in one or another of the system's parts does not usually cause such a general disturbance as that caused in a narrow and deep scientific theory by changes at sufficient depth.

Let us now turn to Klug's reaction to the claim (of the adherents of the doctrine of free judgment) that in certain cases the judge is forced to make arbitrary decisions. Klug replies that such "arbitrariness" does not mean the absence of consideration: the judge even in such cases does not reach a decision "by tossing a coin" but rather on the basis of unwritten principles. In this part of the debate as well, a clear distinction between actually existing law and perfect law is lacking. Here too Klug sees himself absolved from directing the discussion to the possible and the desirable. Owing to the oversimplified and misleading interpretation he gives to the basic thesis of the two doctrines he criticizes, he believes that it is possible to refute it merely by pointing out that in every instance — also when following the recommendations of the "opponents of logic" — the judge offers arguments and hence requires logic. However, it is clear that his reply, insofar as it refers to existing law, misses the point. The unwritten principles serving as a basis for judicial arguments in the cases under discussion are not deduced from the law. Consequently, they are not unlike the new premises discussed earlier. Their very formulation is a nonlogical operation. Such operations are unavoidable in adjudication — *this* is the fundamental "antilogical" thesis, not "the paradoxical claim that adjudication is possible without the aid of logic". Implicit in Klug's reaction is the assumption that there are sufficient "unwritten principles" to solve all the complex questions for which the ordinary "free" intuition of justice does not provide an unequivocal solution. In support of this assumption, which is essential to his reply, he gives no reasons whatever, nor does he explain how these principles are established and protected against chance. It appears again that his defense of legal logic leans tacitly upon his undefended aprioristic stand.

The evaluation of the two "antilogical" doctrines can be summarized as follows. Their basic position seems acceptable insofar as it concerns the state of adjudication today. However, it appears exaggerated if construed as casting serious doubt on the possibility of extensively rationalizing adjudication through the development of legal structures and through their progressive adaptation to social conditions. The difference between good law and good science, from the point of view of the importance of logical operations in their practical application, is not as great as it seems at first glance. Also the difference between them from the point of view of their relative stability is not significant enough to justify the relinquishment of the logical development of law and of its improvement as a system of applied theory.

The only merit with which Klug credits the two doctrines is that they have shown "that in deriving conclusions from existing law it is necessary to take into consideration, aside from the legal premises laid down in legal stipulations, some initial material" (12). Such an evaluation ignores the essential. The great merit of the two doctrines is that they have analyzed the social function of law and emphasized its empirical foundation. Here, as in other spheres, the antiaprioristic trend has often been, owing to misunderstanding, regarded as "antilogical". Klug, with his aprioristic tendencies, would presumably be reluctant to recognize this merit, even if he saw the problem of legal confirmation as relevant to the debate on legal logic. In any case, the framework of his discussion is limited, from the outset, by his narrow and faulty conception of applied logic.

Though, admittedly, the *discovery* of evidential premises for adjudication "is not a task of legal logic" (12), there seems to be no justification for excluding the syntactic and semantic aspects of these premises, and of the legal system as a whole, from the scope of legal logic. Moreover, an investigation of such logical questions as those discussed by Klug should not be separated from their wider methodological and pragmatic background: a discussion of the nature and scope of legal argument and legal logic can hardly be enlightening if it fails to deal with the characteristics of law as an applied theory, the circumstances of its development, etc. Klug ignores both these considerations, and by subjecting his discussion to excessive limitations renders it superficial and sterile.

I shall now turn to the part of Klug's book dealing with the "special arguments of legal logic". These are, according to the order of the sections: inference by analogy, inference by inversion, arguments *a maiori ad minus, a minori ad maius, a fortiori, ad absurdum,* and arguments of interpretation[5]. Klug explains that the use of the special forms of argument involves difficulties, unlike the easy use of "the fundamental form of legal inference", i. e. the traditional form *barbara:* "The fundamental form of legal inference is characterized by the fact that the major premise includes the general legal directive, while in the minor premise the concrete situation is subsumed. The concluding sentence gives the concrete judgment of obligation as following from both premises" (49). It has already been pointed out that Klug regards sentences which include expressions of obligation ("judgments of obligation") as belonging to the scope of the ordinary, nondeontic "logic of science".

3. Analogical Inference. (Formal) Logic and Heuristic "Logic". Creative Judgment and Semantic Interpretation

Klug characterizes the use of analogical inference (or *argumentum a simile*) in the following manner: Analogical inference occurs when a legal rule whose explicit formulation refers to a certain state of affairs is applied to a different state of affairs, congruent with the first "in all essential respects". In other words, by means of analogical inference a given legal rule is brought to bear upon an unforeseen case which corresponds, nevertheless, to the "basic idea" of the rule. The difficulty in the use of analogical inference, Klug points out, lies obviously in the obscurity of the distinction between essential and unessential respects or between basic and unimportant ideas.

The form of *argumentum a simile* is this:

All M are P; all S are N; therefore, all S are P,

----

5 Only the first two of these modes of reasoning will be dealt with in this chapter. The next three will be dealt with in pt. II, sects. 4, 7, and 8; in particular, Klug's own account of *argumentum a maiori ad minus* will be discussed in pt. II, sect. 7.

with "*M*", "*N*", "*S*", "*P*" serving as predicates, and the meaning of "*N*" being: similar to *M* (or, to be more exact, similar to all *M*) in all essential respects. This similarity in itself "is not a fundamental logical relation" (123). The argument as it stands is not valid, but becomes valid on the substitution of "*M-or-N*" for "*M*" in the major premise. The class of individuals with the property *M-or-N* is called "the circle of similarity of *M*". For example, certain statutory rules in German law refer explicitly to contracts of sale, i. e. contracts concerning the transfer of material property. Here analogical inference permits the application of these rules to contracts of transfer of a commercial establishment, including goodwill, etc. It is sufficient to interpret the original rules as applicable not only to contracts of sale in the narrow sense, but also to contracts which are contracts-of-sale-or-contracts-similar-to-contracts-of-sale ("similar" to be read as "similar in all essential respects", thus also subsequently in every suitable context), since contracts of transfer of a commercial establishment are similar to contracts of sale. In the form given above: *S*, contracts of transfer of a commercial establishment; *P*, contracts to which the original rule is applicable; *M*, contracts of sale; *N*, contracts similar to contracts of sale. After the amendment of the major premise, the minor premise is subsumed under it as in any syllogism constructed in accordance with the fundamental form of legal inference. It follows that we should agree with those logicians who refuse to attribute to analogical inference a special logical structure of its own.

Analogical inference, Klug advances, may also be used when legal assumptions are a necessary but not a sufficient condition for legal consequences. In Klug's own convenient terms, analogical inference may be used not only when the legal assumptions *extensively* imply the legal consequences, but also when they imply them *intensively*. (In Klug's terminology "extensive implication" denotes the propositional connective "if", with the characteristic *TFTT*, whereas "intensive implication" denotes "only if", *TTFT*.) Let it be assumed, for example, that the law stipulates that only government officials possess the right to receive tax-free expense money. Being a government official is thus a necessary condition, but not a sufficient one, for enjoying the aforementioned right. Do notaries, who are considered semigovernmental officials, also fulfill the necessary condition for the same right? This depends upon the resolution of the question of whether or not semigovernmental officials may be said to belong to the circle of similarity of the class of government officials.

Klug concludes:

On the basis of the formal-logical structure of analogy developed above, one can show the possibilities available in its practical application for deciding when a certain analogical inference is admissible and when inadmissible. But the criterion for this question, so essential in practice, is not provided by the figure of inference as such, but rather by the definition of the suitable circle of similarity. Depending on whether the definition is broad or narrow, it will be possible to draw more or less numerous analogical inferences. Without a precise definition it is impossible to draw any conclusions. ... The purpose in view is decisive here. Before us is a teleological binding force. Hence, as long as the appropriate circle of similarity has not been defined, the criteria for the admissibility of an analogical inference are not logical, but rather teleological. But when the circle of similarity has already been defined, the analogy takes on an exact shape, and the question of whether an inference of similarity is admissible can be unequivocally resolved (128).

Klug's analysis of *argumentum a simile* is worth discussing in some detail. As we have seen, he distinguishes between two forms of it — the primitive one which is inexact:

(1) All M are P; all S are N (similar to M in all essential respects); therefore, all S are P;

and the amended one:

(2) All M-or-N are P; all S are N; therefore, all S are P.

He explains that only the latter is formally valid.

One can attempt to imagine the opinion that would be held in this matter by an unbiased representative of the jurists. He would argue as follows:

The amended form (2) does not correspond at all to what we call "analogical inference". Moreover, even the primitive form (1) represents only the final stage of the entire argument. Its initial and essential stage is constituted — in our opinion — by the establishment of the minor premise "all S are N". Indeed, this premise, as opposed to the major premise "all M are P" which appears in the law, is not a datum, but should be inferred through the comparison of the meanings of S and M. According to our conception, therefore, *argumentum a simile* is composed of two partial arguments:

(3) Through the comparison of the meanings of S and M (e. g., contracts of transfer of a commercial establishment and ordinary contracts of sale) it is inferred that all S are similar to M in all essential respects or, in short, that all S are N.

(4) The legal rule which determines that all M are P is extended also to S on the basis of the essential similarity, and thus it is inferred that all S are P, in accordance with Klug's primitive form (1).

The arguments referred to in (3) and (4) are not formal and seem, moreover, unsuited to formalization. In the former, the statement of essential similarity is based on substantive considerations, whereas in the latter a formally invalid rule of inference is used, viz. the special, material legal rule that permits the transition from "all M are P" to "all N are P". This transition is essential to *argumentum a simile*, no less so than the inference of the essential similarity in the first stage (3). Yet Klug excludes both these steps from the argument on the pretext that the discovery of premises is not a task of legal logic. But the premises in the amended form (2) are clearly the results of the analogical argument, not its points of departure. The formal inference (2) is unimportant in comparison with the material inferences (3) and (4), and it is implausible to view it as the gist of the argument.

Klug does not in fact discuss such a position. However, to the extent that a reply is implicit in what he says, it is not only too brief, but erroneous as well. Before turning to this, it will be useful, for the purpose of appraising the jurists' stand, to try to unravel the two partial arguments pointed out by their imaginary representative in (3) and (4). The following minimum assumption relative to the use of the terms "argument" and "inference" as logical terms seems acceptable to both sides: Inference and argument involve a relation between certain sentences (the premises) and another sentence (the conclusion), the nature of that relation being determined by logical rules, i. e. by nonempirical rules that refer only to the sentences involved and to their meanings. In this general characterization, suitable to both deductive and inductive argument, the crucial question concerning the specific nature of the logical rules, whether material or purely formal, is left undecided.

The conclusion of the argument referred to in (3) is:

(5) All S are N (i. e. are similar to M in all essential respects).

What, then, are its premises? Clearly, premises analyzing the meanings of "S" and "M" are needed. In a schematic and very simplified

3*

manner, but adequate for our discussion, let it be assumed that the
two premises are:

(6) All M are (have the properties) A, B, C;

(7) All S are (have the properties) A, B, D.

These meaning rules can be seen as explicitly or implicitly involved
in the legal system. Can (5) now be deduced from (6) and (7)? Certainly not; a third, complementary premise is still required:

(8) A and B (or one of them) are essential properties of all M,
and these are all the essential properties of all M.

The metatheoretical nature of (8) is prominent, and it is now clear
that the entire argument by which (5) is inferred from (6), (7), and
(8) is an argument in metatheory. Accordingly, for the sake of
accuracy, (6) and (7) should likewise be formulated in metatheoretical language:

(6*) "All M are A, B, C" is a meaning rule;

(7*) "All S are A, B, D" is a meaning rule.

The premises still require supplementation by appropriate metatheoretical meaning rules, especially by meaning rules for "essential
similarity". Obviously, (5) must also be understood as a metatheoretical proposition.

Let us try to determine the meaning of (8). It is quite clear that
the relativization of the concept of the essentiality of a property is
required here. It should not merely be said that A is essential to
all M, but rather that A is essential to all M with respect to the
explicit law:

(9) All M are P,

or with respect to the legal consequences P, or even to one specific
end ("basic idea", "intention") of the law. To say that A and B are
all the essential properties of all M with respect to the explicit law,
means — in our schematic case — that property C is not relevant
to law (9), in the sense that the following rule, of which law (9)
is a special case, is sound:

(10) All (objects having the properties) A-and-B are P.

Consequently, we accept in metatheory not only the proposition:

(9*) The rule "all M are P" is sound,

but also the proposition:

(10*) The rule "all A-and-B are P" is sound.

It is also clear that (10) is not dependent, in the logical sense, on (6) and (7), and that (8) and (10*) are not dependent on (6*) and (7*). We accept (10) (in the legal system), as well as (8) and (10*) (in metatheory), not merely on the basis of the analysis of the meanings of "M" and "S", but because we understand or interpret the "intention of the legislator" or the will determining the "basic idea" of law (9). Proposition (8) — relativized with respect to law (9) — follows, in a metatheoretical argument, from (6*), (7*), (9*), (10*), and suitable meaning rules. It is important to stress that (10*) is a premise essential to (8). Hence, (10) too precedes (8) in the pragmatic sense: it is impossible to accept (8) as true without first accepting (10*) in metatheory — that is to say, without first accepting (10) as a sound rule, the improvement of law (9). Now, the metatheoretical proposition (5) — likewise relativized with respect to law (9) — can no longer be viewed as resulting, according to some material rule, "from the comparison of the meanings of M and S", as the representative of the jurists maintains [see (3) above]. As explained, (8) is necessarily one of the premises. Hence, (5) cannot be accepted prior to the acceptance of the amended law (10). Thus, the sound generalization (10) now clearly appears not only as the centre of gravity of the entire analogical argument, but also as the key to its understanding: the acceptance of (10) establishes the essential similarity of S and M.

The important point is this: *logically*, the legal finding (10) is not established by the legal data (9), (6), (7), and further meaning rules. It does not follow from them, nor is it supported by them — to an extent even prima facie sufficient for its acceptance — by any rules, whether formal or material, deductive or inductive. It is dependent on them and "follows" from them, as it were, only in a *psychological and heuristic sense*. The comparison of the meanings of "M" and "S", with the aid of (6) and (7) and with respect to law (9), constitutes an *occasion and stimulus* for the reduction of law (9) to its relevant elements. The amended law (10) is unobtainable from the legal data in any argument. In particular, (10) is unobtainable from the legal data in a nonformal argument, if the term "argument" is used in its logical sense, involving a nonempirical relation between premises and conclusion[6]. There is, of course, the possibility of rule (10) being supported by other legal rules and by paralegal scientific considerations, especially sociological ones. Its acceptance could also be defended with the aid of methodological principles. Such considerations, inasmuch as they are induced by the comparison of S with M, are obviously relevant to the purpose of clarifying the concept of analogical argument. However, is it possible to view them as real arguments in the logical sense? A moderate inductivist would reply: in principle, yes; in practice today, no; in the future, perhaps; the matter will depend on the practical possibilities of developing appropriate inductive procedures that would enable the jurist to assess (compare, estimate, determine) the support lent to legal rules by other legal rules, scientific statements, and methodological principles. At any rate, for the time being at least, the logical-inductive element can play no role in the explicatum of the concept of analogical argument.

For the purpose of illustration, let us examine the example of contracts. The law stipulates that legal consequences P apply to ordinary contracts of sale. The question arises whether they are also applicable to contracts of transfer of a commercial establishment. We compare the meanings of the terms "ordinary contract of sale" and "contract of transfer of a commercial establishment". The contracts of the former type have the properties A, B, C, with "C" specifying that sale in the ordinary sense applies only to material objects. The contracts of the latter type have the properties A, B, D. On making this comparison, it occurs to us that property C of the ordinary contracts of sale is irrelevant to the "basic idea" of the law, in the sense that the properties A and B alone justify the consequences P. Indeed, under the influence of (a clear intuition of) the strong support lent to our hypothesis by the rest of our legal, paralegal, and methodological considerations, we amend the law accordingly. The formulation of the amendment is thus caused psychologically by the investigation of the given law and of the meanings

---

6 It is worth emphasizing that the inductive support lent to (10) by the conjunction of (6), (7), and (9) *alone* is very slight and hence useless for the explication of the concept of legal analogical argument as a concept of logic. Indeed, the very establishment of the analogy involves the acceptance of (10) on the basis of *adequate* support.

involved in the problem; but it can by no means be affirmed that the amended law results logically, whether formally or materially, from these data. The generalization of the original law obviously precedes the statement of essential similarity, with respect to the original law, between the two types of contract: the very function of this statement is the expression of the fact that the two types of contract both belong, as special cases, to the scope of a well-established generalization of the original law.

Now it will be easy to conclude our critical examination of the position current among jurists set forth above. After generalization (10) of the original law (9) is accepted, the following conclusion is immediately deduced from it with the aid of meaning rule (7):

(11) All S are P.

This is the final result of the analogical argument. Thus it has become evident that the metatheoretical propositions (8) and (5) do not at all serve as premises in the argument and in this respect are redundant. It follows, therefore, that the two nonformal considerations (3) and (4) in the analysis under examination are also wholly redundant. The deduction of (11) from (10) and (7) constitutes an integral part of the process of establishing (11) by analogical reasoning. However, the corresponding argument:

(12) All A-and-B are P; all S are A, B, D; therefore, all S are P,

does not in itself constitute an adequate logical explicatum of the concept of legal analogical argument. Rather, it should be seen as constituting only the terminal, deductive component for such an explicatum, the completion of which will depend on the possibility of assessing the inductive support that the relevant data lend to (10).

Therefore, as long as no adequate method of setting out and appraising such inductive arguments is available, only a pragmatic explication of the concept of analogical argument is possible. The terms *"argumentum a simile"*, "analogical inference", as usually employed, are not designations of a genuine mode of argument, in the logical sense, but rather refer to what is in fact a heuristic process. Such current use of the words "argument", "inference", and the similar use of other logical terms, such as "premise", "conclusion", and even of the terms "logic" and "logical" themselves, can hardly be disqualified. But it should be remembered that their meaning as terms of legal heuristics and as expressions in the current general usage differs greatly from their logical meaning. Such a heuristic "argument" or "inference" is of course by no means formal. But this is not to say that it is a nonformal argument or inference, in the genuinely logical sense.

Let us now return to Klug's considerations and examine his two forms (1) and (2). They are:

(1) All M are P; all S are N; therefore, all S are P.

(2) All M-or-N are P; all S are N; therefore, all S are P.

Klug makes the transition from (1) to (2) by amending the given law "all M are P", which serves as the major premise in (1). He is right in maintaining that the analogical argument in one way or another involves the amendment of the original law; but he is mistaken in proposing the version "all M-or-N are P" as the amended law. Its weak point, of course, is "N" (which symbolizes, it will be remembered, "similar to M in all essential respects"). The essential similarity is "not a fundamental logical relation" (124), as Klug himself admits; moreover, "N" is not a predicate in the legal object language, as are "M", "P", or "S", but is a predicate in the semantic metalanguage. Its meaning is rather complicated, since it depends, as we have seen, on a certain valid generalization of the original law, a generalization which Klug does not even formulate. Therefore, since in the formula under discussion — "all M-or-N are P" — expressions of the object language and of the metalanguage are intermingled, the formula and its substitution instances are not well formed. The minor premise — "all S are N" — suffers from a similar deficiency. It follows that argument form (2), proposed by Klug as a formalization of the analogical argument, must be disqualified for formal reasons, and this despite the fact that it appears formally valid at first.

I now turn to Klug's claim that it is possible to carry out analogical inference not only when the legal assumptions in the original law constitute a sufficient condition for the consequences ("all M are P", cases of "extensive implication"), but also when they constitute a necessary condition for them ("only M are P", "intensive implication"). His example, already cited before, is this. If a law stipulates that only government officials have the right to receive tax-free expense money, do notaries, who are considered semi-governmental officials, also fulfill the necessary condition for that right? Klug replies that the matter depends on the answer to the question of whether or not semigovernmental officials belong to the circle of the class of government officials. This answer raises serious reservations, since, if the notaries only resemble government officials without actually being government officials, it cannot be ruled, unless the aforementioned law is disregarded, that they fulfill the necessary condition stipulated in it. There is indeed an important difference between the two cases: while in the "extensive" case the amended version "all M-or-S are P" is a logical *reason* for the law "all M are P" (for example: M, ordinary contracts of scale; S, contracts of transfer of a commercial establishment), in the "intensive" case the amended version "only M-or-S are P" is the logical *consequence* of the law "only M are P" (for example: M, government officials; S, notaries or semigovernmental officials). (I am of course assuming that "only M are S" means that no non-M is S and does not entail "all M are S"). In other words, in the former case the amendment of the law involves a generalizing, reductive operation, while in the latter case it involves a deductive operation which limits the scope of the law. While the generalization of the original law does not permit decisions opposing it, such decisions are rendered possible by its limitation: "S-which-are-not-M are P" is compatible with "only M-or-S are P", but not with "only M are P". Hence, the similarity between S and M here does not seem relevant to the unravelling of the basic idea of the law as it stands.

Still, one is inclined to say that notaries, as semigovernmental officials, do resemble government officials and that the law "intends" perhaps after all to include them in the scope of the term "government officials". This, however, is only a false dilemma. In order to resolve it, it will be useful to distinguish between creative judgment and semantic interpretation. Instead of viewing an act of adjudication as involving an amendment of the law itself, it is often preferable to view it as involving only its semantic interpretation — that is to say, the formulation of meaning rules for the terms which appear in it. In an ideal system the terms are unequivocal, and therefore the meaning rules for a term are not dependent on the particular law in which that term occurs. In existing systems, on the other hand, the meaning of the terms varies at times from law to law, and the meaning rules are in this sense relative. This is expressed by phrases such as "for the purpose of the application of this law, ..." prefacing the meaning rules. It is important to emphasize that the meaning rules themselves need not be formulated in the form of an equivalential definition: "*M* and ... are identical" (as a meaning rule for *M*). On the contrary, there are great theoretical and practical advantages, related to the open texture of theoretical terms, in meaning rules formulated as conditional or subsumptive sentences: "all *M* are ..." — such as rules (6) and (7) above — or "all ... are *M*". The law in Klug's example can thus be interpreted with the aid of the rule:

> For the purpose of the application of this law, notaries are (or: are to be considered) government officials.

In such a manner it is possible to apply the law to notaries without altering its wording, and thus without disregarding it. But this is made possible not by the inclusion of the notaries in the *circle of similarity* of the class of government officials, as Klug maintains, but by their inclusion in this class *itself*. "Essential similarity" here becomes "essential subsumption".

Yet, aside from this, there is another similarity of a more abstract nature between notaries and government officials, which also contributes to the inclination mentioned at the beginning of the preceding paragraph. This similarity is not relative to the given law and to its "basic idea", but rather is related to the entire set of laws in which the terms under discussion occur. With respect to a fairly large number of legal rules a notary is a government official, while with respect to others he is not. Moreover, there are numerous rules which apply, according to their explicit phrasing, to both government officials and notaries. This is the actual meaning of the saying that notaries are semigovernmental officials. Since the relativity of his "essential similarity" escaped him, Klug failed to distinguish between the two kinds of similarity. This circumstance presumably further strengthened his mistaken belief that the "intensive" and the "extensive" cases are alike with respect to "essential similarity" and to the legal reasoning relative to it.

There are, however, noteworthy differences between the two cases. In the "intensive" case, only the semantic-interpretation kind of legal analogy is admissible, since creative judgment involves a plain contradiction of the law. In the "extensive" case, on the other hand, neither kind of legal analogy is disqualified in principle, and creative judgment is often plausibly replaceable by semantic interpretation. Thus, in the example of the contracts, the original law can be interpreted by ruling that, for the purpose of the law's application, contracts of transfer of a commercial establishment are to be considered contracts of sale. While leaving the wording of the law unchanged, such an interpretation is compatible with the open texture of the term "contract of sale". Klug represents the analogical inference as involving the actual extension of the law. He speaks, as we have seen, of the original law being supplanted by its amended version, which serves as an essential premise in the proposed formalized argument. Yet, while such a conception corresponds in principle to the "extensive" cases, Klug is obviously mistaken — as has been explained — in applying it to the "intensive" cases as well. Jurists rightly emphasize that the distinction between arguments of creative judgment and arguments of semantic interpretation is not sharp. In cases in which neither alternative is excluded, the preference for semantic interpretation over creative judgment — this preference being desirable for practical reasons — depends on the possibility of so formulating meaning rules, for the purpose of applying a given law, that these rules will not contradict other laws or more general meaning rules and that the term's new meaning will not differ too much from its meanings with respect to other laws. Yet, on the whole, the substantive considerations for or against the introduction of a new meaning rule closely resemble considerations for or against a corresponding amendment of the law itself.

The findings of the foregoing discussion of the legal analogical argument can now be summed up schematically as follows:

1. *The clarification of the explicandum as a heuristic concept.* Let l be a law referring explicitly to all M. The question arises whether it is also (implicitly) applicable to all S; that is, whether formula f, obtained by substituting "S" for "M" in l, is sound. The answer to this question is affirmative, for logical reasons, in either of the following cases: (*a*) there is an expression "R" such that formula g, obtained by substituting "R" for "M" in l, represents a sound generalization of both l and f; or (*b*) a meaning rule m for "M" is accepted, stipulating that for the purpose of applying l all S are M. Under such circumstances it is customary to say that M and S, and in case (*a*) also R, are similar to each other "in all essential respects" relatively to (the "basic idea" or the "true intention" of) l. The process of the discovery of g (or of the conjunction of l and m) and of f as sound, with the considerations which lend intuitively adequate

support to g (or to the conjunction of l and m), and with the deductive consideration in which f is inferred from g (or from l with the aid of m), is called *"argumentum a simile"* or "analogical argument (inference)".

2. *The clarification of the explicandum as a logical concept.* The formulation of the logical explicatum of the concept of analogical argument depends on the possibility of adequately formalizing and appraising the aforementioned supporting considerations by means of a sufficiently developed inductive logic. Should this possibility materialize, the corresponding inductive forms and procedures will constitute the main part of the explicatum, whereas the rule of inference corresponding to the aforementioned deductive consideration will serve as a correlative component.

In evaluating Klug's considerations as discussed in this section, it can be said in summary that he has not succeeded in clarifying the nature of what jurists call "analogical inference" or *"argumentum a simile"*. His claim as to the formal nature of analogical inference is based on a serious distortion of the accepted use of these terms, and his analysis suffers, moreover, from rather serious logical errors.

4. Legal Inference by Inversion.
The Metalogical Character of Its Conclusion

Further on in his book, Klug represents the legal inference by inversion as follows. The law stipulates that if a state of affairs fulfills legal assumptions a, then legal consequences c apply to it. By means of an inference by inversion (or *argumentum e contrario*) it is inferred that if a state of affairs does not fulfill assumptions a, then consequences c are not applicable to it. Such an argument is also called *argumentum e silentio*. For example, from the rule permitting several legal residences to people, it is inferred that several legal residences are not permissible for corporations.

The inference is invalid whenever the legal assumptions are a sufficient but not a necessary condition for the consequences (cases of "extensive" implication); the inference is valid whenever the legal assumptions are a necessary or a necessary and sufficient condition for the consequences (cases of "intensive" or reciprocal implication). Sometimes the legal formula itself permits a decision as to the nature of the implication. The "intensive" interpretation, in particular, is valid with respect to rules negatively formulated, subsidiary rules which lay down exceptions to the main rule, or rules which include expressions such as "only if". "However, when it is impossible unequivocally to determine what the character of the appropriate implication is, teleological analysis is required. Then it is possible to agree on the basis of teleological principles — in adjudication and in jurisprudence — as to what should be considered as determined (defined) on the basis of the teleological axioms" (134). Clearly then, in Klug's opinion *argumentum e contrario* is none other than the ordinary formal inference by inversion:

Only if *a* then *c*; therefore, if not *a* then not *c*,

with "*a*" symbolizing the legal conditions (assumptions), and "*c*" the legal consequences. Accordingly, he disqualifies argument by inversion as invalid whenever the assumptions in the original law only "extensively" entail the consequences — that is to say, whenever the original law prescribes that if *a* then *c*, and not that *only* if *a* then *c*.

Klug's contsrual of the term "*argumentum e contrario*" deviates from the usage customary among jurists even more than his construal of the term "*argumentum a simile*". In the "intensive" case, when *only* M are P, it is impossible — as we have seen — to generalize the law by extending the scope of "M". Consequently, whenever we come across an S which is not M, we can be assured that this S is not P; on this point Klug is of course correct. But this is a trivial case of an ordinary, safe formal inference which jurists do not generally view as constituting a "special argument" in legal logic. The situation is different in the "extensive" case: when a given law *l* stipulates that all M are P (or, alternatively, are non-P), and the judge is confronted with an S which is not M but is similar to all M in certain respects, the question may arise whether or not an S qua S is similar to all M "in all essential respects", and hence is P (or is not P, respectively). If the analogical argument succeeds, the conclusion is that all S are P (non-P) or — metalegally speaking — that *l* is applicable to all S. If, on the other hand, the analogical argument fails, *l* is thereby found to be inapplicable to an S qua S, and the conclusion then is that an S qua S is not P (is P), *insofar as the applicability of l is concerned*. (This reservation will be explained in the following paragraph.) It is the latter type of reasoning process, suitably describable as "argument from the absence of analogy", which is referred to as *"argumentum e contrario"* or "inference by inversion" by jurists.

The explanation of the foregoing reservation involves the distinction (made here under the simplifying assumption that the legal system is consistent) between *unconditional* and *conditional* applicability of a legal rule or conclusion. Whenever a given law *l* either explicitly stipulates or analogically implies a certain rule *r*, then the addition to *r* of a qualification such as "by virtue of *l*" does not in itself constitute a reservation as to the applicability of *r*. It can be said, accordingly, that both explicit legal rules, and conclusions of successful *argumenta a simile* are always unconditionally applicable. When, on the other hand, a tentative rule *r* misses the analogical subsumption under a given law *l*, it may still be vindicated by appeal to some other law. Consequently, unless there are sufficient grounds for holding that *r* is not thus vindicable, its denial, obtained by inversion from *l*, cannot be considered applicable. In sum, the applicability of a legal conclusion as established by *argumentum e contrario* is always conditional. This explains the need for the reservation. Accordingly, whenever a conclusion by inversion is couched in the object language without reservation, its formulation must be regarded as elliptical. Whether the elliptical formulation is grammatically negative or affirmative, its real import is always metalegal and negative. More definitely, the two formulae (1) "an *S* qua *S* is not *P*" and (2) "all *S* are *P*", if they are obtained by inversion from *l* and hence are elliptical, should be construed as meaning that *l* neither explicitly stipulates nor analogically implies (1′) that all *S* are *P* and (2′) that an *S* qua *S* is not *P*, respectively. Again, the situation is different with *argumentum a simile:* the conclusion of a successful analogy can be adequately rendered in the object language and does not call therefore for metalegal reservations.

Parallel to the characterization of the analogical argument as given at the end of sect. 3, legal argument by inversion can now be characterized schematically as follows:

1. *The clarification of the explicandum as a heuristic concept.* Let *l* be a law explicitly referring to all *M*. The question arises whether it also (implicitly) applies to all *S*; that is, whether formula *f*, obtained by the substitution of "*S*" for "*M*" in *l*, is sound. Let the following twofold assumption be made: (*a*) no expression "*R*" can be found so that the formula obtained by substituting "*R*" for "*M*"

in l would constitute a sound generalization of both l and f; and (b) it is impossible to accept a meaning rule for "M" which would prescribe that for the purpose of the application of l all S are M. Then the answer is a qualified negative: it is not the case that all S are P, insofar as the applicability of l is concerned — that is, it should not be ruled by virtue of l that all S are P. Under such circumstances, it is customary to say that M and S are not similar to one another "in all essential respects" relatively to (the "basic idea" or the "true intention" of) l. The process of the discovery of this result, with all the considerations which lend intuitively adquate support to it, is called "*argumentum e contrario*" or "inference by inversion".

2. *The clarification of the explicandum as a logical concept.* The formulation of the logical explicatum of the concept of *argumentum e contrario* depends on the possibility of adequately formalizing and appraising the aforementioned supporting considerations by means of a sufficiently developed inductive logic. Should this possibility materialize, the corresponding inductive forms and procedures will constitute the main part of the explicatum.

Klug's analysis, entirely ignoring cases in which inversion is not formally valid, is very far from being adequate, since from a legal point of view these are precisely the cases of interest, corresponding — as Klug himself admits — to the generally accepted conception. The manner in which he emphasizes the formal-logical nature of the "special arguments of legal logic" is certainly oversimplified and does not properly take into consideration the "antilogical" positions and the views of the various adherents of "nonformal logic". He relates inference by inversion to the well-known adages: "Qui dicit de uno, negat de altero" and "Exceptio firmat regulam in casibus non exceptis" (130) — which he, however, quotes only incidentally and fails to analyze or explain. Indeed, these adages, as well as the designation "*argumentum e silentio*", do not suit his conception: they do not point to a formally valid mode of inference but to procedural principles and heuristic devices which can be analyzed along the lines of the foregoing critical considerations. This is also the case with Kelsen's "negative norm", which is quoted by Klug in the same connection: "One is free with respect to that which one is not obliged to do or to refrain from doing" (130).

Kelsen's principle is particularly interesting for two reasons. Firstly, it can be interpreted both as concerning ordinary, conditional inversion and as concerning, more importantly, what might be called *unconditional* (or *absolute*) *inversion*. In the former interpretation, the principle is taken to mean that if a given law *l* neither imposes nor prohibits a certain action *a*, then both *a* and non-*a* (i. e. both the doing of *a* and the refraining from doing *a*) should be regarded as conditionally permitted by virtue of *l*, i. e. as permitted insofar as the applicability of *l* is concerned. In the latter interpretation, the principle under discussion is taken to mean that if *no* law either imposes or prohibits *a*, then both *a* and non-*a* should be regarded as unconditionally permitted, i. e. as permitted by virtue of the entire legal system. In this more important sense, the "negative norm" is a kind of principle of completeness of law with respect to all possible actions. Secondly, involved in Kelsen's principle, whether explicitly or implicitly, are the deontic concepts of obligation, prohibition, and permission and the logical relations between them, such as the equivalence between the obligation of *m* and the prohibition of non-*m*, and so on. Klug, who limits the discussion while distorting its object and who believes that the ordinary logic of indicative sentences is sufficient for law, is not prepared to discuss these aspects of the "negative norm", although he calls it "a noteworthy application of inference by inversion to legal philosophy" (130). He only remarks: "This is not the place for a discussion of this thesis. But the example shows the importance of *argumentum e contrario* for the overall legal sphere" (130) — without any further explanation.

5. *Conversion of Law Into a Calculus. Legal "Teleologics"*

The last section of Klug's book — "Logic, Science of Law, and Philosophy of Law" — can be summarized as follows.

Observing the rules of logic is a necessary though insufficient condition for making the domain of law scientific. "Hereby both something negative and something positive are expressed. Negatively, the thesis states that we are to reject all *logicism,* insofar as by this term the philosophical trend that overemphasizes the logical aspect is meant. Positively, it follows from the thesis that the construction of scientific theories is possible only with the aid of logic. Logic serves as an indispensable tool for the progress of knowledge and for the development of theory" (147—148). "It should be emphasized that no connection with any *metaphysical* or *antimeta*-

physical system results in any way from the recognition of the
necessity of applying modern logic to these sciences [the science of
law and the philosophy of law], since all that is meant here is that
the use of a tool is required. The object to be treated is not yet
determined by the choice of the tool" (148). In particular, the use
of logic must not be confounded with positivism. The application of
modern logic to legal science should be directed towards the calculization *(Kalkülisierung)* of existing systems of positive law. When
the legal system is formulated in exact language, legal logic will
serve as the logical syntax of that language. The conversion of law
into a calculus will not lead to its removal from life but, on the contrary, will bring it closer to life, owing to clarity and exactness. The
analyses of the legal inferences given in the book are barely "cal-
culizations of very small sections of the systems of positive law"
(150).

Authors such as Engisch, who cast doubt on the possibility of
applying the axiomatic method to law, should be answered as follows: "Thought should be given to the fact that, according to the
state of contemporary science, logically unobjectionable foundations
are conceivable only as axiomatic. Also when 'basic ideas', 'principles', 'commonplaces', 'special circumstances', 'concrete situations',
'substantive logic', etc. are referred to, inferences are made. But
inferences are only possible in an axiomatic system. Therefore the
jurist has always acted — also in the case-law method! — in at
least a quasi-axiomatic manner. Theoretically, it is not a far step
to a legal calculus. The fact that the practical difficulties are very
considerable does in no way affect the possibility in principle" (150).

Though, Klug explains, from a purely logical point of view the
axiomatic legal system can be altered or replaced, it is nevertheless
subject to teleological principles. The development of a teleological
system for the purpose of directing legal systems is the task of the
exact philosophy of law. The basic form of a teleological axiom is:

For all *x*, if *x* is behavior of type *A*, then *x* is obligatory behavior.

Here "obligatory" can be replaced by "useful", "desired", "ordered",
"proper", and so on. To use Carnap's expressions, "the logical construction of the world" should be supplemented by its "teleological
construction". Among other contributions to teleological systems,
G. H. von Wright's deontic logic is mentioned in the context.

Finally, Klug touches on the problem of the relativity of logic and teleologics. He disagrees with Carnap's "principle of tolerance", according to which "everyone may construct his own logic, i.e. his form of language, as he desires". His objection is that "an argument of this sort refutes itself, since its correctness is incompatible with the existence of a criterion for its own general validity" (155). A similar argument is offered with respect to the relativity of teleologics: "The claim that there is no meaningful and generally valid behavior refutes itself, since if it were true, the establishment of that very claim could not be generally valid and meaningful behavior" (156). There is thus a limit to logical and teleological relativity. Klug remarks that "the determination of logical calculi is teleologically bound" (156). It is impossible to construct a logical system without teleologics, just as it is impossible to construct a teleological system without logic. "It follows, then, that between logic and teleologics there is a reciprocal functional dependence, whose exact analysis still constitutes an open problem" (156). With this the book ends.

One may not accept Klug's use of the terms "science" and "cognition", a use according to which law is a science or a sphere of cognition, and still agree with the emphasis he places on the close link between law and logic. Admittedly, it is the link with logic which transforms law into a domain of argument. Klug's answer to Karl Engisch's sceptical objections is also plausible. Law is a domain of rational argument only to the extent that it can be formulated as a rigorous theoretical system. Adjudication that requires intuitive reasoning cannot be considered logical unless its arguments can be tested through formalization within the framework of the system. It is true that the formalization of law constitutes a very difficult practical task; but, again, we are not entitled to attribute a rational nature to legal argument unless we view this task as feasible.

Legal logic is now seen by Klug as the syntax of the language of law. This conception, which should be properly extended by the addition of semantics to syntax, is strikingly different from that represented in the body of Klug's book and explained in his Introduction. The few "special arguments of adjudication", through which legal logic was there defined in its entirety for the purpose of "exact delimitation" (see sect. 1 above), are now thought of as "very small sections of the systems of positive law". In this manner, the lip service paid to the new conception reflects the fact that Klug only began — to the smallest extent and without much success, as we have seen — the study of the field he intended to encompass when he wrote his Introduction.

Against the background of Klug's general demand for rigor and exactitude, his reservation as to "logicism", understood as overemphasis on logical aspects, may seem surprising. For, indeed, what does "overemphasis" mean here? This reservation should apparently be related to the view that logic *alone* is not sufficient for the development of the legal system: in his Preface to the first edition Klug admits that in dealing with complicated legal problems "it is impossible to reach the goal by means of logical analysis alone" and that "much scope has been left to intuition"; he adds that a correct logical process constitutes only a necessary condition but not a sufficient one for "legal cognition" (IV). However, he in no way points to the character of law as an applied field requiring empirical confirmation. Klug, who regards law as a science and a domain of cognition, paradoxically ignores the essential dependence of law on the sciences, in particular on psychosociology. What he emphasizes is the dependence of "legal science" on "legal philosophy" or "teleologics", which is also considered a "scientific" field inasmuch as it too requires logic.

His view that the demand for the "calculization" of law should not be made dependent on any particular philosophical position requires qualification. This view is in fact unobjectionable to the extent that it points to the basic indifference of logical form to content, to put it briefly. From the point of view of legal methodology, however, a philosophical position such as Klug's own, which assumes an a priori foundation for law, hardly seems compatible with a proper conception of the process of "applying modern logic" to law. Whether "positivism" is more appropriate depends on what is meant by this much abused word; and Klug fails to clarify this. At any rate, the demand for the rationalization of law may be taken to presuppose that only empirical control can vouch for the soundness of legal prescriptions. Law is "close to life" to the extent that it is properly connected to the sphere of practical application and is empirically confirmed. Mere "calculization", even on a "teleological" basis, is not enough.

There is no room for a special, "philosophical" enterprise of basing law on extralegal principles of obligation. A prescriptive principle accepted as determinant with respect to law should be seen as belonging to the legal system proper. The separation of "teleologics" from law itself is related to the fact that Klug's legal logic, inasmuch as it is the ordinary predicative (nondeontic) logic, does not permit the convenient formulation of orders, prohibitions, and permissions. Klug sees von Wright's deontic logic as relevant to the philosophy of law, but not to law itself. The development of law belongs, in his opinion, to "the logical construction of the world", requiring completion by its "teleological construction". But "the logical construction of the world" is descriptive, whereas law is essentially prescriptive, and in this sense law is already "teleological". The renouncement of philosophical "teleologics" as a basis for law naturally ensues from the recognition of the empirical character of legal confirmation, on the one hand, and of the deontic character of legal logic, on the other.

The remarks concerning Carnap's principle of tolerance, too, involve a misinterpretation of his view. The argument by which Klug attempts to show that the principle is self-contradictory is based on the mistaken assumption that it refers to the content of propositions and to their truth (their "general validity"), whereas it actually concerns only the form of the sentences through which the propositions are formulated. "A criterion for the general validity" of a synthetic proposition is always empirical, never purely logical. It is an additional error to view the principle of tolerance as an ordinary synthetic proposition. The argument concerning the relativity of norms of behavior is also deficient. The mistaken identification of general validity with a priori validity, and the confusion of the truth of a proposition with the ethical correctness of its affirmation, are especially outstanding. The view that there is a limit to the relativity of logic seems acceptable, but for reasons other than those which Klug had in mind. It is possible to extend this view to a field complementary to logic, if for this purpose methodology is substituted for teleologics. Under the same condition it is also possible to provide a plausible account of the "reciprocal functional dependence" between the two fields. However, there is no need for such a discussion in the present context.

In conclusion, it can be said that Klug in his book did not succeed in properly presenting legal logic and properly analyzing the formal character of legal argument. It is no wonder, therefore, that his views met with opposition and that his shortcomings seemingly strengthened the positions of those who contend that legal argument does not belong to the scope of formal logic.

Chapter 2

Two Nonformalistic Positions: Engisch and Simitis

1. *Engisch on Law and Axiomatics*

In his essay "The Meaning and Scope of Legal Systematics", 1957 [13], Engisch attempts to show that there are serious obstacles to the development of a legal system with the aid of the axiomatic-deductive method. So much empirical content is enmeshed in legal concepts, he explains, that they cannot be reduced to a small and closed set of basic concepts, as can mathematical concepts. Moreover, law differs from mathematics not only as a system of concepts, but also as a system of sentences. The main difference is this: in mathematics deduction is "almost the matter itself", while in law it serves "merely as a conceptual scaffolding" (176). In law every deductive step involves the wielding of so much material that the purely deductive element seems insignificant as compared to the required "cognitive operations". In sum, there is only "seeming deduction" in law; hence, the scientific ideal of the axiomatic-deductive method cannot be realized in the legal sphere.

Engisch is right in observing that it is impossible to define all legal terms with the aid of a small set of primitive terms. But neither his account of this fact nor the conclusion he draws from it seems acceptable. In his account he ignores the distinction, essential here, between a pure legal system, without interpretation, and an applied legal system. He fallaciously compares applied law to pure mathematics. Correctly but needlessly, he points out the multiplicity of empirical elements that contribute to the meaning of theoretical terms. The remark holds with respect to applied legal systems, in which rules of interpretation bear upon the meaning of open legal terms. This is also true, however, of the terms used in applied mathematics. On the other hand, the purely theoretical meaning of a term, in any sphere, is determined by the basic sentences (axioms, postulates) in which it occurs. However, the basic sentences need not constitute a system of definitional equivalences; the possibility of developing a theoretical domain as an axiomatic-deductive system does not depend on its terms being erected into a scaled order of explicit definitions. Moreover, the primitive terms need not be few in number. Their number depends on the nature and purpose of the system and certainly is incomparably greater in law than in such basic mathematical fields as elementary arithmetic or geometry. So far, then, Engisch's observations do not bear out his pessimistic conclusion.

His appeal to the very function of deduction is no more convincing. Deduction is "almost the matter itself" not only in pure mathematics, but also in pure law considered in abstraction from its application. On the other hand, deduction is "merely a conceptual scaffolding" not only in applied law, but in applied theoretical systems in general, including branches of mathematics as applied in science or technology. Not only jurists concerned with the application of law, but — generally — theoreticians engaged in the construction of systems with a view to some application, unavoidably require appropriate "cognitive operations".

2. Engisch on the Nature of Legal Knowledge

In "The Tasks of a Logic and Methodology of Legal Thinking", 1959 [14], Engisch discusses both "legal cognition" and "legal logic". I shall examine his views on legal cognition in this section and his views on legal logic in the following section.

Engisch begins his essay by arguing that legal knowledge is less dependent on its object than is the knowledge of nature or history. The part played by "subjective" operations in interpreting and supplementing an explicit law is decisive. Accordingly, Engisch maintains, the view that legislative legal thinking involves the cognition of an object placed before the cognizant subject requires qualification. However, as there are objective factors in law, there is room to speak of legal knowledge and thus also of legal logic and methodology. Legal knowledge is essentially normative: legal cognition by its very nature involves the valuation of the desirable, and the propositions it tries to establish are statements of obligation.

Engisch's reluctance to identify "legal knowledge" with scientific knowledge, though sound in itself, is not based on sufficiently clear reasons. The reference to the normative character of law is of course in place, but only as a start of the analysis. In associating knowledge with "statements", Engisch seems to consider valuative "statements of obligation" as if they were genuine statements of fact. However, the usual indicative grammatical form of deontic legal sentences is misleading, since their primary use is not descriptive but prescriptive. Still, law requires confirmation, and in this respect legal rules are based on sociological and technical knowledge about the general will of society and about the means of realizing social aims in accordance with that will. True, the general will is flexible, and legal confirmation is particularly indefinite. Engisch, however, though he recognizes social dynamism, tries to account for the imperfections of legal knowledge on the grounds of its being a mixture of "subjective" and "objective" elements. Accordingly, he allows room for a special legal logic: like Kant's transcendental logic which established synthetic a priori propositions about nature, "this logic too is a material logic" (78—79). To the extent that an objective foundation of law is possible, he considers that one can speak of "true" legal statements of obligation, such as the statement that a murderer is to be punished by life imprisonment in Germany today.

Clearly enough, this comparison of law to science is but a gratuitous allowance to the tradition of German philosophy. Such "true legal statements" as the one cited should be construed either as true historical statements of fact or as prescriptive rules corresponding to the general will. In either case they are empirically established. In point of fact, Engisch offers no example of a synthetic legal "statement of obligation" with a priori validity.

Engisch points out that in many legal cases objective certainty cannot be achieved; in particular, it is often impossible to determine in an unequivocal manner whether or not a legal concept is applicable in given circumstances. With regard to this, Engisch recalls a conversation he had with Klug, who maintained that every legal proposition can and should be unequivocally established on an axiomatic foundation. In Klug's opinion, the number of axioms does not matter, and even a judicial sentence of, say, five months imprisonment should be deducible from the axioms. For Klug, the axiomatic method coincides with deduction. Engisch himself, on the other hand, maintains that axiomatics involves "a specific 'ideal type' of deductive operations, characterized by the fact that new theories are derived from relatively few axioms in a purely logical manner, without the aid of material knowledge, as if merely through the fixed rules of a game. In comparison with this ideal type, legal deduction appears less complete, less safe, and always requiring support through material cognitions" (86).

In this controversy neither Klug nor Engisch seems entirely right. Both recognize correctly that a legal system does not conform to the "ideal type" of purely formal systems in which all the findings may be deductively derived from relatively few axioms. Klug insists on the purely deductive character of legal systems and considers that what differentiates them from the narrow and deep systems of pure mathematics is their possession of an incomparably greater number of axioms. Engisch, on the other hand, vaguely senses the open texture of applied legal concepts as qualifying the formal character and the "objective validity" of legal argument, both in actual practice and in principle. As they make no appeal to the idea of inductive support, there appears to be no room for a compromise between them. Klug, in maintaining that in a sufficiently developed legal system the unequivocal deductive derivation of a just sentence is possible, ignores the radical open texture of legal rules and the dynamic character of the circumstances relevant to the sentence. Engisch, on the other hand, though he correctly recognizes the unsuitability of mere deduction for adjudication, concludes from this that the precise determination of the sentence must remain "subjective" and arbitrary. It is of course true that in an empirical system there are no strictly certain findings. Nevertheless, it may be contended that the idea of the rationality of such a system must in principle involve the possibility of assigning a value to a variable so as to maximize inductive support. More generally, it may be maintained that in order to promote the effective rationalization of adjudication, the development of law as an axiomatic system must be combined with basing its application on appropriate inductive procedures. At any rate, the identification of the rationality or "objectivity" of argument with its *deductive* nature is a mistake common to both Klug and Engisch.

3. Engisch's Concept of Material Legal Logic

In the middle section of his 1959 essay [14], Engisch expounds his thesis that legal logic is "material" in nature. Just as mathematical logic develops in close dependence upon the special requirements of mathematics, so, he maintains, legal logic must grow from the specific material structures of legal thinking. "Here we are faced by the difficult question of how it is in principle possible to correlate material-logical investigation significantly with the positions of formal logic" (81). The difficulty is that formal logic purposely ignores all content, whereas material logic tries to take into consideration the nature of the subject matter peculiar to its domain. The modes of correspondence between content and form should therefore be examined. Though in a sense it is correct to say, with Carnap and Klug, that material logic is applied formal logic, "still I am inclined to think that legal logic, as a form of material logic, should break the circle of applied logic thus conceived and assume some further tasks" (83). In particular, "can we not expect of *material* legal logic that it should reflect the reciprocal relationship between the logical forms and the special material which goes into these forms? This of course is not possible without an analysis of the special premises, and finally also of the special axioms and basic concepts with which jurisprudence has to deal. Herewith it appears also that material logic passes, without a clear boundary, into legal methodology" (83).

Here, for example, is a syllogism from Klug's book: "A murderer is to be punished by life imprisonment; *A* is a murderer; therefore, *A* is to be punished by life imprisonment." This is the form *barbara,* reducible to *modus ponens;* formal logic ensures that such a syllogism is valid. But where do the premises come from? "The question we must elucidate within legal logic as material logic is, in what fashion and manner the premises are formed as such; though in doing this we must not, of course, get lost in details" (83).

Since such material logic, Engisch points out, endeavours to analyze the structure of legal thinking, it involves formal logic, methodology, and the theory of knowledge. He considers this syllogism: "All guilt is guilt of volition; negligence is guilt; therefore, negligence is guilt of volition." The intention here is to establish that the punishment of negligence is just. Formal logic stipulates that the inference is valid according to *barbara,* whereas legal logic immediately inquires as to the origin and proof of the premises. "The questions we now encounter are methodological and epistemological" (85). The conceptual material itself requires "material-logical consideration": concepts such as "guilt", "guilt of volition", and "negligence" belong to a special area, the "normative and valuative" area. How, then, can it be proved that all guilt is guilt of volition? What is the meaning of this proposition? Can it be derived from other propositions as a theorem, or is it perhaps an axiom? And if it is an axiom, does this mean that the proposition is evident? Does

it serve as a postulate or simply as an assumption? "Problems of subsumption and 'construction'" also arise: how can the distinguishing
marks of guilt of volition be brought out in negligence? "When one
considers such ways of posing questions, it can be clearly seen that
penetration into these problems of legal logic is not simply a matter of 'technique' with which it was misidentified. Legal logic is truly
philosophical logic. The problem involved is not to teach devices with
the help of which tasks of legal thinking may be mastered as easily
as possible, but rather to consider what has to be done when one
thinks in a legal manner. The problem involved is to come to terms
with oneself as jurist, and yet to keep the limits of the power of
legal cognition in sight" (85).

Substantive criticism of Engisch's very broad conception of legal
logic is somewhat hindered by its lack of clarity. On the one hand,
he maintains that legal logic is primarily nonformal. On the other
hand, however, he characterizes the nonformal parts of legal logic
as methodological and epistemological. Thus it would appear that
his disagreement with the formalistic conception of logic is merely
terminological: he chooses to apply the term "logic" to several fields
combined, only one of which is so designated by the formalists. Yet,
this terminological preference involves much confusion. The affirmation that "material legal logic passes, without a clear boundary,
into legal methodology" may seem gratuitous, if not badly circular, as
long as the respective fields have not been adequately characterized.
When logic is conceived as syntax and semantics, and methodology
as the investigation of the rational development of the system, the
two fields are indeed found to be closely interrelated, but the distinction between them remains nonetheless clear-cut. Engisch disregards
this distinction in the domain of law. His major error seems to
reside in the view that material legal logic — in his own comprehensive conception of it — is capable of "breaking the circle of applied
logic" in some deeper sense, and of "assuming some further tasks"
in an organic way, and not just by a simple conjunction of applied
logic, methodology, and the theory of knowledge. The modes of
application of logic to the legal domain can and of course should
be investigated. However, the methodological and practical aspects
of constructing a legal system and of legal reasoning, whether or
not we regard them as belonging to the subject matter of logic,
are perfectly compatible with both the intrinsic distinctness of legal
syntax and semantics and the formal nature of legal argument.

Pure logic, when properly applied, must of course conform to the domain of application, and adequate system construction requires sufficient acquaintance with the subject matter. To the extent that this is what Engisch wishes to emphasize, he is of course right. The rationalization of law must rest on the descriptive study of legal practice, and there is particular importance in the study of such accepted types of legal thinking as analogical argument, free valuation, etc. Engisch is likewise right in his opposition to the conception of legal logic as "technique". What he does not seem to have shown, however, is in what respects his conception of extended material logic is preferable to the conception of legal logic as applied formal logic. Indeed, nothing in his essay contributes to the elucidation of "the difficult question of how it is in principle possible to correlate material-logical investigation significantly with the position of formal logic", or of "the question we must elucidate within legal logic as material logic", viz. "in what fashion and manner the premises are formed as such". Up-to-date methodology is capable of elucidating such questions, and, to the extent that we do not wish to "get lost in details", satisfactory answers do exist. However, they rest on precisely those principles which Engisch rejects or about which he expresses reservations, in particular on the clear-cut distinctions between logic and methodology and between general and special logic and on the notions of pure theory, interpretation, and confirmation. In relation to the example concerning the punishment of negligence, he points to some genuine methodological topics, in particular to "the questions of subsumption and 'construction'". However, he divides the major problems into an indefinite series of fragmentary and mostly obscure questions, such as those concerning the nature of the legal "conceptual material" and its "areas", the "origin and proof" of legal premises, or the nature of legal axioms. Only a few of these questions are tentatively answered in his essay, in the spirit of his intended material logic, but his answers are not any clearer than his questions. Thus he tells us that the concepts of negligence and guilt belong to the "normative and valuative area", but he does not satisfy our curiosity as to what other "areas" there are in the legal sphere. As regards the question of the nature of legal axioms, he vaguely hints at the possibility of answering it by means of a distinction between postulates and mere "assumptions", but he does not at all explain this distinction itself.

4. Simitis on "the Problem of Legal Logic"

Spiros Simitis holds that legal logic is essentially nonformal. In his widely documented and pungent essay "The Problem of Legal Logic", 1960 [68] and [69] [7], he opposes Klug's conception of legal logic. On the whole his criticism is sound: he correctly points out that Klug unduly limits the scope of legal logic to a few modes of argument, which, moreover, he distorts in his analyses. However, some of Simitis's objections appear mistaken or irrelevant, and his belief that the nonformalistic tenet is borne out by the failure of Klug's analyses is totally unwarranted. I shall not discuss his criticism here, as the details of his opposition to Klug are of less interest in the present context than is his own conception of legal logic.

Simitis characterizes logic in general as "the science of laws of (all) correct thinking" (61). This formula of qualified psychologism is, at the least, misleading. Indeed, the reference to "thinking" is likely to give the impression that a branch of psychology is implied. Yet Simitis can hardly be taken to hold that logic is an empirical science. As a matter of fact, he refers to "*correct* thinking". But at the same time he refuses to admit that the laws of correct reasoning are formal. For him, "formal logic is only a phenomenon of logic and not logic as such" (72). Thus, between the formalist Scylla and the empiricist Charybdis, the "science of correct thinking" entices him, as many others, into an illusory escape.

Though proposing to investigate the relationship between logic and law as well as the general conditions and specific functions of legal logic, Simitis does not provide an adequate methodological basis for such an investigation. Not only is he far removed from admitting that law as a rational sphere should be conceived, in principle, as an axiomatic system, but he also seems to misconceive the distinction between general and special logic, as well as the notions of a pure theoretical system and an applied theoretical system. True, he states in the conclusion of the essay that "it is the task of legal logic to prevent legal order from becoming a disconnected juxtaposition of varied norms" (93) and to ensure "the logical consistency of a well-ordered system of legal reasoning" (94); but even in these rather conciliatory formulations his hypostatic conception of legal logic as a factor external to law is apparent. He rejects "logicism",

---

7 [69] is an English translation of the German original [68]. My quotations are taken from the English version.

which demands the subordination of law to formal logic. Logic is only "one of several ways of fulfilling the task of law", and the function of logic with respect to law "is exclusively instrumental" (89). Hence, there is no need and no reason to decide whether it is classical or modern logic that is more suitable for law. Not only is it useful to combine various forms of logic, but "legal logic is impossible without this combination" (93). It would seem that Simitis regards the various forms of logic as comparable, as it were, to a set of tools: just as an artisan does not limit himself to one tool, since the use, e. g., of a pair of pliers of one sort can neither prevent nor replace the use of a pair of pliers of a different sort in other circumstances, so there is no basis whatsoever to "the claim of exclusiveness of an individual form of logic" (93).

A major point that Simitis tries to bring out, though he does not properly express it, is this: law is not a pure theoretical field, but an applied one that requires both proper connection with the domain of application and adequate confirmation. Thus he emphasizes the "concrete *telos*" of law, its "social substratum", its "ties with life", its "relationship to reality", etc. This point cannot be contested; but Simitis misrepresents it as implying the nonformal nature of legal logic. Formal logic, in his opinion, gives rise to "the danger of law being fixed in unreal abstraction, hostile to reality" (75), whereas "legal logic is not the field of operation of arbitrarily exchangeable formulae of axiomatics. Here it is absolutely impossible to separate the predicate from the content" (91). Legal logic should investigate and foster such nonformal modes of reasoning as "valuation", "material decisions", "analysis of substance", "endowing norms with a meaning", "consideration of the object", etc. Simitis believes that "the knowledge of the ties that bind all logical reasoning to reality", knowledge that in his opinion characterized Aristotle's views, is forgotten in modern logic. He thus disregards precisely those philosophical and methodological principles which provide a proper understanding of the aforementioned ties. In several places in the essay, the formalistic conception of logic is misrepresented as involving the preservation of the stability and rigidity of the system, contrary to the progress of law. In particular, *argumentum e contrario,* inasmuch as it aims at the prevention of an analogical application of the law, is characterized as "corresponding to a strictly formal logical view" (76—77) and as "the classical example of the dangers of formal argumentation in legal science" (80).

Simits conceives legal logic as directly concerned with the actual practice of reasoning in the courts. Consequently, he strongly criticizes the formalistic doctrine of legal conclusions as a blatant distortion of the facts. The following central passage is worth quoting:

> Legal conclusions, therefore, do not prove themselves to be a part of applied general logic. What legal conclusions seem to have in common with logic is merely the name. Argumentation with the help of legal conclusions is only pseudological argumentation. "Wrapping up a legal argument in the form of a syllogism is nothing more than a kind of window dressing." It is only a proof for the fact that courts and authors "are able to present the growth of law as 'logical' . . . even while they make a choice before which logic itself stops short". — On the basis of this argumentation, therefore, no legal logic can be founded. Legal logic begins where the pseudologic of legal conclusions stops.
>
> It is not by mere accident, however, that specially the courts have tried again and again to impart to their arguments the forms of logical argumentation. The fiction that the rules of logic are observed in judgments has great importance, for it tries to avoid the impression that interpretations are arbitrary. The true reason for a judgment, namely the valuation, is concealed and the way of pseudological argumentation is chosen (85—86) [8].

It is indeed the case that the heuristic modes of reasoning customary in the courts today (*argumenta a simili, e contrario, a maiori ad minus,* etc.) "do not prove themselves to be a part of applied general logic"; they are not genuine arguments, in the logical sense, and to that extent they can be qualified as "pseudological argumentation". Simitis, however, completely ignores the regulative importance of "the fiction that the rules of logic are observed in judgments". Further on in the essay, he rejects both "the idea that each judgment must be the inevitable logical result of a given legal rule" and "the conception that a legal order comprises the complete and perfect solution of any number of possible cases" (86). But this idea and this conception can hardly be understood as directly concerning the existing deficient legal system: they should rather be construed as applying to an ideal system of law and thus guiding the amelioration of the existing system. Accordingly, Simitis's declaration that "true legal logic will never foster pseudological argumentation but destroy it" (87) would seem worth subscribing to if the said "destruction" were meant as involving the substitution of genuine arguments, in the logical sense, for heuristic modes of reasoning. Like-

---

8 Simitis's quotations are from a jurisprudential source.

wise, his wish that legal logic may "succeed in freeing itself from that illusion of certainty which is given by a formal-logical interpretation of the law" (87) would seem acceptable if the said "liberation" could be understood as involving the continuing conversion of illusion into truth — that is to say, as involving the increase of legal certainty precisely through the promotion of systematic formalization. This is, of course, a continuous process: owing to the dynamic character of society it is impossible to ensure beforehand, once and for all, "the complete and perfect solution of any number of possible cases". Simitis, however, at the close of his essay expresses the hope that the liberation of law from "hypostases, mock legal problems, and fictions" (94) will be actually attained, provided that legal logic will have been appropriately supplemented by the addition of nonformal elements.

A further objection, closely related to the former, concerns the unquestioned identification of formal logic in general with deductive logic alone; in other words, it concerns the failure to distinguish, and even to mention the distinction, between induction and deduction. Simitis is right in opposing the identification of the judicial argument with the syllogistic deduction terminating it. The gist of the argument is indeed not in the syllogism itself, but rather in the considerations supporting its premises. According to Simitis, such support cannot, by its very nature, be formal, since it involves "valuation" and "axiological arguments": genuine legal logic "begins where the pseudologic of legal conclusions stops"; the decisive step in the arguments of the application of law "cannot be taken by means of formal logic but only by axiology" (77).

Admittedly, as long as the formalization of nonconclusive argument in empirical fields remains a debatable problem, a student of legal reasoning may be reluctant to admit that nonconclusive legal argument is formal-inductive in nature. He is free, indeed, to regard such argument as fundamentally nonrational or merely heuristic. Simitis, however, holds that typical legal argument is both nondeductive and rational, and he entrusts its study and amelioration to a nonformal, axiologically oriented "legal logic". In these circumstances, his failure even to consider inductive logic as an open problem may be deemed a shortcoming, the more so since he fails to clarify the axiological criteria which he envisages for legal logic. In fact, he makes no attempt to reveal the deeper nature of these axiological considerations. In particular, the idea of relating them to assessments of inductive support seems altogether foreign to him. Yet, his position would certainly not be weakened if it were possible to interpret his demand for complementing formal logic by axiology as a demand for complementing deductive logic by inductive procedures. On the contrary, such interpretation would render some of his questionable central formulations both lucid and plausible. His claim that "the guiding principle for an analogy stems from the evaluations on which legal order is based and not from a formal logical operation, be it exact as it may" (78) would then become: "The guiding principle for an analogy stems from the assessments of the inductive support on which legal order is based and not from deductive operation, be it exact as it may"; and his belief that "the knowledge of this secondary role of logic in legal reasoning would stifle all attempts to substitute formal-logical processes for valuation" (87) would become: "The knowledge of this secondary role of deductive logic in legal reasoning would stifle all attempts to substitute deductive processes for induction". Indeed, it may be held against Simitis that it is precisely the *formalization of legal valuation* which should constitute a "major task of legal methodology" and that it is appropriate inductive logic which could eventually best serve as the *"novum organum dialecticum"* (93) for law. Accordingly, the claim that "an axiomatic legal science, freed from values, cannot exist" (88) could be replaced by the claim that a purely deductive legal system is not possible; and the claim that "the task of the law is not to produce logically exact but reasonable judgments" (87) may be found more enlightening when "logically exact" is interpreted as "deductively derived from the system", and "reasonable" as "inductively well-supported".

Simitis would presumably reject such an interpretation of his position, for it is entirely opposed to the antiformalistic character of his discussion. The question therefore arises of how he himself understands the nature of the nonformal logical operations he views as essential to legal argument. As indicated, he gives no clear answer to this question, though he emphasizes the "rational" and "logical" character of legal argument: "Law is rational. Reason is the basis of all logical reasoning. Legal science can, therefore, not afford to do without logic. Feelings and emotional factors are useless as standards for a legal system" (91). He considers that valuation involves "arguments based on the scope of the law" (87) and "examining the principles on which every individual rule is based"

(80). He does not renounce even exactness: he demands "exact valuation of the conflict of interests in each particular case" and "a valuation based on an exact observation of the interests involved" (81). Yet, he remarks that "to realize that formal-logical reasoning is necessarily incomplete does not mean that material reasoning is perfect" (91). However, one cannot be sure whether he intends to say that material legal reasoning happens to be deficient at present or that it is somehow inherently deficient. On one occasion he describes legal analogy as "the result of an axiological observation" (79), but there is no evidence that he means observation as opposed to reasoning. At any rate, he does not intend all those casual hints to constitute an adequate analysis of the subject under discussion. On the contrary, he regards the examination of "the boundaries between axiological and formal-logical reasoning in law" (87) as a task for the future and considers that legal logic should "elucidate the possibilities of an exact realization of a valuating judgment" (87).

An apparently important attempt to undertake such a task was made by Theodor Heller in a book that appeared a short while after the publication of Simitis's essay.

Chapter 3

An Axiologistic Position: Heller

1. The Logicians' and the Lawyers' Analogical Inference. The Inductive Nature of Legal Argument

Heller's book *The Logic and Axiology of Analogical Adjudication* [29] appeared in 1961. At the beginning of its first, introductory part, devoted to a general discussion of "the concept and the logical structure of analogy and of analogical inference", the aim of the work is said to be: "by the example of analogy to show the points of contact between the problems of the application of law, and formal logic, and to make a contribution towards the necessary separation between the logical and the axiological elements in the application of law" (1). Implicit in the basic distinction between the logical and the axiological elements of legal analogy are two assumptions of unequal plausibility. The first one, unobjectionable, is that the mode of induction known in general logic as "analogical inference" does not exhaust the jurists' concept of analogical inference. The second assumption, on the other hand, seems confused and dubious: it is that the residue is entirely or mainly nonlogical. For Heller the residue in question is "axiological": it involves the "spiritual acts" of "valuation", "preference and rejection", and "choice between several possibilities". The axiological elements, however, are not properly analyzed. In the weak hints as to the nature of value and valuation, idealistic and aprioristic echoes can be heard. The act of valuation "is not determined solely by its underlying real factors" (2), since it also hinges on "thought relating to the matter" or on "consideration of the 'nature of the matter'", inasmuch as such consideration involves "the possibility of seeing existence in a rank order". Heller justifies the avoidance of all philosophical treatment of valuation by pointing to the methodological character of his investigation. This justification is unacceptable, especially since the axiological concepts play a major role in the book. The very distinction between philosophical and methodological treatment lacks clarity here. In any event, insofar as a philosophical approach involves the clarification of obscure basic concepts, the methodologist ought to be a philosopher.

It can be plausibly maintained that "the axiological elements" of legal analogy do have a logical aspect that escapes Heller's attention, viz. the inductive support lent to the argument's conclusion by the relevant legal data and sociological knowledge. Consequently, though Heller is right in emphasizing that "the procedure of analogical inference in logic is unable to exhaust the sense and meaning of legal analogy" (2), he appears to be mistaken or dogmatic in assuming that the residue is nonlogical and that its analysis would be methodologically uninteresting. This coupling of a correct opinion with a questionable one entails another such coupling, concerning the adequacy of induction for law. Heller, of course, is right to the extent that he intends to say that the very weak support given to the conclusion by the premises in the logicians' analogical inference is insufficient for legal argument. But he is apparently prejudiced in maintaining that legal argument can and always should be absolutely compelling and, hence, that "it would contradict the essence of the legal norm to allow only a 'probable' obligation for the legal consequence it determines" (20). One senses confusion between the acceptance or rejection of a legal norm and the question of how strongly it is supported. Those charged with legislation and adjudication must of course establish and accept certain norms as legally valid and must make unequivocal decisions. It is misleading, though perhaps usual, to characterize norms in this respect as "absolutely binding". It is, however, an obvious mistake to identify the legalistic validity of a rule with its soundness. Since legal rules are not established a priori but call for empirical confirmation, their soundness is never absolute but is in principle subject to assessment. The public is certainly entitled to expect legislators and judges to provide the strongest possible support for legal rules and decisions. But a poor, weakly supported ruling, too, is "absolutely binding", as long as it is not amended.

The assumption that the "spiritual act" of valuation is capable of bestowing some genuine, primitive rational force, let alone absolute certainty, upon legal conclusions is a major weakness of Heller's position. What is involved here is the unwarranted belief that there are nonlogical modes of legal reasoning that are essential to law and, moreover, are preferable to logical arguments.

In opposition to the logicians' analogical inference, unconvincing as it is, the successful legal analogical inference is accompanied by a clear intuition of its adequate strength. For this reason the former can justifiably be viewed as a "provisional inference" guiding the elaboration of the latter. But the transition from the first inference to the second does not come about, as Heller maintains, through the completion of the logical modes of argument by some more efficient, as it were, nonlogical modes of argument, but rather through the extension, distinct or indistinct, of data lending support to the conclusion. The improvement of legal argument depends on the rationalization of the legal system; as long as sufficient progress has not been made in this undertaking, legal analogical argument must indeed remain intuitive in nature. In this sense it is possible to agree with Heller that "the states of affairs bearing upon the analogical inference must somehow be internally weighed" (54). But this may be seen merely as a practical necessity. Heller's considerations are deficient because he fails to distinguish between the actual imperfect state of law and logic and their ideal, perhaps amply realizable nature: he seems to regard the existing limitations of legal argument as characteristic of law in principle. The straying of the legal analogical argument "beyond the sphere of logic" to axiology is, in his opinion, unavoidable, and he does not consider it a defect that can and should be coped with. Accordingly, he main-

tains that modern calculi of probabilities "do not provide a fulcrum
for the establishment of legal analogy" (143). In particular, under the
influence of the fiction of "the certainty of the *particular case*" (47)
in law, he regards the statistical method as being in principle of no
interest for legal argument. He thus ignores the hardly deniable
suitability of mathematical statistics to the psychosociological research that is basic to legal confirmation.

2. Legal Logic Is Essentially Deontic. The Problem of Subsumption. The Intuitive Character of Legal Argument in Practice

The second, main part of Heller's book deals with "analogy and
the application of law". Its first chapter is devoted to "a logical
analysis of the legal proposition and the problem of the analogical
application of law".

Like Klug and Engisch, Heller mistakenly believes that ordinary
predicative logic is adequate for law. In describing legal rules —
such as "murder is punished by death" — as true or false, he confuses the legal norm with a historical statement, viz. the statement
that the norm does or does not belong to one or another legal
system. The historical statement is indeed descriptive and therefore
true or false, but this is irrelevant to the fact that the norm itself
is not descriptive, so that the distinction between truth and falsity
does not apply. A legal rule can be good or bad, just or unjust,
more or less strongly confirmed; but justice should not be identified
with truth, nor legal confirmation with historical confirmation. Heller maintains that no special logical symbols or rules are needed to
represent the imperative character of legal sentences, since it can
be agreed once and for all that every legal consequence is imperative. This allegation is implausible. To begin with, as legal language
requires ordinary descriptive conditionals, there is a need, in order
to prevent confusion, for a means of distinguishing between the descriptive sentence "if a, then b" and the legal rule "if a, then b is
obligatory". Moreover, law requires, aside from sentences of obligation, sentences of prohibition and of permission as well. The two
latter forms of sentences can indeed be reduced to sentences of
obligation as follows: "a is prohibited" means "non-a is obligatory", and "a is permitted" means "non-a is not obligatory". But if

we accepted Heller's proposal and relinquished the expression of obligation, we would no longer be able to distinguish, e. g., between "non-*a* is obligatory" (i. e. "*a* is prohibited") and "*a* is not obligatory" (i. e. "non-*a* is permitted"). Aside from this, we would be unable to retain all the laws of ordinary propositional logic. Thus, in order to distinguish between "not non-*a*", as the short form of "non-*a* is not obligatory" (i. e. of "*a* is permitted"), and "*a*", we would have to renounce the law of double negation. Finally, law requires conditionals in which deontic expressions occur not only in the consequent but also in the antecedent, such as "if *a* is permitted, then *b* is obligatory", and the like. The acceptance of Heller's proposal would therefore entail an unbearable ambiguity.

Heller rightly emphasizes the importance of the distinction between the concrete *state of affairs* and the legal *findings:* the former is described in nonlegal language, the latter in the technical language of law. Likewise, he rightly points out that the problem of the subsumption of states of affairs under the corresponding findings is not a purely logical problem. Indeed, the problem is primarily methodological. In particular, the very possibility of such subsumption is dependent on the existence of appropriate interpretative rules. For practical reasons, the legislator cannot be expected to formulate all the rules of correspondence required for the efficient application of law; to connect the legal system with the domain of application is largely the task of adjudication. In any event, the interpretation of a theoretical system cannot be derived from the system itself, and in this sense it can be granted that "logic by its own means cannot finally determine" (66) the proper correspondence and that the subsumption of states of affairs under legal rules "cannot be exhausted through the means of pure logic" (67). In this respect law is like any other applied system: the formulation of rules of observational interpretation is empirically controlled by the consequences of their application. Heller, it is important to note, says nothing positive about the logical aspect of the subsumptive operation. He maintains that subsumption rests on "legal valuation" and on "axiological considerations". Insofar as he means "nonlogical" reasoning, his view seems untenable. Interpretative operations can be carried out either by pure intuition, i. e. without any distinct argument at all, or with the aid of more or less distinct substantive and methodological arguments, enthymematic or complete, unformalized or formalized, But one does not seem entitled to speak of nonlogical and yet rational consideration or valuation unless criteria are available for the distinction between good and bad operations, criteria that in the context of justification would replace the rules of logic.

In a detailed discussion of the analogical application of law, Heller extends his remarks about subsumption to parallel norms and maintains that their formulation is not "a primarily logical procedure", but rather rests on "a special mode of legal consideration that bursts the sphere of pure logic", viz. "the general axiological-teleological consideration" (75). Again, he does not sufficiently clarify the nature of this "mode of consideration"; he does not indicate its rules, nor do his illustrations throw any light on the matter. For example, on the basis of suitable relating rules certain laws of sale are extended to barter trade by the replacement of several expressions. But what is the allegedly nonlogical "special axiological consideration" that justifies such a simple extension of the original norm? In other cases the analogical application of a rule necessitates far-reaching changes in its original wording. But, again, *what are* the reasons that require such changes and determine their details? Had Heller properly analyzed his examples, he would have realized that the special reasoning procedures, insofar as they contain any distinct reasons whatever, have proper logical counterparts, i. e. deductive or inductive arguments, in the context of justification. Indeed, to the extent that the reasoning procedures in question cannot be set out as proper arguments, they constitute indistinct intuitive operations escaping rational control. Far from playing a positive role in legal argument, the alleged nonlogical modes of reasoning can be viewed as weaknesses.

Heller rightly opposes attempts to clarify the concept of legal analogy with the aid of such obscure concepts as "legal similarity", "the spirit of the law", and the like. However, his own analysis suffers from a heavy dependence on different obscure concepts, often veiled by plausible wording. Thus, when he asserts that the objective will of the legislator should be discovered through social valuation, this seems at first sight to be an acceptable view. But, for Heller, social valuation depends on the aforementioned "axiological deliberation" and on "thought relating to the matter", and not, as it should, on adequate confirmation by sound sociological research, making use, in particular, of the statistical method. Heller, in placing legal analogical argument in the "metalogical sphere" (82), accords preference to intuition over research.

Is a parallel norm enforceable? Schematically, if the law stipulates that consequence x follows from the conjunction of assumptions a, b, and c, does it also follow from the conjunction of a, b, and d? This question confronts the judge who employs the analogical argument. Heller's claim that the calculus of probabilities is irrelevant to the problem is not unequivocal. He is right insofar as he refers to the impossibility of deriving the parallel norm from a few premises only, i. e., in the schematic case, from the original norm stipulating that a, b, and c warrant x and from the meaning rules for c and d: probabilistic calculations are indeed of no avail here. However, neither the majority of jurists nor Heller himself understand the analogical argument in this manner. To establish their conclusions by analogy, lawyers do not refrain from considering any reason that seems relevant, including sociological as well as methodological reasons. In practice today such arguments are carried out in an indistinct manner; they lack explicit formulation, and the arguer has no clear awareness of the total sum of data and background knowledge that pragmatically "supports" his conclusion. Under such circumstances there is, of course, little room for calculation. But the actual situation is not necessarily final. In principle, the rationalization of the legal and paralegal domain may be seen to involve the employment of appropriate mathematical, in particular statistical methods.

This point escapes Heller, who makes a given analogy depend on the "valuation of the substantive meaning" of the data, on the examination of the "sense" and "internal configuration" of the law, on "argumentation that no longer belongs to logic" (89), and the like. To the extent that he intends to describe the existing situation and in particular to emphasize that legal analogical argument does not in fact constitute a primarily logical operation today, his account is on the whole acceptable. However, there is not doubt that he regards the nonlogical elements of legal argument as in principle its positive elements.

Yet, paradoxically, his position, in a way, is less opposed to the rationalization of law than it would seem at first. Indeed, there are two faces to the allegedly nonlogical reasoning which he discusses but fails to analyze rightly. On the one hand, what he seems to mean is a kind of intuitive reasoning in which the arguer's awareness of the conclusion is accompanied by a striking feeling of evidence. On the other hand, however, he occasionally expresses the view that the modes of consideration and deliberation in question can and should be improved by the explicit formulation of implicit premises. He does not seem to have realized that the two characteristics he ascribes to legal argument — i.e. its radically intuitive, nonlogical nature and the improvability of its rational quality through the formulation of implicit premises — are to a large extent incompatible. Moreover, his insistence on the practical implications of the latter characteristic harmonizes well with the requirement for the rationalization of legal argument with the aid of appropriate inductive methods. These internal strains in Heller's position are due to his failure to draw a clear distinction between what exists in actual fact and what is desirable and possible in principle, as well as to his failure to envisage the prima facie inductive nature of legal argument and to admit the suitability of mathematical statistics to legal psychosociology.

3. The Empirical Nature of Legal Confirmation

The second chapter in the main part of Heller's book is a discussion of "legal analogy as axiological law finding". Heller begins this chapter by putting forward two complementary theses. The first is that law does not have a "purely logical" or "purely conceptual" nature. This view is not problematic: a legal system, inasmuch as it applies to society, is an empirical system, not a pure one. The second thesis is that law is essentially an axiological field and as such involves the nonempirical cognitive activity of valuation. This, as it stands, does not seem acceptable. The concepts of value and valuation require clarification. Their proper analysis links them to volitionary factors in society and to prescriptive elements in language. Law involves valuation inasmuch as it is intended to express the effective social will regarding certain aspects of society. Only in this sense can it be maintained that "the legal norms contain anticipated value judgments about legal cases which are to be decided according to them" (144). But this is not to say that law strays beyond the empirical sphere. A priori guarantees for value judgments are impossible, and all valuation within a legal system requires empirical support.

Heller, however, appears to relate the dependence on valuation to a supraempirical sphere of validity. Though it is true, in a sense, that "the application of the law does not represent an exclusively cognitive operation of thought, but rather is a *willed* decision" (103), such a decision requires empirical, especially sociological support; introspective volitional evidence is not enough, since it is not the individual will of the judge that is determinant, but the general will, which can be scientifically studied. In particular, the interpretation of legal terms is subject to empirical control. Heller rightly insists on the distinction between the legal and the extralegal meanings of explicit legal terms. But he is mistaken insofar as he holds that substantive questions of interpretation can be decided on the basis of nonempirical criteria. For example, was a reported accident in the mountains a "guiltless accident", in the sense of some appropriate legal rule? Should a leashed fox brought into a grocery shop be considered a "dog" in order to make a certain rule applicable? Answers to such questions will not be weighed, in the final analysis, on the basis of abstract scales of values, but according to their conformity to the manifestations of the effective will. Thus, in the case of the fox it is hygiene which forms the decisive factor, as Heller himself remarks. But how should this be understood? Clearly enough, the judge has sufficient empirical acquaintance with both the society in which he lives and its legislators in order to know that the interdiction against bringing dogs into a grocery shop is not meant to refer to dogs as such but only to dogs insofar as they are noxious with respect to food. Moreover, he is sufficiently versed in the elements of empirical science in order to know that foxes are similarly noxious. Accordingly, he rules that the legal analogy holds. To the extent that all his findings are well confirmed, his decision is a good one, and the interdiction, generalized to include foxes, is considered to be a just, well-founded ruling.

To point, as Heller does, to the difficulty of determining the exact term of imprisonment in a given case is also of no avail as support for his axiologistic thesis. Precise rational sentencing is indeed very complicated, inasmuch as it depends on many parameters which cannot be easily disentangled. The precise sentence is therefore intuitively determined; if the judge has both a sound social intuition and sufficient experience, such a method is likely to be satisfactory in practice. But with respect to the ideal of perfected adjudication the intuitive method is only a lesser evil. The rationalization of legislation and adjudication may be seen to involve the furtherance of both the empirical control of law and its systematic formalization; it has certainly nothing to do with the fostering of nonlogical and supraempirical thinking.

As has already been remarked, certain parts of Heller's argument suggest that his position is not purely aprioristic, but rather constitutes a paradoxical blend of apriorism and empiricism. Indeed, he emphasizes now, correctly of course, that the meaning of legal rules and the force of the underlying valuations change with time. He recognizes that the validity of the axiological inference depends on changing social conditions, on legal precedents, and on the subjective will of the legislator. Thus it appears that he does not deny the need for empirical confirmation of the judicial conclusion. But what are the specific nonempirical, axiological criteria of the rational force of the inference? He provides no clear reply to this question, which is so crucial to his main position. He explains, to be sure, that analogical reasoning in law involves the perception of "axiological equivalence" between the relevant states of affairs, but this is hardly more than an empty phrase as long as the criteria for the recognition of such equivalence have not been determined. In order to bring out the specific axiological nature of the equivalence, Heller insists that it cannot be determined through a "purely external" comparison of the states of affairs, but only through their valuation. What he takes to be the supraempirical character of legal analogy is in fact its essentially prescriptive character. For example, in order to establish the analogy between a fox and a dog with respect to the interdiction against bringing them into a grocery shop, an exhaustive descriptive analysis of these two animals, including their hygienic aspects, is not sufficient: a prescriptive finding is also required, viz. the interdiction against bringing noxious animals into a grocery shop. *Pace* Heller, the "axiological equivalence" cannot be nonempirically perceived in any "spiritual act" of abstract valuation. Moreover, the "axiological equivalence" — the counterpart, in fact, of Klug's "essential similarity" — can by no means be regarded as constituting the basis of analogy, for it is established only as a *result* of a cogent analogical argument.

It is worth developing the last point in some detail. The opposition between the logicians' and the jurists' analogical inference is relevant here. In logic, Heller points out, from a partial correspondence between states of affairs, their complete legal congruence is only problematically inferred, whereas the axiological inference provides certainty: "The axiological mode of consideration aims precisely at the establishment of the equivalence of two or more legal cases that are to be compared. All the rest is then a matter of logical inference: legally equivalent states of affairs entail equal legal consequences; states of affairs *A* and *B* are legally equivalent; so, they entail equal legal consequences" (118). Heller explains that the logicians' problematic analogical inference is only tentative : it constitutes the initial stage of the entire argument and is subsequently replaced by the conclusive axiological inference. The latter is "an *aliud* which does not evolve exclusively according to formal laws of thought, but the results of which again create a condition of departure for the application of formal laws of thought and thus ensure that in the logical constructions built upon them the formal structure of the analogical inference is entirely eliminated" (119).

This analysis must be rejected as inadequate and confused. The distinction between the tentative and the improved analogical argument can be correctly represented as concerning (1) the short but explicit argument in which the parallel norm is "induced" with almost vanishing inductive support, from the original norm and the meaning rules for the homologous terms and (2) the enthymematic argument in which the parallel norm, often accompanied by a striking feeling of evidence, is intuitively "inferred" from all the relevant data, both legal and extralegal, of which the arguer has only a fragmentary and indistinct awareness at the time of drawing his prima facie rational and inductive conclusion. Heller rightly regards the former of these arguments, which he calls "analogical in the logical sense", as a provisional, merely heuristic means of reasoning, the role of which is to suggest a possible conclusion for the latter argument. However, as has already been remarked, he does not clearly realize that the transition from the first argument to the second primarily involves a vast extension of the set of "premises" which becomes largely indistinct and therefore necessitates intuition. He misconceives this transition as primarily involving an essential improvement of the apprehension of the premises and conclusion, the "mode of consideration" of which he regards as changing from logical to "metalogical" and from tentative to conclusive.

What, in fact, is inferred in the main stage of the legal analogical argument is not any sort of "axiological equivalence", but a generalization encompassing both the original norm and the projected parallel norm. The latter is then derived from the generalization, whereas the assertion of the legal equivalence of the cases is a *metalegal* statement of the legal finding obtained. Consequently, the syllogistic argument, which Heller considers an essential complement of the axiological inference, is metalegal. As quoted above, this argument is: "Legally equivalent states of affairs entail equal legal consequences; states of affairs A and B are legally equivalent; so, A and B entail equal legal consequences". The major premise of this syllogism is analytic, and the acceptance of the minor premise depends on the prior acceptance of the conclusion. Hence, this syllogism can by no means serve as an authentic creative stage in analogical reasoning.

Thus, once again, the question arises as to the nature and structure of the axiological inference itself, of that "*aliud* which does not evolve exclusively according to formal laws of thought". It is precisely this major link in Heller's analysis, located between the preliminary heuristic step and the plain metalegal deduction, that remains a mystery. Since the point is central and decisive, it is worth illustrating. In the example of the noxious animals, the tentative argument is this: it is forbidden to bring a dog into a grocery shop; a dog, among other properties, has the properties A, B, C; a fox too, among other properties, has the properties A, B, C; so, it is perhaps forbidden to bring a fox into a grocery shop. The terminal syllogism here is: legally equivalent states of affairs entail the same legal consequences; the bringing of a dog into a grocery shop and the bringing of a fox into a grocery shop are legally equivalent; so, both entail the same legal consequences. But what is the central link, i. e. the allegedly nonlogical axiological "consideration" by means of which the legal equivalence of the two animals can be conclusively established? Heller casually remarks that hygiene is the determining factor. The following reasoning is thus suggested: it is forbidden to bring a noxious animal into a grocery shop; a fox is a noxious animal; therefore, it is forbidden to bring a fox into a grocery shop. This, however, is a plain syllogism. While its minor premise is a statement of fact, its major premise constitutes an interpretative paraphrase of the original norm, in which "dog" is construed as "noxious animal". The confirmation of both premises is essentially empirical and calls for inductive arguments. The special "axiological foundation" which, according to Heller, is alone capable of granting the required "legal certainty" to the conclusion of a legal analogical argument, escapes all attempt at identification and analysis: the alleged nonlogical and nonempirical "*aliud*" appears simply not to be there.

Conclusion and Supplementary Observations

Comparison of the views discussed so far reveals basic similarities no less than basic differences. All four authors — Klug, Engisch, Simitis, and Heller — are united in the opinion that law is a domain of knowledge. Accordingly, they disregard the deontic character of legal logic. They do not deny the dependence of law on its social background, and they sometimes even emphasize its links with "life". Nevertheless, they tend to regard legal confirmation as a matter of nonempirical cognition. All four authors agree that legal argument is rational.

On this common background differences of opinion about the nature and scope of legal argument and legal logic stand out boldly. Klug takes legal argument to be formal-deductive and leaves teleological considerations outside the scope of legal logic. In Engisch's broad conception legal logic includes both "material logic" and applied formal logic. Simitis holds that legal argument and legal logic are nonformal. Heller, who refuses to recognize nonformal logic, distinguishes within the domain of law between logical and hence formal argument, and axiological argument, which he considers to be outside the province of logic.

These differences of opinion, which should be regarded as both terminological and substantive, derive from erroneous considerations and deficient analyses, the result, to a large extent, of adherence to an outdated methodology. The authors under review do not distinguish between the properties of reasoning as it is practised in fact and its rational nature in principle. Insofar as they consider induction, statistics, or probability, they reject them as improper for legal argument. Empirical data is not regarded, as it should be, as providing inductive support for law, but as the object of such special axiological or teleological "considerations" as contribute to quasi-certain legal knowledge. Intuitive reasoning, whether called "teleological", "material-logical", or "nonlogical", is taken to be rational, although nothing clear is said about the nature, rules, or criteria of rationality. The properties of law as an applied system are thought to need special emphasis, and the nonpure character of the field is taken as testifying to the essentially nonformal character of its arguments. Briefly, one finds a substantial lack of clarity in the views of the German authors on the nature of applied theoretical systems, as well as much confusion between the context of discovery and the context of justification, between logical and methodological matters, between theory and metatheory, and so on.

The following supplementary remarks concern intuitive argument and legal confirmation, in turn.

In view of the prominence of the intuitive character of legal argument in practice and in relation to the ambiguity of such terms as "argument", "premise", "conclusion", and "logic", which are used either in the heuristic or in the genuinely logical sense, it may be enlightening to point out a more radical and somewhat puzzling ambiguity in the expression "intuitive argument". The ambiguity is that a so-called intuitive argument is, or is conceivable as, both an intuitive "argument" and an "intuitive" argument, i. e. both an intrinsically intuitive act and a genuine, though nonformalized and enthymematic argument. As a very simple example, consider the case of a woman who, having heard somebody approaching, says: "It is my husband." She can be said to have *intuited* in what she has heard that it is her husband who is approaching, and she can also be said to have *inferred* this *in a flash* from what she has heard. In the former account no argument at all is meant, whereas in the latter account an enthymematic argument is alluded to, involving among its implicit premises some such assertion as: "Whenever on previous occasions I heard similarly sounding steps, it was usually my husband who was approaching." It might be objected at this point that unless the woman has kept a record of her previous experiences and knows, in particular, the exact numbers of the correct and incorrect past statements in question, the formalization of her inference will be frustrated by the indefiniteness of the corresponding inductive support. This objection is met by remarking that the formalization of an inductive argument need not involve precise quantification. That roughly estimated inductive support is nonetheless formal in nature is clearly illustrated by the foregoing example, in which the premises, "a large proportion of S are P" and "x is S", formally support the conclusion, "x is P."

The arguments framed in the actual process of legal reasoning combine some explicit premises and conclusions with some latent links. The way of improving such aborted, fragmentary arguments depends on how their latent links are viewed: if they are seen as involving intrinsically intuitive acts (of valuation or the like), the arguer will be advised to try to concentrate more intensely, so as to intuit more acutely; if, on the other hand, they are seen as involving genuinely logical but undeveloped stages of argument, the advice will be: try to unravel those links so as to bring in some further explicit premises. Both viewpoints and both methods can be adopted conjointly. What cannot be properly said, however, is that the links in question are intrinsically intuitive qua genuinely logical, or vice versa. Nor can this be properly said of an entire argument. A fine-grained mosaic may be misperceived as grey when composed in fact of black and white elements. The (nontrivially construed) claim that legal argument, though rational, is essentially nonformal seems largely due to a similar illusion. (The trivial point that legal argument qua an intrinsically intuitive process cannot be considered formal is of course not called in question.)

Legal confirmation, inductive in principle, is highly intuitive in practice. Both legislation and judicial interpretation depend on three kinds of grounds — viz., legal grounds supplied by the existing system, methodological grounds, and empirical grounds regarding the pertinent aspects of the general will. The first two kinds mentioned are kinds of *legalistic grounds;* they may overlap inasmuch as practical legal methodology is partly governed by law. Whereas legalistic grounds are proper to warrant the *prima facie legitimacy* of a decision, only empirical, *paralegal grounds* are capable of establishing its *soundness.* Grounds of the latter kind are provided by primarily psychosociological information which may contain diverse, intricately entangled, and largely overlapping elements — political, economical, historical, educational, ethical, administrative, medical, technological, and so on. The intricacy of the problem of legal confirmation is due to a great extent to the complexity, indefiniteness, and variability of the effective general will. The confirmation of a judgment, moreover, combines data concerning the particular case with the aforementioned kinds of grounds. To provide appropriate methods for adapting all such crude supporting material to the purpose of rational legislation, interpretation, and judgment, is a major task of legal methodology. On the theoretical level, this task involves the construction of an adequate system of inductive logic. It is true that, in a sense, the progress of legal psychosociology is capable of alleviating the difficulty of the problem: as paralegal knowledge relevant to legal confirmation grows more comprehensive and more precise, it may become less difficult to devise an adequately sharp apparatus for the assessment of inductive support. It must be noted, however, that the progress of legal psychosociology appears itself to depend on the development of such anticipated inductive methods as the progress in question would permit to dispense with or simplify. This somewhat paradoxical situation is accounted for by the fact that the interrelations between law and legal psychosociology are so intimate that legal logic must, indeed, embrace the entire paralegal domain together with the legal system proper.

The confirmation of a legal rule, under an assumed or tentative interpretation, naturally involves statements about the direct utility of the rule as well as about the expected indirect effects of its enforcement and the desirability of those effects, according to standards of utility and desirability conformable to the general will. The confirming information may, for example, contain statements to the effect that the legislator intended the interpretation in question; that specified majorities of such and such official bodies or public associations, or specified proportions of the entire population or of some sections of it, or certain noted personalities, either favor or oppose the rule as envisaged or some anticipated effects of its enforcement[9]. A difficulty arises, however: statements of fact appear *formally* unsuitable to support a prescriptive rule. There are two ways to solve this problem of the *logical gap between fact and law*. One way would be to replace the rule under confirmation by the factual statement to the effect that its enforcement would be conformable to the general will. The alternative way would be — roughly speaking — to replace every factual statement about an attitude of approval or disapproval toward a state of affairs by an appropriately weighted prescription-like or optative sentence in which the prescriptive operator would apply to the description of the approved or disapproved state of affairs; the weighting would in principle involve assigning to every such sentence a numerical coefficient, positive or negative, determied on an empirical basis, according to the relevant characteristics of the respective volitional attitudes. Both ways seem virtually equivalent to one another with respect to the research problems, both theoretical and practical, they would involve. In particular, calculations of weighted averages seem, at any

---

9 As is suggested by such examples, suitably elaborated forms of the *teleological argument* and of the *argument from authority* seem to be in place in legal reasoning.

rate, essential to legal confirmation. To be theoretically adequate, the method of weighting must be very complex. Some scant hints are sufficient to bring out the subtlety of the task of devising such methods. For example, it can be seen that, in view of the diversity of the relevant factors, the operations of weighting and averaging must be so devised as to avoid plural reckoning of the same factor. Reiterated averaging on several levels thus appears appropriate. The method of weighting must allow for what is at stake in case of misestimation. A particularly thorny problem is that of combining empirical with legalistic support. In brief, rationalized legal confirmation can be seen to require a thorough acquaintance with the legal system, a vast body of sufficiently elaborate psychosociological information, and adequate mathematical tools, including statistical methods. The most difficult theoretical problems of inductive confirmation, it is worth noting, are not peculiar to law, but are well known to and actively tackled by methodologists of science, both social and natural, and of various fields of action.

The foregoing remarks are not intended as countenancing attempts at a thoroughgoing realization of those theoretical possibilities and requirements to which they point. Effective rational control of the intuitive links in legal reasoning cannot be humanly achieved beyond a certain limit and may, moreover, cease to be worthwhile long before that limit is reached. The very characteristics of the general will that render legal confirmation so complex in theory facilitate its execution in practice. As actually performed, legal confirmation is extremely selective. It is largely governed by current routine procedures or explicit legal rules, including such stereotyped principles — ethical, ideological, and so on — as often make it possible, when used as premises, to derive a legal conclusion deductively. The soundness of such premises can of course be called in question unless they have been adequately confirmed. As long, however, as the operative routine procedures, rules, and principles are not seriously challenged, they contribute to the apparent smoothness and reliability of legal confirmation. In those very frequent cases in which rough estimates are sufficient to determine a decision, intuition can surely be trusted, the more so as comparative rather than absolute evaluations are normally required in adjudication. In many other cases, especially when relatively little would be at stake in case of misjudgment — and hence quite generally in the determination of precise details within secure limits, as in sentencing — arbitrary decision may seem preferable to elaborate deliberation. A very partial explicit use of the available relevant information and recource to such rough and fragmentary inductive methods are those involved in random selection of juries, decision by voting, averaging of proposals, and trial and error, prove satisfactorily workable.

Between a perpetual status quo and unrestricted attempts at thorough formalization there seems to be, from the practical point of view, enough scope for a judicious project of rationalization of the domain of law. Nevertheless, in view of the apparent adequacy of the actual modes of legal confirmation, it is possible to argue that any such undertaking is superfluous. It would also be possible to argue that, from the philosophical point of view, both the claim and the regulative principle of the rationality of legal argument are worth relinquishing altogether. This, at any rate, seems to be an intelligible and tenable position. But to regard legal argument or decision as rational without being able to point, as the legal inductivist does, to a general way of bringing out and analyzing the presumed rationality is gratuitous if not senseless. Whoever claims that there is such a way, other than that of inductive logic, and that there are, in particular, nonformal standards of the rationality of adjudication, must elucidate his claim. That attempts at such elucidation involve either a misconception of the formalistic position or some substantively mistaken views will be the main conclusion of the present inquiry.

Part II

The Belgian Discussion

Introduction

A group of lawyers and logicians, headed by Chaïm Perelman and Paul Foriers and forming the legal section of the Belgian Centre National de Recherches de Logique, has been promoting discussion on and research into legal logic since 1953. As is attested by Foriers, "it all began in August 1953, at the time of the International Colloquy in Logic which was held in Brussels", when "in a very animated and occasionally even passionate debate certain logicians, who tended to see the formal sciences as a model to be followed by all other sciences, were ranged against certain philosophers and scholars, who maintained that this outlook could not withstand confrontation with the methods by which those fields really develop" ([22], p. 23). In the part of the Colloquy devoted to "Proof in Law", papers on legal reasoning were read by Norberto Bobbio, from Italy, and by Marie-Thérèse Motte, of the Belgian group, and there was a general discussion. A brief account of these papers and of the discussion will now be given. (See [73].)

In his paper entitled "Introductory Considerations on the Jurists' Reasoning" [06], Bobbio distinguished between two types of investigation which, although distinct in principle, are closely interrelated in the jurists' practice: theoretical investigation which requires deductive "arguments of the logical and systematic type", and empirical investigation which requires inductive "arguments of the historical and teleological type" (81). Investigation of the former type aims at the systematic development of the legal system and involves operations of theoretical construction besides those of deduction proper. Investigation of the latter type aims at unravelling the pragmatic circumstances of legislation and is undertaken with a view to determining the legislator's intention in every case of theoretical perplexity. Investigation of either type is "demonstrative". The jurist's reasoning thus differs radically from that of the moralist, who has recourse to a persuasive rhetoric, involving "arguments of a suggestive character which escape the domain of logic and of science in general" (71). The jurist replaces valuation by judgments of legal validity. Occasional confusion notwithstanding, Bobbio tends to distinguish between the logical and the pragmatic aspects of legal argument. His analysis points to the prescriptive nature of legal rules and to the prima facie inductive aspect of their interpretation. However, his recognition of the empirical nature of legal confirmation seems only partial: declaredly influenced by Kelsen's legalistic doctrine of justice, Bobbio tends to underestimate the need for continuous reinterpretation of legal rules on the basis of extensive paralegal information reaching beyond the circumstances of legislation.

In her paper entitled "The Rigor of Reasoning in Legal Debates" [55], Mlle. Motte distinguished four kinds of courtroom reasoning which differ in specific "degrees of rigor", viz.: (1) deductive reasoning, the simplicity and rarity of which points to basic differences between the legal system and "the deductive systems studied by the logician" (86); (2) inductive reasoning, used only to establish factual statements; (3) interpretative reasoning, which is "metatheoretical" in that it "compares, estimates, develops systems" (89) and which may, in particular, involve analogical extension; and (4) rhetorical reasoning, used to convince the judge. This analysis, carried out mainly on the level of descriptive pragmatics, suffers from the vagueness of the term "degree of rigor" and from the confusion of logical with procedural formality, of the rational force of argument with soundness, of argument with heuristic procedures, methodological operations, and psychological influence.

In the general discussion (of which only a scant account is here given, without critical comments), Perelman distinguished between rhetoric (of which he is reputed to be the renovator) and logic as follows: "We propose to give the name of 'rhetoric' to the study of *all* forms of argumentation, and we oppose it to logic which would be the study of formalizable and mechanizable and, from this point of view, impersonal demonstration" (93). Yehoshua Bar-Hillel, from Israel, complained of "the rapid deterioration which the word 'logic' is undergoing nowadays" (98); referring to the question "whether argumentation by jurists is essentially different from argumentation by natural scientists", he pointed to the fundamentally imperative and hence "indexical" or context-dependent character of legal rules. Paul Bernays, from Switzerland, pointed out that logic is primarily a matter of consistency, that law is methodologically similar to science, and that it depends on "a philosophical science of law" which he charges with "the appraisal of the positive principles according to the standard of justice" (101). A. J. Ayer, from England, distinguished between the question of the lawfulness of a legal decision and that of the legitimacy of the law upon which it rests. He characterized the latter question as "purely a matter for decision" and the former as "partly a question for a decision, partly a question of fact", and maintained that "in both cases it is hopeless to try to formalize the reasons for the decisions". He therefore concluded that "the only way out of our problems is to study what is actually done" (104). Robert Feys, of the Belgian group, argued that "legal logic should enter a metatheoretical way rather than undertake the development of a calculus of legal modalities" (105).

In 1956, several members of the Belgian group published a collective study, entitled "Essays in Legal Logic, Apropos of the Usufruct of a Debt" [15], in which legal argumentation is examined as exemplified in an actual discussion of a definite legal problem — "whether the usufructuary of a debt has the right to receive the principal which has become due, without the consent of the owner of the principal" (261 c). The summary account which follows is limited to considerations about the reasoning exemplified and to conclusions about legal reasoning in general, whereas the specifically legal discussion is disregarded[1]. The study, as published, consists of a preface, three central essays, and a concluding essay.

The preface, by Robert Feys [18], attests to variations in the basic terminology within the Belgian group. The term "logic" is now used in the comprehensive sense in which Perelman used the term "rhetoric" in 1953, i. e. as equivalent to "theory of argumentation"; the term "logic" in Perelman's narrow sense of 1953 is

---

1 Consequently, this account may appear somewhat obscure. It is given both as historical background and for subsequent reference. It is more likely to be found comprehensible if reread after pt. II. For a fuller account of the "Essays", see my article [32].

replaced by the term "formal logic" whereas "rhetoric" now desig-
nates that part of the theory of argumentation which is neither formal nor inductive logic. Feys's brief remarks are impaired by the
use of the obscure concept of "specific rigor" and by the confusion
of logic with heuristics and methodology and of argument with
persuasion; these deficiencies were already noted above in the 1953
paper of Marie-Thérèse Motte.

Mlle. Motte is the author of the first essay [56]. To resolve the
legal problem at issue, she proposes the interpretation of a certain
rule of the Belgian code as an analogical extension of another rule
of that code. She considers her attempted solution to be an illustration of "metatheoretical" reasoning which, though not dependent
on "the old formal logic" (262 c), possesses a high degree of rigor
inasmuch as it involves a kind of "self-asserting" extension (265 c)
and "quasi-formal" analogy, resting on "a veritable isomorphism"
(264 b). These notions are due to a misconception: what are regarded as "nonformal" or "quasi-formal" modes of reasoning are in
fact methodological operations, guided by heuristic principles and
involving short deductive arguments.

In the next essay [21], Paul Foriers examines three legal doctrines with a view to resolving the legal problem. He finds that two
of them primarily involve "compelling" arguments the conclusions
of which are not acceptable. In representing the third doctrine as
involving such rhetorical reasoning as corrects the unacceptable
"results of a compelling logic" (270 b), he confounds the validity of
a deductive argument with the soundness of its conclusion. The
"rhetorical reasoning" to which he refers appears to consist of
various operations, such as pointing to laws and to their properties,
giving a name to a concept, analyzing legal relations, and proposing an amendment of a law, which are not purely argumentative in
themselves but are interlaced with arguments the formal nature of
which is not denied by Foriers.

In his "Reflections on a Tool" [10], R. Dekkers sets forth a modified version of a legal doctrine of which he is a coinventor. Insofar as the analysis of legal reasoning is concerned, this essay seems
less open to objection than the others; in particular, it avoids con-
founding logical with pragmatical matters to too great an extent.

In the concluding essay, entitled "Problems of Legal Logic" [59],
Chaïm Perelman, purporting to single out "the peculiarities of legal
reasoning as they appear to someone who is chiefly familiar with

formal logic" (272c), points to some characteristics which law in fact shares with other empirical fields. Under the ancillary influence of the confusion of the rational force of argument with its soundness and of the substantively legal context with the methodological and the evolutionary, he misrepresents the dissimilarity of law with respect to pure logicomathematical fields as involving a special, "rhetorical" kind of logic.

In sum, insofar as the authors of the "Essays" intended to illustrate the allegedly nonformal nature of legal argument, they cannot be said to have made their point.

Foriers reports that in 1958[2] a Colloquy in logic, organized by the Belgian Center in Louvain, assembled "formalistic logicians, philosophers of law, and lawyers. The clearest results of that colloquy were to convince the members of the Center of the inopportuneness of all premature attempt at formalization" ([22], p. 27). A summary of the colloquy was published in Logique et Analyse, the organ of the Center. A discussion of the problem of the specificity of legal logic developed subsequently in a series of articles which appeared in the same periodical. It is to this discussion, as conducted in Logique et Analyse from 1959 to 1962, that the main body of pt. II is devoted. Sect. 1 deals with the interventions of Perelman, and of B. H. Kazemier (from the Netherlands), in the Louvain Colloquy. Both consider legal logic "specific". Sect. 2 deals with an article by Georges Kalinowski, in which this Polish logician (presently living in France) denies the specificity of legal logic. A second article by the same author is here divided into two parts which are discussed successively in sects. 3 and 4. Sect. 5 is devoted to an article by Robert Feys and Marie-Thérèse Motte, in which they give a rather evasive answer to the question at issue, whereupon Perelman, in an article which is dealt with in sect. 6, reaffirms the specificity of legal logic. In this respect he is followed, on the whole, by Jan Gregorowicz, from Poland, an article by whom is discussed in two parts, in sects. 7 and 8[3].

---

2 In the same year there appeared [63], the main founding work of "the new rhetoric", conceived as "nonformal logic". See [64].

3 With only a few exceptions, the quotations in pt. II have been specially translated from the French. The exceptions are: the previous brief quotations from Bernays, which have been translated from the German, and those from Bar-Hillel and from Ayer, whose interventions were made and recorded in English. As a point of translation, it is worth noting that

1. *Perelman and Kazemier on the Logical Specificity of Law*

In the published summary of the Louvain Colloquy of 1958 [37], we read:

> In addressing himself to Mr. Bar-Hillel, who in his intervention had declared himself unable to grasp any difference between legal definition and definition in the other sciences, Mr. Perelman, in order to elucidate the specificity of law in this domain, distinguished between three types of systems: (1) *the given formal system:* congealed, it is not subject to modification; therefore, some of its problems are insoluble; (2) *the natural or technical sciences:* in this domain, the scientist, in order to solve a difficulty, seeks to modify the system; however, there is no *urgent* necessity for this attempt to succeed; (3) *law:* in all lawsuits, the judge *must* decide; he has no right to leave the controversy in suspense, alleging that the law is not clear. The means for deciding must therefore be given to him. Hereby the judge, more than the scientist or the mathematician, will be master of his techniques of reasoning, and it is thus that he collaborates in the formation of law. As he cannot escape the given legal system, he has recourse to reasoning by analogy. But it is not enough for him to decide: his decision must also be *reasonable*. He therefore introduces some techniques of argumentation into legal reasoning that are not altogether specific to law and are likewise used in the sciences in the making. The demonstration of the decisive element in legal practice thus leads us to ascertaining this central fact: the primary impossibility of separating will and intelligence in the analysis of law (39).

Perelman's observations can be seen to suffer from the confusion of logical with pragmatic concepts. The context makes it clear that "the given formal system" is a plainly logical concept: what is meant is a system given by its axiomatic basis. "Congealed", on the other hand, is a pragmatic characteristic: a system is said to be congealed as long as its basis is not altered. Perelman is wrong in maintaining that the property of congealment differentiates mathematical from scientific and legal systems. Indeed, scientific systems, such as Newton's mechanics or Einstein's theory of relativity, can certainly be subjected to the proviso that their basis should not be altered during a period of investigation, and this of course applies likewise to any "given", i. e. definite, legal system. On the other hand, purely

---

the French word *"raisonnement"* has been rendered as "reasoning" or as "argument", according to context. Indeed, it is used to refer to argument as involving some premises and a conclusion, whereas the French word *"argument"* is more often used to refer to arguments in the sense of reasons advanced in support of a thesis.

mathematical or logical systems may be dealt with for the purpose of alteration and especially with a view to extending, splitting, or uniting systems.

Regarding the difference between the insolubility of certain mathematical problems and the solubility of scientific and legal difficulties, Perelman seems unaware of the ambiguities of "problem" or "difficulty" and of "solubility". In ("congealed") mathematics, the so-called decision problems concern "decision" in a logical sense, and solubility too is here a purely logical concept. Scientists and lawyers, on the other hand, are mainly concerned with problems of extension, with difficulties of application, and with solubility primarily in the pragmatic sense, especially so whenever the difficulty is eliminated by the judge's decision. Though "congealed" empircal systems are not, indeed, typical domains for investigating logical decision problems, such investigation is not excluded in principle. On the other hand, problems of extension may be successfully solved in mathematics as well as in science and in law. Problems of empirical application, to be sure, are not dealt with in purely mathematical systems: this is precisely what distinguishes pure mathematics from both empirical science and law. This manifest difference, however, cannot be accounted for in terms of "congealment" and "solubility".

The suggested comparison of law with empirical science seems no more cogent. Again, in the sciences as well as in law, certain difficulties, in particular difficulties of application, can no doubt be eliminated by an alteration of the system. However, the view that the logical specificity of law with respect to science can be accounted for by reference to the "urgency" with which solutions are required does not seem sound. Moreover, the very assumption that law differs considerably from science in this respect seems questionable. Just as jurists and judges are often expected to remove the lacunae of law promptly, so scientists too are urged to activate research. Scientific solutions, in point of fact, are not always quickly forthcoming; but it happens likewise that legal proceedings are of long duration. The questions of fact on which judicial decisions normally depend may be very intricate. A verdict of "not guilty" due to insufficient evidence ("the benefit of the doubt") is not so much the result of reasoning as of the relinquishment of further inquiry. Specifically legal (not plainly factual) investigations, too, can be lengthy and can lead to varying conclusions in several instances.

The confusion of logical with pragmatic elements is again involved in the claim that the urgency of decision in law determines specifically legal "techniques of reasoning" and "means for deciding". Accelerated scientific inquiry differs in many respects from inquiry at a normal rate; similarly, accelerated legal proceedings, e. g. under special military law, differ considerably from proceedings at a normal rate. But such pragmatic differences are not relevant to the logical aspect of reasoning, i. e. to the question of the rational force of arguments in the context of justification. Neither science nor law possesses a special inferential apparatus for urgent reasoning. Hence, even if the claim about the greater urgency of legal reasoning were admitted, it would make no difference regarding the nature of legal as compared with scientific argument. It is a mistake to hold that the pragmatic circumstances of discovery bear upon the rational force of justification. Nobody would think of speaking — in ordinary, nonmetaphorical language — about rapid validity, urgent relevance, or accelerated justice. Perelman, indeed, eschews such an explicit paradox in remarking that the judge's decision must be "reasonable". But his point remains nevertheless basically pragmatic.

The remark that the judge, to ensure the reasonableness of his decision, uses "techniques of argumentation that are not altogether specific to law and are likewise used in the sciences in the making" considerably attenuates the main claim about the difference between law and science. Implicit in this remark seems to be the view that a legal system is not as stable as a mature and well-confirmed scientific system, but rather resembles a young science in its dynamism. This view in itself seems quite acceptable, but is no more relevant to the question of the logical differences between law and science than are the former remarks about the obligation to decide and the corresponding "techniques of reasoning". As regards "the primary impossibility of separating will and intelligence in the analysis of law", Perelman's intention does not seem sufficiently clear. It can perhaps be assumed that "will" here represents the pragmatic elements of law and "intelligence" its logical elements. Insofar as this assumption is correct, the quoted expression can be seen as epitomizing Perelman's basic error regarding legal logic.

Further on in the published summary of the Louvain Colloquy we read:

After a brief intervention by Mr. Bar-Hillel who declared himself incapable of distinguishing what differentiates the situation of the judge from that of the scientist, Mr. Kazemier attempted to clarify this difference by contrasting the nature of the judge's decision with the nature of the physicist's decision. In a lawsuit, the judge must decide and he is not free to do this *indifferently* in favour of either party; his decision becomes integrated in a legal system; the judge considers such a system as a whole, but an *open* whole, and seeks to demarcate what should be added to it. The specificity of decision in law appears therefore when an element should be *added* to a given system (40).

Kazemier's remark is not clear. It seems to refer to the contrast between law qua undergoing a continuous process of formation and mature science qua constituting a flawless framework for smooth deductions. Consequently, his remark too must be construed as concerning the methodological and heuristic rather than the logical specificity of law. Yet, Kazemier seems to be impressed much more than Perelman by the fiction of a stable science: he ignores "the sciences in the making", in which, no less than in law, decision is required "when an element should be added to a given system" and in which, moreover, the scientist is not free, either, to decide "indifferently" but rather must, like the judge, try to "integrate" his decisions into the "open whole" of the evolving system.

It appears evident that Perelman's and Kazemier's observations ([60], [44]) fail even to establish the claim about the methodological, let alone the logical, specificity of law.

2. *Kalinowski's Denial of the Specificity of Legal Logic*

In his article "Is There a Legal Logic?", 1959 [40], Georges Kalinowski refers to the "Essays in Legal Logic" of 1956 (summarized above). His aim is to inquire whether those essays, in particular that of Marie-Thérèse Motte, provide evidence for the claim that there is a specific legal logic. He concludes that they do not.

Kalinowski distinguishes between "theoretical logic" and "normative logic". He regards them as two parallel versions of logic in general. Theoretical logic consists of logical laws, such as these:

(1) If, for all x, x is f, then a is f.

(2) If all the known essential properties of A resemble the known essential properties of A' and if A, moreover, has the property n, then A' probably has the property n' which resembles the property n of A.

Normative logic, on the other hand, consists of practical rules of reasoning, warranted by the laws of theoretical logic. For instance, in accordance with the foregoing examples we have:

(1′) From the premise "For all x, x is f" the conclusion "a is f" ought to be drawn.

(2′) Whoever admits that all the known essential properties of A' resemble the known essential properties of A and that A, moreover, has the property n, is bound to admit that A' probably has the property n' which resembles the property n of A (49).

As can be seen from the two examples, Kalinowski regards logic in general as applying both to deductive and to inductive reasoning, the latter category comprising analogy. He rejects Mlle. Motte's view that the extension of a legal system is a kind of reasoning, though he admits of course that extension can be justified by reasoning. At any rate, he points out, neither extension nor reasoning by analogy is specific to law. "In our opinion, there is only one logic: logic *tout court* (whether it be conceived in the theoretical or in the normative sense)" (53). Though it is most interesting and useful to investigate the applications of the rules of logic in the various branches of law, "it is vain to try to study legal logic in the proper sense of the word, as it does not exist" (53).

Kalinowski's position seems acceptable in the main. Still, two critical remarks are in place. First, the manner in which nonconclusive argument is presented leaves room for reservations. The wide conception of logic, encompassing inductive logic, is of course sound in principle, but it is impaired by the unqualified use of such obscure expressions as "resemble" or "essential properties" and of such plainly pragmatic expressions as "known properties". Analogy, inasmuch as its primary function is heuristic, is indeed a bad example of logic proper (cf. above, pt. I, ch. 1, sect. 3). Second, "normative logic", though perhaps useful for didactic purposes, seems to lack any deeper philosophical interest. Moreover, the term itself is clearly misleading, since the "normative", i. e. practically prescriptive, aspect of the rules in question is not essential to their logical content.

3. Kalinowski on Interpretation: (i) Authenticity, Meaning, and the Resolution of Contradictions

I now turn to a second article by Kalinowski, entitled "Legal Interpretation, and the Logic of Normative Propositions", which followed the earlier one in the 1959 volume of Logique et Analyse [41][4].

Kalinowski classifies the rules of legal interpretation thus: (1) rules for the determination of the authentic tenor of legal norms, (2) rules for the determination of their meaning, (3) rules for the resolution of inconsistencies, and (4) rules for the elimination of lacunae. In surveying these classes of rules in turn, he attempts to test his claim that there is no specific legal logic[5].

(1) The rules of the first class serve the purpose of establishing, for example, that a certain statute or a certain gazette are authentic sources of law. It is obvious that such rules have hardly anything in common with the logical rules of argument.

(2) The second class comprises rules of verbal interpretation and rules of real interpretation; the former are used to ascertain the "letter" of the law, the latter to unravel its "spirit". Both these sub-classes depend on the rules of legal language, i. e. rules of vocabulary and syntax. Particularly important are the rules for the use of definitions. Other rules serve the purpose of determining the exact meaning of ambiguous or vague terms. The rules of real interpretation are subordinated to a "superior rule of interpretation", which prescribes the principle to which interpretation should conform, such as "equity", "the objective content of the norm", "the legislator's will", or the like. A special rule enjoins that the interpretation of any norm should take into account the norms to which it is related in meaning. Further rules direct the interpreter to the "causes" of the norms — whether external, such as *occasio legis,* or internal, viz. teleological, psychological, historical, etc. — and to the "logical reason" of the law, i. e. to the more general norm from which the law is derived. Kalinowski concludes: "As an outcome of the foregoing analysis,

---

4 Incidentally, "logic of normative propositions" must not be confounded with "normative logic" in the sense of the previous article; indeed, the logical investigation of normative utterances can remain purely "theoretical", as will appear presently.

5 Only the first three classes will be dealt with in this section; the appropriate part of the article will be summed up briefly, then commented upon. The fourth class will be discussed in the next section.

we find that the rules for the determination of the adequate meaning of legal norms are, in general, essentially different from the logical rules of reasoning, although the latter too, in particular the rule of substitution, find application there" (134).

(3) In the third class, several kinds of rules for the resolution of inconsistencies are distinguished. Territorial inconsistencies, i. e. contradictions between norms applying to the same persons in different territories, are resolved according to the rules of private international law. The resolution of temporal inconsistencies is governed by the rule "Lex posterior derogat legi priori"; of hierarchical inconsistencies, by the rule "Lex superior derogat legi inferiori"; of extensional inconsistencies, by the rule "Lex specialis derogat legi generali". These rules are also used to resolve contradictions between common and statutory law. The resolution of the remaining kinds of inconsistencies, in particular of "horizontal" contradictions, is governed by the aforementioned superior principle of interpretation. "In conclusion, one is led to ascertain that these rules, like those examined above, differ essentially from the logical rules of reasoning; however, here too legal interpretation requires the application of certain currently used logical rules of reasoning" (135).

Kalinowski's analysis clearly establishes the practical-methodological character of the rules of legal interpretation. Even when explicitly stated in statutes, rules of legal interpretation are not addressed, as ordinary legal rules are, to the general public, but to those charged with the administration of law. Moreover, they are inessential in principle, in the sense that, although they are necessitated in practice by the imperfections and the dynamic character of the existing systems, they would not be needed in a perfect, unambiguously formulated, consistent, and complete legal system, conformable to a stable social reality. The actual function of rules of legal interpretation is to direct the identification of the existing system and its continuous construction and readjustment. However, Kalinowski rightly implies, identification, construction, and readjustment are not logical operations. To confound the logical rules of argument with the practical rules of interpretation is no less improper than to confound, say, the rules for the specific use of a mechanical device with the rules for its construction, identification, or repair.

Kalinowski also correctly observes, though perhaps with insufficient clarity, that the use of the nonlogical rules of interpretation nevertheless involves logical operations. This is obviously true inasmuch as interpreters of law employ methodological arguments; for example, the premises "a later law abrogates an earlier one with which it is inconsistent" and "law *A* is later than law *B* with which it is inconsistent" entail the conclusion "law *A* abrogates law *B*". Such practical arguments of interpretation must not be confounded with primary legal arguments.

In the second class, the rules of *verbal* interpretation can be regarded as directives for the formulation of legal meaning rules, including equivalential definitions. But, again, though using a meaning rule as a premise is a logical operation, the amending of a deficient meaning rule or the introduction of a new one are not logical but methodological operations. A system with obscure, ambiguous, or exceedingly vague meaning rules is a bad logical instrument: it makes flawless argumentation hardly possible. The rules of *real* interpretation seem to constitute the main part of practical legal methodology: some of them are heuristic rules guiding the elaboration of a definite interpretation for the theoretical formulae of law; others are rules of confirmation. When a certain principle is singled out to serve as the "superior rule of interpretation", no a priori justification can be given for such choice. Kalinowski's analysis thus points to the empirical foundation of rules for the determination of meaning in general. This remark also applies to rules for the resolution of inconsistencies, as well as to rules for the elimination of lacunae.

4. Kalinowski on Interpretation: (ii) The Elimination of Lacunae

The category of rules that serve the purpose of removing lacunae includes those means of interpretation which are generally known as "logical": the two *argumenta a fortiori*, viz. *argumentum a maiori ad minus* and *argumentum a minori ad maius; argumentum a simili ad simile;* and *argumentum a contrario.*

Argumentum a maiori ad minus assumes that there is an implicit obligation, or permission, to do anything that is "less" than what is explicitly imposed, or permitted. For example, if it is explicitly permitted to divulge the proceedings of the public sessions of the parliament in print, then, *a fortiori,* it is implicitly permitted to divulge them orally, as oral anouncement is "less", namely less efficacious, than publication in print. *Argumentum a minori ad maius,* on the other hand, assumes that there is an implicit prohibition to do anything that is "more" than what is explicitly prohibited. For example, if it is forbidden to tread on a lawn, then, *a fortiori,* it is forbidden to tear up the grass, the latter action being a more efficacious way of destroying the lawn than the former.

Kalinowski enumerates the judge's grounds for arguing *a fortiori* as follows: first, a general rule of interpretation which imposes the obligation of eliminating lacunae; second, a superior axiomatic rule of interpretation, such as "interpretation should conform to the public good" or the like (cf. preceding sect. 3); and third, the judge's conviction that the norm obtained by the argument satisfies the superior rule of interpretation. The legislator, in order to draw attention to the most common and typical cases, occasionally formulates a particular norm instead of a more general one. It is precisely the task of *a fortiori* interpretation to pass from the given particular norm to the general one that is implicit in it and then from the latter norm to derive norms similar to the former.

Kalinowski's account of the *argumenta a fortiori,* like his treatment of the rules discussed in the preceeding section, brings out the practical-methodological character of these means of interpretation and the small part that logic plays in them. Yet, his discussion also suffers from certain weaknesses; in particular, it does not provide an adequate analysis of those quantitative or comparative aspects of actions which are estimated as "less" or "more". Such an analysis, instead of merely referring to the "efficacy" of actions, would have to take into account the degree of their danger or harmfulness. Another reservation concerns the legislator's alleged intentional abstention from the formulation of adequately general norms. Indeed, as the formulation of a general norm need not prevent the supplementary indication of the typical cases to which it is meant to apply, it can hardly be seen why the legislator should conceal his "true intention" from those charged with the application of law, thus imposing upon them the easily dispensable task of generalizing (as distinguished from particularizing) interpretation. On the contrary, it seems that a better case can be made out for reducing the indication of more definite cases in the formulation of law: indefinite, highly theoretical rules are more easily applicable to changing social conditions. At any rate, it seems highly desirable that legislators should always attempt to express the entire *ratio legis* according to their "true intention". The rational construction of law should systematically endeavour to reduce the judicial search for "implicit grounds".

Argumentum a simili ad simile, or argument by analogy, is likewise presented as governed by the general obligation of eliminating lacunae and by the superior rule of interpretation. But it is conceived as a kind of genuine argument, in the logical sense. By means of this argument, Kalinowski explains, it is possible to establish a norm similar in content to an explicit norm, provided that the two norms concern situations which are similar in all respects, except that only one of them is covered by an explicit law. The underlying principle is expressed by the well-known maxim: "Ubi eadem legis ratio, ibi eadem legis dispositio."

As in his preceding article (see sect. 2), Kalinowski classifies argument by analogy among the inductive modes of reasoning: he now divides reasoning in general inexhaustively into "deductive, analogical, etc.". The imputation of logical impurity made in sect. 2 also applies in the present context. Kalinowski now appears, in a way, to be even less cautious than before. Indeed, in the first article, analogy concerned situations similar in their "essential properties", whereas now it concerns situations similar "in all respects". Such total resemblance between two situations is obviously a misconception, inasmuch as the situations, not being identical, necessarily differ in some respects. The *ratio legis* that two situations may have in common is a heuristic rather than a logical concept.

Argumentum a contrario can be used, we are told, whenever the word "only", whether explicitly occurring or only assumed, prevents an appeal to analogy with respect to the element to which "only" applies. Two cases are distinguished: (1) the qualification "only" applies to the agent; (2) it applies to the action. In either case, *argumentum a contrario* allows two conclusions from the given text: one affirmative, which is obtained by the omission of the word "only", and one negative, by inversion. Case (1) is illustrated by the rule: "Novations are permitted only between persons capable of contractual bonds". From this, two conclusions are drawn in *argumentum a contrario*: first, that those capable of contractual bonds may carry out a novation, and second, that those who are not capable of contractual bonds may not carry out a novation. Case (2) is illustrated by the following rule: "If the seller was not aware of the defects in the goods, he will be bound to refund only the amount of the price." Here the two inferences are: first, that a seller who was unaware of the defects in the goods is bound to refund the amount of the price, and second, that he is not bound to refund more than the amount of the price.

This treatment of *argumentum a contrario* is far from satisfactory. The distinction between the two cases seems inadequate and uninteresting. In ordinary language, the word "only" has many uses. It can apply to any object and to any property, relation, number, place, or time, not only to agent and action. Expressions of the form "only *P* are *Q*" are often used in the sense "for all *x*, if *x* is not *P*, then *x* is not *Q*". In such cases, "only *P* are *Q*" does not allow the conclusion "*P* are *Q*", in the sense "for all *x*, if *x* is *P*, then *x* is *Q*". One may therefore seriously question the view that the omission of "only" in such rules as "novations are permitted only between persons capable of contractual bonds" yields a valid consequence. Accordingly, there seems to be no good reason for construing the connective "only if" in legal texts as having the characteristic *TFFT* ("if and only if") rather than *TTFT*. At any rate, as long as ordinary language continues to carry its weight on legal formulations, its ambiguities must be noted and tackled with due caution. A further objection: it seems very unusual and terminologically improper to regard the first of the coupled inferences — the one yielding the affirmative conclusion — as an inference *a contrario*. Finally, the second inference, inasmuch as it constitutes a formal logical inversion, is not *argumentum a contrario* in the proper sense of legal heuristics (cf. above, pt. I, ch. 1, sect. 4). In brief, the analysis under examination appears to be a vain attempt to represent *argumentum a contrario* as a kind of straightforward logical argument.

Kalinowski's main aim is to show the dependence of law on "the logic of normative propositions". The underlying view is of course sound: being essentially prescriptive, law cannot be adequately couched in the framework of ordinary predicative logic but requires deontic ("normative") logic[6]. The details of his account, however, call for a few critical remarks. A certain artificiality and unnecessary complexity are apparent in the formulae advanced; e. g., the formula

---

6 The logic of normative propositions and deontic logic, which virtually coincide in the context of Kalinowski's article, are not identical, but rather the former presupposes and, in a way, generalizes the latter. See [02], [03], and [53].

given as the logical basis for *argumentum a maiori ad minus* reads verbally: "If every agent of class X is permitted to do every action of class A and if every action of class B belongs to class A, then every agent of class X is permitted to do every action of class B." Moreover, the terms "permission" and "permitted" are used in an unusual manner; e. g., *argumentum a contrario* is analyzed as involving the following laws of logic: "the negation of the permission to do some action is equivalent to the alternative between the obligation to do it and the obligation not to do it" and "the negation of the obligation to do something is equivalent to the alternative between the permission to do it and the obligation not to do it". In ordinary use, "it is permitted to do x" is equivalent to "it is not forbidden to do x" and to "there is no obligation to refrain from doing x"; so, the disjunction "it is permitted to do x, or it is forbidden to do x" is a tautology. In Kalinowski's use, on the other hand, "it is permitted to do x" is equivalent to "there is no obligation to do x, and it is not forbidden to do x"; consequently, the tautological disjunction is: "there is an obligation to do x, or it is permitted to do x, or it is forbidden to do x", and it also follows that "it is permitted to do x" and "it is permitted not to do x" entail each other. In legal language it is the ordinary sense of "permission" and "permitted" which is usually intended; moreover, this also appears to be the best way of construing Kalinowski's own examples so as to avoid some otherwise unnecessary complications in their analysis. Thus, in order to pass from the rule that novations are permitted only between those capable of contractual bonds to the conclusion that those who are not so capable cannot carry out novations, he has need of an odd assumption which he regards as implicit in the law, viz. that those who are not capable of contractual bonds have no obligation to carry out novations.

Kalinowski concludes his discussion of the last class of rules of interpretation by stating: "As regards the rules for the elimination of lacunae in law — excepting the one which imposes this task — they constitute an application of logical rules of reasoning" (140). In his general conclusion, he points out that the logical rules are only one means of solving various problems of interpretation: "The above problems are resolved by means of multifarious actions, such as verification of the promulgation of a given legal norm in the Official Gazette or some argumentation, most often deductive or analogical" (141). He emphasizes that the rules of interpretation are by no means special rules of reasoning and expresses reservations regarding the appellation "legal logic" as applied to legal interpretation: the connection between legal interpretation and logic is an indirect one that arises because arguments of interpretation lean on some generally employed logical rules. These are largely the syllogistic rules associated with certain laws of the logic of normative propositions, which also have application outside of the domain of law — in the sciences, in fields of practical knowledge, and in everyday life. This last claim may be regarded as misleading with respect to the sciences. To the extent that coordinated activity in technical fields or in everyday life involves using prescriptive language, appropriate logic, imperative or deontic, is indeed required. But the unqualified attribution of such logic to the sciences may encourage the confusion of the logical context with the pragmatic: it is the language of the practical methodology of the sciences which is prescriptive, whereas the specifically scientific language serves the purpose of making factual statements, not of formulating commands, directives, or norms.

It thus appears, in more than one way, that Kalinowski does not clearly and consistently maintain the very distinction on which his analysis could be expected to hinge, i. e. the distinction between logical and pragmatic elements. On the whole, the second part of the article considerably weakens the impression produced by both its first part and the previous article, viz. that in his examination of the current modes of legal interpretation he had succeeded in duly separating the two kinds of elements and in submitting them to proper analysis. Agreement with his basic tenet, i. e. with his denial of the existence of nonformal legal logic, need not involve the unqualified acceptance of his analysis in its entirety.

5. Feys and Motte on "Legal Logic, Legal Systems"

The article "Legal Logic, Legal Systems", 1959 [19], by Robert Feys and Marie-Thérèse Motte relates the Kalinowski's two articles, especially to his basic thesis that there is no specific legal logic. In their conclusion, they claim:

It seems obvious to us that logical deduction in law should not be limited to a play of syllogisms embellished by "probable" arguments and to the work of the interpretation of texts. Systems of law, to be sure, all share the same logic; nevertheless, each of them has its own structure or, one might say, its own internal logic, which is rendered by a set of rules of a syntactic type. And they can be "logically" developed only by a play of analogies exactly respecting the internal logic of the systems to be transposed. We believe we have clearly specified in what definite sense and for what purpose it could be useful to reason logically in terms of "legal systems" (147).

Contrary to the belief expressed in the last quoted sentence, whatever its exact meaning may be, the central claims and basic ideas of the article suffer from lack of clarity.

Some confusion is caused at the outset by the presentation of the problem of the specificity of legal logic as a terminological one: "The choice of terminology is a matter of usage and can be largely left to everyone's personal preferences. The term 'legal logic' can serve as a 'noncommittal' designation of the study of legal reasoning, of the method of law" (143). Although the discussion subsequently enters a more objective course, the "noncommittal" use of the term "legal logic" blurs the dividing line between substantive questions and merely terminological ones. On the one hand, as we have just seen, Feys and Motte do not discard the use of the term as a designation for legal methodology. On the other hand, however, they countenance "close criticism" of "the arguments, perhaps venerable, that are found in actual practice" (144) and declare that they themselves, in contrast to some others (the hint to Perelman is here transparent), do not refer to "the personal element" in legal reasoning, but rather to "the element of strict and impersonal rigor". Should this declaration be construed as involving the relinquishing, at least for the purpose of the discussion, of the formerly admitted use, on account of the authors' "personal preference" for a use according to which legal logic is a formal inquiry? Or perhaps what is meant is a comprehensive field, combining, if not indeed closely interconnecting, the formal investigation of the legal system with the empirical investigation of the existing practices and methods? One may search in vain for a sure answer to this query in the article, in which the very distinction between formal-logical and pragmatic elements, insofar as it is implicit in a general context relating to "reasoning and method", fails to go beyond some casual indistinct references to "impersonal rigor" and the like.

Having mentioned the possibility of applying intuitionistic logic to law, Feys and Motte proceed: "But let us confine ourselves to different legal systems, all admitting classical logic as underlying formal logic. The comparison of such systems will permit one to reason accurately on extension, on analogies of syntactic structure (rigorous analogies, isomorphisms) of which these systems are capable. Extensive reasoning is always conceived in relation to a definite deductive system; a rigorous analogy refers to the structure of a definite deductive system" (145). It is a mistake, our authors explain, to think that analogical argument is always merely probable; for example, a rigorous argument from proportion can be based on identity of structure. Mlle. Motte, in the essay to which Kalinowski refers in his critical observations (see above, sect. 2), dealt with "structural or 'rigorous' analogy". There, "the concern was not to discover a mechanical means of constructing or even verifying deduction through legal structural analogy. But it is interesting to formulate the conditions of such structural analogy accurately, so as to be able to distinguish, on verifiable grounds, between an analogy which is conclusive and one which is not" (146).

An example is given to illustrate the point. Is it possible to patent a new kind of rose? Such cases are not explicitly mentioned in legal texts, and there is hardly any reason for ascribing such intention to the legislator of a century ago. Nor is any precedent available. Consequently, there is apparently room for extension here. Indeed, there seems to be a close similarity between animate and inanimate objects with respect to patentability. "But does this similarity permit one, *de lege lata,* within the framework of the *existing legal system,* to extend patentability to this kind of product? Usual analogy gives no soundly based answer to this question. Rigorous analogy alone, based upon an exact correspondence of legal conditions, will justify extension within the framework of the existing legal system" (146). With a view to extension, "the internal logic of the law" must be considered: "Let us say that the internal logic of a law of social defense will be different from the internal logic of a penal law; the difference in deductive structure or in internal logic will lead to diverging and perhaps practically incompatible measures in the two cases" (147).

One must try to grasp the nature of the "extensive reasoning" and "rigorous analogy", which hold such a central place in the authors' conception of legal logic. As for the former, undoubtedly a kind of "metatheoretical", i. e. methodological, investigation is intended. The latter, on the other hand, is clearly meant to serve as a rigorous mode of reasoning "within the framework of the existing system", the rigor of this reasoning being regarded as based on its essential connection with "the structure of a definite deductive system". Legal logic appears thus as an indistinct blend of methodology and applied logic.

But "rigorous analogy" can apparently in no way be considered a genuine kind of argument in the formal-logical sense. Indeed, we are facing a dilemma here. Either the parity between the domain of application and the domain of comparison, within a single legal system or between two systems, is laid down explicitly and adequately by the law itself or it is not so laid down. In the former case there is no need at all for reasoning by analogy, but only for ordinary derivation. In the latter case there is room for an analogical inference, but of the usual, nonrigorous kind. In any case, genuine inference by "rigorous structural analogy" is obviously impossible. Isomorphism is, to be sure, a formal relation. However, to constitute an adequate basis for deduction, it must be actually and entirely given, for no such isomorphism can be "discovered" or "inferred" on the basis of data that fail to establish it in the strict sense. The criteria that would permit us "to distinguish, on verifiable grounds, between an analogy which is conclusive and one which is not" would naturally have to include formal relations the knowledge of which would remove all need for analogical inference. The notion of "conclusive analogy" thus appears to be merely illusory.

The example of the patenting of roses makes this clear. The judge may either permit or prohibit the patent, but neither decision can be "rigorously" established. Indeed, if, as assumed, ordinary analogy is powerless here, no "exact correspondence of legal conditions" can be expected. For such relation could not be claimed unless the patenting of roses were provided for in legal texts; but then the original problem would not arise at all, and any appeal to analogy, whether ordinary or rigorous, would be superfluous.

And as there can be no inference by "conclusive analogy", so there can be no extension based on such analogy and yielding a "soundly based answer" to the question of extension *de lege lata*. It can be seen that in the concepts of analogy and extension, as set forth in the article, heuristic elements and a formal element are intertwined. The formal element, viz. isomorphism, is incapable of providing a basis for either a mode of genuine inference or a kind of extension strictly derivable from the existing system. The aprioristic idea of both creative and conclusive law making is an obvious misconception.

There remains "the internal logic" of a legal system (see the quotation at the beginning of this section). As explicitly stated, the system's "own structure" in hereby intended. But such structural specificity is hardly relevant to the genuine problem of the specificity of legal logic. Indeed, the "set of rules" by which the structure is determined is not restricted to rules of inference alone, and not even to rules "of a syntactic type", as our authors maintain, but includes semantic rules as well; moreover, what is specific to a given legal system is the entire set of its rules rather than certain rules in particular. In the sentence in which it is said that systems of law "can be 'logically' developed only by a play of analogies exactly respecting the internal logic of the systems to be transposed", the word "logically" occurs in quotes, and it would be interesting to find out the true intent of this reservation. But the obscurity of the whole sentence would in any case frustrate any attempt at adequate interpretation and constructive criticism.

As for the central question under discussion, i. e. the question of the specificity of legal logic, it appears to consist of two different questions which have not been clearly distinguished in the article: (1) Is legal logic a special kind of logic — deontic, intuitionistic, or the like? (2) Are there special logical categories, in particular special, possibly nonformal modes of inference, appropriate only or mainly to law? There seems to be no disagreement on the first question. Indeed, though confining themselves to "classical logic", Feys and Motte do not oppose Kalinowski's view that law requires deontic logic; moreover, they recognize the applicability of intuitionistic logic to law. On the other hand, in answering the second question in the affirmative, they are apparently opposing Kalinowski, who answers it in the negative. However, their contention actually amounts, as we have seen, to two claims that nobody would seriously dispute, viz. that law has proper methodology and heuristics and that legal systems may differ in structure. But they have not shown, and in fact did not claim to show nor presumably even mean to maintain, that there are modes of inference, either formal or material, specific to law. It can therefore be said, in conclusion, that their article does not seem to have made any positive contribution to the elucidation of the problem of the specificity of legal logic.

6. Perelman on "Formal Logic, Legal Logic"

Perelman's article "Formal Logic, Legal Logic", 1960 [61], is directly relevant to the preceding discussion. "Is there logic other than formal and, more particularly, is one justified in speaking of legal
logic?" (226). Several authors have been engaged in controversy on
this question. "In the opinion of some of these authors, such as
Mr. Kalinowski, logic is, by definition, a formal science. But what
entitles one to impose a definition accepted by oneself upon another? Mr. Feys and Mlle. Motte merely retort in reply to M. Kalinowski that 'the choice of terminology is a matter left to personal
preferences'. Is this really so? Are there no reasons for which it is
preferable to adopt such or such other definition and, in consequence, to limit or extend the scope of a twice millenary field of
study?" (226—227). Bocheński and Church are also named among
those who identify logic in general with formal logic. "But, indeed,
there are highly honorable reasons for this identification, though
they are not compelling and do not depend on formal logic" (227).
These reasons concern the mathematician, for whom "logic becomes
a field of study which ceases to be philosophical and acquires the
respectable status of a rigorous science studying the structure of
logistic systems or of uninterpreted calculi" (227).

In one respect at least, Perelman states the problem of the specificity of legal logic clearly: nonformal logic alone is to be considered
specific legal logic; it follows that those who regard all logic as
being formal are thereby bound to admit that there is no specific
legal logic. Perelman rejects this position, since he takes it to rest
on a conception of logic that confines it to the province of mathematics. It should be remarked immediately that formalists such as
Church, Bocheński, or Kalinowski would presumably be very reluctant to admit formality as a defining characteristic of logic. They
define logic as an investigation into the general conditions of the
rational force of arguments. These conditions are found by them to
be formal; they hold, that is, that the rational force of arguments,
either in or out of mathematics, never depends on nonformal conditions; in particular, they see no room for "material" rules of inference in any field whatsoever. Consequently, as they see logic, it
is indeed irreducibly formal, though not "by definition". At any
rate, there are no grounds for charging them with an arbitrary pre-
conception of logic outside mathematics. The quoted remark that

the "highly honorable reasons" for the restriction of logic to formal logic in the mathematical field "are not compelling and do not depend on formal logic" ignores formal induction; moreover, it seems to imply that the formalists expect formal logic alone, as it were, to vouch for the soundness of arguments.

Perelman, to be sure, in opposing legal logic to formal logic, does not point to any nonformal rules of inference in the legal sphere. Although he does not provide an explicit definition of logic of his own, it is clear that he regards logic as investigating "modes of reasoning". His conception seems to be nonformalistic in two respects: (1) the study of reasoning is concerned not only, nor even mainly, with the rational force of argument, but rather with all aspects of reasoning; thus conceived, logic is a largely pragmatic, mainly psychosociological investigation; (2) reasoning and argument do not necessarily involve an inferential process or relation, but may consist of heuristic and methodological operations. (Perelman himself does not employ the terms "pragmatic", "heuristic", "methodological" for the purpose of characterizing logic.)

Nobody, of course, will deny the "nonformal", i. e. empirical, character of legal pragmatics and practical methodology. It appears therefore that Perelman is primarily concerned with the use of the term "logic", which he claims as a designation of those fields. But at the same time he disregards both the specificity of the formal study of argument and even the very distinction between formal and nonformal elements and aspects. The controversy is thus not merely terminological, but also substantive. The resulting confusion in Perelman's conception seems too high a price to pay for the extension of "the scope of a twice millenary field of study", even if its "philosophical" nature is thereby preserved, whatever the exact meaning of this epithet may be.

The confusion is well illustrated by the expression *"forme de raisonnement"*, i. e. "form of reasoning" or "form of argument". As used in the article, does it relate to a pragmatic concept ("reasoning") or to a formal-logical one? The proper answer seems to be that it relates indistinctly to both. Among the "forms of reasoning" peculiar to law Perelman names "the arguments *a fortiori, a pari, a contrario,* and the argument by analogy", the use of which "never occurs in the form of a formally correct or incorrect demonstration" (228). He systematically refrains from elucidating the ambiguities of *"raisonnement"*, and he opposes Kalinowski's attempt at such elucidation. True, Kalinowski — as we have seen — did not succeed in properly separating pragmatic and formal elements in legal reasoning. But whereas Kalinowski's analysis is defective, Perelman entirely ignores the very distinction between disparate elements. He charges logicians with the task of "examining the structure of arguments foreign to mathematics" (230), but he conceives "the structure of arguments" as involving such pragmatic elements as "the adoption of a position" (228) or "the judge's freedom and independence" (229).

"Mathematical logic" itself hardly seems to escape this confusion. When it is said to be "a rigorous science studying the structure of logistic systems or of uninterpreted calculi", apparent recognition is given to logic as a formal inquiry. But formal logic, as such, does not adequately match Perelman's conception of logic in general as investigating "the manner in which people reason in order to arrive at an individual or collective decision" (230). This is, presumably, why it is stigmatized as nonphilosophical. To conform to Perelman's ideal, mathematical logic would have to investigate the actual "modes of reasoning" of mathematicians. To be consistent, such conception would have to disregard the essential difference between the study of, say, pure or special functional calculi and such studies in mathematical pragmatics and heuristics as those, say, of Hadamard and Polya. The characterization of formal logic as dealing with "mathematical demonstration" or with "purely demonstrative reasoning" (229) seems, indeed, to invite the paradoxical inclusion of pragmatic inquiry into formal logic.

Let us now turn to what appears to be the gist of the article, viz. the claim that a legal argument "is not correct and compelling or incorrect and valueless, but is relevant or irrelevant, strong or weak, in accordance with the reasons that justify its use under the circumstances" (228). Perelman is undoubtedly pointing here to the nonconclusiveness of legal argument in support of his claim that it is nonformal. "Correctness" appears here to connote fromal validity, the point being that legal argument does not owe its rational force to formal validity, i. e. that it is not deductive. This view, of course, is unobjectionable in itself; however, it does not justify the claim that legal argument is essentially nonformal. "Relevance" applies to argument in the sense of a reason advanced in support of a thesis (this being, in fact, the prevalent sense of the French *"argument"*) rather than to argument as a set of premises with a conclusion (better rendered in French as *"raissonement"*). "Strength" may refer either to the soundness of the premises or to the degree of the support they lend to the conclusion.

What, then, are the criteria of relevance and strength? Perelman does not even attempt to answer this question, beyond making an elusive reference to the dependence of legal argument on "the reasons that justify its use under the circumstances". At any rate, there seems to be nothing positive in the article to support the claim that the criteria in question are essentially nonformal. Yet, Perelman does not wish to say that they are merely intuitive: such a plainly psychologistic conception of legal argument would be hardly compatible with his insistence on its rationality. Thus caught between formalism and irrationalism, he maintains that legal argumentation "is not mere calculus, but rather is the appreciation of the strength of such and such reasoning" (229). But, surely, the said "appreciation of strength" will not merit the status of a rational operation as long as the very nature of the rules which govern it remains a mystery. Rejecting the dogmatic restriction of formality to "compelling", i.e. deductive, arguments, one wants to allow that relevance and strength in legal argument may be analyzable as formal relations of inductive logic.

Primarily concerned with legal reasoning and construction in the context of discovery, Perelman plainly confuses argument with the provision of intuitive grounds and logic with empirical study. One need not undertake a detailed investigation into the nature and potentialities of systematic legal pragmatics and practical methodology in order to ascertain both their importance and "specificity" with respect to logic. To be sure, there seems to be no objection to assigning the pursuit of these fields to logicians. Indeed, it is highly desirable that those engaged in the said fields should possess a broad background — legal, psychological, sociological, and logicomathematical. But the advantages of such personal union in professional practice should not be allowed to blur the essential differences between disparate fields.

Concluding his article, Perelman declares that "the logician who prohibits himself from examining the structure of arguments foreign to mathematics, who refuses to recognize the specificity of legal argument and of practical argument in general, renders a bad service to philosophy and to humanity: to philosophy, which, in the absence of a theoretical foundation, is obliged to renounce its tra-

ditional role as an educator of mankind; to humanity, which, unable
to find a guide in any rationally inspired philosophies, cannot help
abandoning itself to irrationality, to passions, to instincts, and to
violence" (230). This conclusion seems wide of the mark. No enlightened upholder of the modern, formalistic conception of logic
would doubt the distinctness, with respect to logic, of pragmatic
and methodological investigations in any field or would request
their restriction. In point of fact, formalistically minded logicians
often contribute to such investigation, e. g. Bocheński in the study
of analogical reasoning and Kalinowski in the field of legal methodology. But the enlightened formalist recognizes basic distinctions
and ensures the proper separation of disparate aspects and contexts.
He thus renders an excellent service to research in a truly philosophical spirit, insofar as fostering exactitude and clarity is a major
task of philosophy. As to humanity, it does not seem easy to detect
any connection whatsoever between the logicians' refusal to incorporate their formal investigation with the primarily pragmatic study
of argumentation, and the abandoning of mankind to the afflictions
feared by Perelman.

7. Gregorowicz on "the Argument a Maiori ad Minus and the Problem of Legal Logic": (i) General Stand, and Views Disavowed

In his article "The Argument *a Maiori ad Minus* and the Problem of
Legal Logic", 1962 [24], Georges Gregorowicz undertakes the analysis of one particular mode of legal reasoning not only for its own
sake, but also for the purpose of clarifying "another both discussible
and discussed problem, i. e. the problem of the independent existence
of special legal logic" (66). Since he shares Perelman's basic views on
argument and logic, Gregorowicz's study displays similar defects. In
particular, his analysis likewise suffers from the confusion of logical
with pragmatic concepts. As presented, the problem concerns a logical explicandum: Gregorowicz intends to inquire whether *argumentum a maiori ad minus* constitutes a general-logical or a specifically
legal kind of inference. His detailed analysis, however, largely concerns the corresponding pragmatic aspects. It does not occur to him
that the *argumentum* under study may not have a sufficiently distinct
inferential character at all. The formulation of the problem can, indeed, be seen as involving the so-called complex-question fallacy,

as long as the explicandum has not been adequately shown to be a kind of genuine logical inference. At any rate, Gregorowicz, who emphasizes the pragmatic characteristics and the methodological function of the *argumentum,* is wrong in believing that he has thereby established "the independent existence of special logic": actually, he is only able to point to legal pragmatics and methodology.

From the outset, Gregorowicz characterizes argument in general with the aid of pragmatic concepts: reasoning, conviction, mind. When he states that argument is "all reasoning by which the conclusion is drawn from one or more premises" (66), he presumably views the "drawing of the conclusion" as a psychological phenomenon. In any case, the psychological aspect is clearly indicated in the sequel of the same characterization: "The argument wishes to conduce the mind to accepting as true what has not yet been so accepted." *Argumentum a maiori ad minus* is then presented as a practical means of applying law. Is this a general-logical inference or a specifically legal one? As will be seen presently, Gregorowicz discusses the views of Ulrich Klug, Z. Ziemba, and Georges Kalinowski as representing the former position, and the views of Tadeusz Kotarbiński, Jerzy Wróblewski, and the coauthors Chaïm Perelman and L. Olbrechts-Tyteca as representing the latter position. His point is that those who regard the *argumentum* as a general inference ignore its essential methodological function: they apparently succeed in presenting it is a general formal inference only at the cost of an artificial separation of the interpretation of the premises from the inference itself; they thus distort the psychological truth, disregarding "what lawyers really do when they argue *a maiori ad minus*" (71). This is Gregorowicz's "principal objection" to them. The truth, he explains, is that lawyers do not in fact carry out the interpretation before the inference and lay out a complete and explicit argument, with premises and conclusion: "they start, on the contrary, directly from the norm formulated in positive law and reach a norm not stated *expressis verbis*" (71). Those, on the other hand, who consider *argumentum a maiori ad minus* to be a specifically legal mode of reasoning, grasp better its true character and function. Their views are "more correct, for they give a better account of what the lawyer does when he infers *a maiori ad minus*. Examples show, in fact, that lawyers pass directly from the norms contained in the propositions of a law to norms not contained in them" (73).

Gregorowicz thus conceives "legal logic" as comprising that part of descriptive legal pragmatics which deals with the crude processes of reasoning in the context of discovery. He outlines the program of research accordingly, adding, moreover, the sociological and historical aspect of reasoning to the psychological. As will be seen later (in the next section), some sound methodological ideas can be distinguished in his conception. Meanwhile, it will be useful to examine the two aforementioned triads of views and to see, in particular, to what extent they really represent the two respective positions regarding the problem of the specificity of legal logic. Let me say, both by way of anticipation and as a summary of the preceding criticism of Gregorowicz's general stand, that, paradoxically, there is no real contradiction between the two positions, because the former concerns the inferential aspect of *argumentum a maiori ad minus,* whereas the latter, which is upheld by Gregorowicz himself, concern its semantic and pragmatic aspect. Forcing a choice between general logic of inference and special semantics and pragmatics constitutes a false dilemma.

Gregorowicz does not discuss each view separately, but rather comments briefly upon either triad collectively. The gist of his remarks has, in fact, already been cited. I shall adhere to his report of the several views but shall considerably expand the discussion of them [7].

Klug, in his *Legal Logic* [45] [8] (in a section not discussed in pt. I, ch. 1 above) illustrates *argumentum a maiori ad minus* by the following example. The law stipulates that a conspirator is free from punishment if he informs the authorities or the persons in danger of the plot in time to prevent its implementation. From this it is inferred, *a maiori ad minus,* that the conspirator who prevents the fulfillment of the plot by his own direct action is also free from punishment. Klug regards the *argumentum* as an instance of the classical argument *ad subalternatam propositionem,* which from the applicability of a predicate to a general class infers its applicability to cases belonging to that class. This is a formally valid inference. This analysis, Klug points out, assumes a tacit premise, viz. a generalization of the given legal rule, sufficiently broad to include the

---

7 The first triad will be dealt with in the remaining part of this section; the second at the beginning of the next.

8 Gregorowicz's account is based on the *second* edition of Klug's work. See above, pp. 18—19, n. 3.

case in question in its scope. Thus, in the foregoing example, the argument is based on the general assumption, regarded as implicit in the law, that a conspirator is free from punishment if he intentionally prevents the fulfillment of the plot. This supplementary premise can be established through "teleological considerations". "Only after a basis for the argumentation has been determined in such a manner, can the logical derivation commence" ([45], p. 140).

Klug's analysis is highly inadequate[9]. To begin with, he speaks of and adduces formulae for the inference *ad subalternatam propositionem* (all *S* are *P*; therefore, some *S* are *P*), whereas what he in fact needs is the subsumptive inference (i. e. the classical syllogism *barbara*: all *M* are *P*; all *S* are *M*; therefore, all *S* are *P*). The main weakness of his analysis is this: provided that, as he requires, the mediation of an appropriate generalization of the original rule is assumed, the subsumptive inference constitutes a formalization not of the entire *argumentum,* but of its terminal stage alone. Klug's explication closely resembles that of the analogical argument as given by him (see above, pt. I, ch. 1, sect. 3), though it does not depend, as does the other, on the defective concept of "essential similarity". Both have one major fault in common: accounting only for the terminal, deductive transition from the generalized law to the special rule applicable to the particular case, they considerably distort their respective explicanda, which, as currently understood by lawyers, are heuristic rather than logical in nature. To the extent that this point of criticism is involved in Gregorowicz's previously quoted "principal objection" to the formalistic views, he may be considered right.

As reported by Gregorowicz, Z. Ziemba[10] regards *argumentum a maiori ad minus* as an enthymeme which, duly completed, yields an argument consisting of three premises and a conclusion, as follows:

(1) If action *x* is "more" than action *y*, and if *x* is permitted, then *y* is permitted.

(2) Action *a* is "more" than action *b*; e. g., to dispose of one's share without one's partners' consent is "more" than to do so with their consent.

(3) *a* is permitted: one may dispose of one's share without one's partners' consent.

---

9 Cf. [31], pp. 134—135.
10 Gregorowicz's source is an article written in Polish [80].

(4) Hence, *b* is permitted: one may dispose of one's share with one's partners' consent.

The inference by which a conclusion of the form (4) is drawn from premises of the forms (1), (2), and (3) is formally valid. In ordinary legal reasoning, premise (3) alone is usually formulated explicitly, whereas (1) and (2) are tacit "extralegal premises", "the first of which establishes the rule of the argument *a maiori ad minus* and the second of which is accepted on the interpreter's own responsibility. The third premise alone is a proposition obtained from the law" ([24], 69).

It will presently be seen that Ziemba's explication, though clearly more faithful to the explicandum than Klug's, is not quite adequate. But, first, it is important to point out that, notwithstanding what Gregorowicz and presumably also Ziemba himself believe, the latter's explication of the *argumentum* does not in fact present it as a general, purely formal mode of inference. Although, admittedly, the schema of argument in question is formally valid, it not only contains a deontic predicate or operator, "permitted", but refers in an essential way to a nonlogical relation, viz. the relation of one action being "more" than another. One can, to be sure, ignore the meanings of "permitted" and of "more" and replace them by predicative variables. However, thus construed, Ziemba's schema ceases to represent the argument *a maiori ad minus* and becomes a derived and, in this sense, redundant rule of inference of the first-order functional calculus. As it stands, the schema clearly points to a nonlogical function of the *argumentum*. Indeed, premise (1), which Ziemba himself singles out as essential, is so qua containing both the deontic expression and the special relational predicate in their specific sense, not qua a pure logical form.

What is the nature of the premises (1) and (2), which are usually omitted in actual reasoning in court? The view that both are "extralegal premises" must be taken to mean that they are not drawn from the code, not that they are nonlegal in nature. Premise (1), at least, should surely be regarded as a theoretical principle of the legal system. Some hesitation is perhaps justified with respect to premise (2), in which only the predicate "more", but no deontic expression, occurs. Indeed, though the defining relation of the *a maiori ad minus* is clearly a comparative theoretical concept, the nature of the parameter concerned is not always apparent. This parameter need not be plainly quantitative: the relation in question may be simply the relation between a compound action and one of its components, or it may be some more complex relation between actions, possibly involving such specifically legal elements as rights and duties. Moreover, to be related as "more" to "less", the actions must be "cognate" or "similar", and these are again very ill-defined concepts. The multiformity and the obscure intuitive nature of the relation in question are apparent in the few examples of it given by Gregorowicz: if the branches of one's trees come down on one's neighbor's property, then to enter his property for the purpose of lopping the trees or gathering their fruit is "more" than to lop those trees or to gather their fruit without entering the neighbor's property; to dispose of one's own share without the consent of one's partners is "more" than to do so with their consent; to prosecute a man after his conviction abroad is "more" than to prosecute him after his aquittal abroad. In the last example one may even fail to find the intuition distinctly convincing. Naturally, then, opinions may differ as to whether "more" is better construed as a specifically legal or as a sociological predicate, and instances of (2), accordingly, as rules of law or as statements of fact. I shall return to this question later (in the concluding section of pt. III).

It is clear, at any rate, that the theoretical principle (1) (or the corresponding principle for obligation[11]) is an essential premise in the *argumentum*. Therefore, the logical explicatum of the *argumentum*, inasmuch as it must essentially involve the special predicate

---

11 Though Ziemba applies *argumentum a maiori ad minus* only to permission, it can be applied to obligation as well, as is implied in the dictum cited by Gregorowicz: "Who may more may less, and who is bound to do more is bound to do less" (67). It is worth noting that the principle as applied to obligation follows from the principle as applied to permission, provided that obligation is defined as the prohibition of, i. e. the nonpermission for, abstention (nonaction) and provided, moreover, that the following meaning rule is accepted: if x is more than y, then non-y is more than non-x. Indeed, let us assume that x is more than y. Then, by virtue of the aforesaid meaning rule, non-y is more than non-x. Hence, according to the principle *a maiori ad minus* as applied to permission, if non-y is permitted, non-x is permitted. Hence, by contraposition, if non-x is prohibited, non-y too is prohibited. So, by virtue of the definition of obligation, if x is obligatory, y too is obligatory. It can be similarly shown that the two principles *a maiori ad minus* are equivalent to the principle *a minori ad maius* as applied to prohibition, which is the principle underlying *argumentum a minori ad maius*.

"more", cannot be a rule of inference, but must be regarded as belonging to legal semantics. Just as, e. g., a psychoanalytical argument, far from being a rule of inference, whether formal or material, is an argument leaning on, i. e. having at least one premise drawn from, the psychoanalytical theory, and a relativistic explanation in physics is an explanation leaning on the theory of relativity, so *argumentum a maiori ad minus* is basically an argument leaning on the legal principle (1). It has an important heuristic function. Just as the search for an explanation of a physical or a social phenomenon is often directed by such practical rules as "look for an electromagnetic explanation" or "look for an economic explanation", respectively, so the search for legal justification is sometimes directed by the practical rule "try to argue *a maiori ad minus*".

One can admit that Ziemba's analysis is not adequate and still disagree with Gregorowicz's objections. The latter's main point is that Ziemba takes little account of the manner in which lawyers actually do argue *a maiori ad minus* and, in particular, disregards the fact that they pass directly from (3) to (4) without the mediation of (1) or (2). The position implicit in this criticism involves a plainly psychologistic conception of the rational force of argument and amounts, therefore, to the relinquishment of all attempts at analysis through rational reconstruction. As I see it, Ziemba's explicatum is inadequate not because it is too ample but, on the contrary, because it is too scant: it covers only one part of the explicandum, viz. the terminal, deductive stage of the entire argumentative process. Premise (2) is the breaking link of Ziemba's schema. He regards it, just as (1) and (3), as a datum. But in fact (2) is not a starting point for the argument, as are (1) and (3), but is one of its results. Indeed, to establish that the action foreseen by the law is "more" than the one under trial is the main task of the *argumentum* conceived as a nontrivial judicial argument. The terminal derivation made possible after the acceptance of (2) is a straightforward matter as compared with the confirmation of (2) by all the relevant data and findings. Like the arguments by analogy and *a contrario* (see above, pt. I, ch. 1, sects. 3 and 4), the argument *a maiori ad minus* and the remaining "special arguments" in law are prima facie inductive in nature. Consequently, as long as appropriate inductive logic is not available, it seems that the logical explicatum of the *argumentum* cannot be adequately formulated. Meanwhile, in the absence of adequate (either strictly quantitative or at least comparative) formal inductive procedures, intuitive and ill-defined heuristic considerations of a prima facie inductive nature are used in judicial practice. A thesis of kind (2) may even be accepted occasionally on the basis of *mere* intuition, without any distinct consideration whatever. But in such extreme cases as well, it is not the easy terminal deduction that forms the main stage of the argument, but the very acceptance of (2) as sufficiently confirmed, albeit only in a "qualitative" and indistinct manner, by the relevant background information at the disposal of the arguers.

In evaluating Ziemba's explicatory attempt in brief, it may be said, firstly, that his schema, properly construed, in fact represents *argumentum a maiori ad minus* not as a purely formal rule of inference, but as a kind of argument characterized, among other things, by a nonlogical expression which occurs in its premises; and, secondly, that he too distorts the explicandum, though to a much lesser degree than Klug.

Next, Gregorowicz gives an account of Kalinowski's view, according to which "the argument *a maiori ad minus* falls under the schema of syllogism of the logic of normative propositions, provided that the major premise is subjected to a certain interpretation" (70). He cites the example concerning divulging parliamentary proceedings (see above, pt. II, sect. 4). Gregorowicz seems to be wrong in classing Kalinowski without reservation among those who regard the *argumentum* as a general-logical mode of inference. As we have seen, Kalinowski advisedly emphasizes both the practical-methodological function of the arguments *a fortiori* and the reduced role of the logical element in them. Though there is, admittedly, no sharp contrast in trend between Kalinowski and the two authors previously discussed, it can nevertheless be seen that whereas Klug and Ziemba, in adducing their respective formulae, profess to provide an adequate explicatum of the *argumentum* as a logical concept, Kalinowski only intends to point out the deontic formula on which it leans.

8. Gregorowicz on "the Argument a Maiori ad Minus and the Problem of Legal Logic": (ii) Views Avowed and Constructive Ideas

Let us now consider the three views taken by Gregorowicz as representative of the thesis — avowed by him — that *argumentum a maiori ad minus* is a specifically legal inference. First, Tadeusz

Kotarbiński's characterization of the *argumentum* is reported thus: "If the law permits an action that presents a disadvantage of a greater scope or intensity, it ipso facto permits all action that presents the same disadvantage to a lesser degree of scope or intensity" ([24], 72). Acording to Kotarbiński, Gregorowicz adds, the *argumentum* leans on "an extralogical relation without universal value" and constitutes "a fallible mode of inference, which lacks a properly logical nature, since it uses extralogical as well as logical constants" (72).

Gregorowicz misses Kotarbiński's main point, which can be rendered thus: the *argumentum* cannot be regarded as a rule of inference in the logical sense, nor even as a "special" rule of legal logic, unless the designation "legal logic" is given to a field that does not fall within the province of logic in the strict sense. Kotarbiński can by no means be regarded as upholding the thesis of "the specificity of legal logic" in any nontrivial sense. His true position is well attested to, among other things, by the title of the very book which is Gregorowicz's source: "A Course in Logic for Lawyers" [12]; that is to say, a course in general logic, adapted in scope to the lawyers' needs and illustrated by examples of the application of logic to law. Gregorowicz may have been misled by the not very happy expression "a fallible mode of inference", which should be properly construed as referring to arguments possibly unsound, because of a wrong link, rather than to arguments possibly invalid. The questionable link is, of course, Ziemba's premise (2) (see preceding section), which states that one action is "more" than another. In Kotarbiński's use, logic proper, since it excludes nonlogical expressions, certainly excludes all special semantics.

Next, Jerzy Wróblewski's view is reported briefly [13]. It "ranges the conclusion *a maiori ad minus* among the quasi-logical consequences. By 'quasi-logical consequences' of a norm all those conclusions are intended which can be drawn from that norm with the aid of rules of inference admitted by the legal system in question or by the given legal language. The quasi-logical consequences, like the logical consequences of binding norms, enter, according to this view, into the legal system" (72). These hints are too scant to permit a proper understanding of Wróblewski's position. In particular, the meaning of the central term "quasi-logical consequences" is far from

---

12 It is a book written in Polish [47].
13 Gregorowicz's source is a book written in Polish [79].

clear. It should perhaps be construed as referring to the conclusions of arguments that depend on analytic meaning rules. This interpretation seems to be suggested by the reference to "rules of inference" that are somehow inherent in "the given legal language". Wróblewski may thus be taken to allude to legal semantics. At any rate, his position cannot be said to imply the recognition of the existence of specifically legal logic but, at most, of specifically legal "quasi-logic".

The last remark applies likewise to the reported view of Perelman and Olbrechts-Tyteca[14], inasmuch as they too use the term "quasi-logical", albeit in a different sense: "The quasi-logical arguments, it is said in this case, are characterized by their nonformal character as well as by the effort of thought required for its reduction to formality." Such arguments "always appeal to logical structures or to mathematical relations, without being their substitutes" (72). In particular, *argumentum a maiori ad minus* leans on the relation between a whole and its part. That this notion of "quasi-logical arguments" is meant to be a pragmatic one is clearly attested to by the reference to "the effort of thought" allegedly required for the said "reduction", whatever the exact nature of this latter may be. Gregorowicz also cites and assents to the main views of Perelman's article of 1960, which has already been discussed (see sect. 6).

In conclusion, it can be said that examination of the six views reported by Gregorowicz provides no support for his claim about the specificity of legal argument. It can be remarked, moreover, that the majority of those views have in fact been misconstrued by him. In the first triad Klug alone, by completely disregarding the true nature of the *argumentum*, "succeeds" in representing it as a general formal inference. Ziemba's analysis is not adequate either; but though it likewise purports to reveal the general, purely formal-logical function of the *argumentum*, it actually points to its special semantic nature and heuristic function. Emphasis on its noninferential aspects is clearly intended by Kalinowski. This is likewise the case with Kotarbiński and presumably also with Wróblewski, both classed in the second triad. Finally, Perelman and Obrechts-Tyteca refrain so consistently from distinguishing between logic and pragmatics and from separating "logic" from "quasi-logic", that they

---

14 The source is [63], pp. 260 ff.

cannot be said to uphold the thesis of the specificity of legal logic in any both clear and notrivial sense.

Gregorowicz chooses to speak of the *argumentum* as belonging to special legal logic, conceived as a nonformal theory of inference, "independent and original" and "subordinate to rhetoric" (74). The paradox here is, in his opinion, "only apparent", inasmuch as the sense of the term "logic" as intended by him differs from "the sense given to it by the representatives of mathematical logic" (74). It does not seem to have occurred to him that this terminological muddle can be avoided by suitably subdividing and renaming the field in question, which seems to consist of portions of legal semantics, pragmatics, and methodology.

In the last part of the article, Gregorowicz demands the formulation of "rules of inference *a maiori ad minus*" in accordance with the general historical conditions and the special pragmatic circumstances. He does not give examples of such rules, but the context seems to indicate that he means nonformal rules that would reflect "what the lawyer does when he infers *a maiori ad minus*" (73), i. e. rules that would make it possible to infer the permission (obligation) with respect to an action "directly" from the explicit permission (obligation) with respect to a "greater" action. To be sure, he does not mean the general and indefinite principle which forms premise (1) in Ziemba's schema (see above, sect. 7). Indeed, he explains, "it is impossible to construct a single rule of argumentation *a maiori ad minus*, valid for a set of entire systems. Rules of this kind can only be constructed for various parts of law taken in isolation" (73). Moreover, the rules in question are characterized as "forms of inference more or less general, fallible, containing extralogical constants in addition to the logical constants" (74). Presumably, then, Gregorowicz means "material" rules that would warrant the inference of "*b* is permitted (obligatory)" from "*a* is permitted (obligatory)" in various cases. That *a* is "more" than *b* need not be mentioned in the rules; but they will not be *a maiori ad minus* rules unless the relation in question occurs in every case, as a matter of fact. Under this proviso, however, Gregorowicz's analysis can be seen, curiously enough, to be equivalent to Ziemba's; in particular, there appears to be a one-to-one correspondence between the set of Gregorowicz's rules and the set of postulates represented by form (2) in Ziemba's schema. Moreover, there are two outstanding advantages to Ziemba's analysis. First, his schema contains an explicit formulation, as premise (1), of the essential general principle *a maiori ad minus*, which is only de facto involved in Gregorowicz's conception. Second, Ziemba requires no "special" rules of inference. These are clearly redundant, inasmuch as they amount, in their inferential function, to an artificial and uninteresting fusion of the general principle (1) and the postulates (2) with the ordinary formal *modus ponens*.

It is worth noting that Gregorowicz closely approaches the idea of theoretical postulates. To illustrate the sense of "logic" in which he speaks of legal logic, he cites the following two adages, which were regarded as principles of logic by Perreau, the French student of law: "Quod nullum est, nullum produit effectum" and "Habilis ad nuptias, habilis ad pacta nuptialia". These can be seen as theoretical postulates involving the legal concepts of a void action and of a capacity, respectively. Gregorowicz does not say that these adages exemplify the rules of inference *a maiori ad minus* which he envisages, but it seems that he takes them to resemble such rules very closely. He points out that they can be couched alternatively in the form of "directives", thus: "if you hold that in the law *L* an act is declared void by that law, admit also (on pain of proceeding differently from the other lawyers or on pain of being ridiculous) that it produces no legal effect", and "if, in accordance with the law *L*, you hold somebody to be capable of marriage, hold him also (in virtue of the same motives) to be capable of concluding matrimonial contracts" (74). He claims in conclusion: "If what I have said above is correct, then in the controversy for or against the existence of legal logic one must side with those who answer in the affirmative. The construction of such logic will involve metatheoretical investigations of what lawyers do de facto. These inquiries will uncover the basis of what lawyers constantly admit. Thus, legal logic will formulate either theses as dictated by those findings or directives corresponding to these theses" (75). It is clear, then, that Gregorowicz admits the possibility of formulating the nonformal "rules of inference" as postulates ("theses"). He couches the corresponding "directives" in plainly pragmatic language ("hold", "admit", "proceeding", "ridiculous"), according to his primarily pragmatic conception of legal argument and legal logic. He marks no preference for either alternative. His illustrations, however, show the naturalness of the theses as against the somewhat ludicrous elaboration of the directives. Moreover, the very fact that the theses are purely systematic, whereas practical elements are involved in the directives, indicates that the two versions are not substantively equivalent: if the theses are adequate, the directives contain elements foreign to "legal logic". The inessential elements can, to be sure, be eliminated through appropriate reformulation; but even so readjusted, the doctrine of the material rules of inference would remain inferior to the doctrine of theoretical postulates, as was pointed out in the foregoing comparison of Gregorowicz's analysis with Ziemba's.

Gregorowicz's terminal reflections thus present two faces. On the one hand, they lean avowedly on the "rhetorical" conception of argument and logic. On the other hand, however, they can be construed as expressing a demand for and as tracing the outline of an extensive and rigorous theorization of law. This theorization would involve systematic unravelling of what is implicit in legal theory, abstractive elimination of pragmatic elements, formalization of seemingly material relations, and careful formulation of postulates, rules, and underlying principles. In the light of such methodology, *argumentum a maiori ad minus* and the other special legal arguments will no longer be represented as rules of inference, whether formal or material, but rather, in the context of discovery, as heuristic devices capable of foreshadowing the said theorization and, in the context of justification, as kinds of complex arguments, characterized by certain kinds of premises and by prima facie inductive stages leading to the terminal deduction. "The controversy for or against the existence of legal logic" will thus reach a happy ending or, at least, will decline in vehemence, in that the controversy which today is both substantive and terminological will turn into a merely terminological one, limited in scope and lacking deeper philsophical importance. Indeed, when the legal system is abstracted and disjoined from its pragmatic aspects and is conceived as involving no material rules of inference, the terminological need to distinguish between the different contexts makes itself apparent, while the motives for speaking of nonformal or rhetorical logic are considerably weakened. There still remain, however, two apparently conflicting ways of answering the question as to "the existence of legal logic". On the one hand, the characterization of logic as the theory of the rational force of argument can be understood, narrowly, as implying the absence of nonlogical expressions from the rules of logic. This conception involves the denial of the existence of legal, as distinct from general, logic. On the other hand, it seems both convenient and unobjectionable to regard the comprehensive syntactic and semantic theory of the legal system, possibly including a suitable theory of inductive support, as constituting legal logic; meaning rules in particular, owing to their conceptual tenor and special role in arguments, seem most fittingly designated as rules of logic. With respect to this alternative, law is of course no exception among special fields. The issue, as has been pointed out, is merely terminological.

If Gregorowicz's position is interpreted as involving a preference for the latter alternative, his terminal reflections appear all the more acceptable — excepting what is implied by the notion of nonformal rules of inference and the concomitant relegation of logic to rhetoric. He cites Perreau's characterization of the adage "Habilis ad nuptias, habilis ad pacta nuptialia" as "doubtlessly a principle of logic, but how annoying in actual fact". This remark can be construed as jocularly expressing the difference between the laws of general logic, which are rigid and lack all legal content, and the special meaning rules, which are flexible and closely related to the prescriptive content of law. Gregorowicz himself can be taken to point to the same difference when, in outlining the envisaged reconstruction of law, he remarks that "naturally, the theses obtained will not be analytic propositions as are, for example, those of the propositional calculus, and the directives will not be infallible. They will, however, be rational and useful" (75). Indeed, the analyticity, in the general sense, of the meaning rules differs from the purely formal analyticity of the laws of general logic. As for the "fallibility" of special logic, it can be seen as referring to hesitations and differences of opinion in the context of discovery, to the possibility of change in the historical context, and to the prima facie inductive nature of arguments in the context of justification. Furthermore, when Gregorowicz writes, in the conclusion of the article: "The construction of such logic will involve metatheoretical investigations of what lawyers do de facto. These inquiries will uncover the basis of what lawyers admit constantly" (75), these remarks too — in contrast to some apparently similar ones in the central part of the article — can be interpreted in the spirit of a judicious methodology as countenancing rational reconstruction of law ("metatheoretical investigations", "uncovering the basis") in close connection with actual legal practice.

In conclusion, then, it can be said that Gregorowicz, towards the end of his article, corrects an important part of his erroneous views and deficient analyses. His progressive attitude finds a concise expression in Francis Bacon's aphorism which closes the article: "Optima lex quae minimum relinquit arbitrio judicis, optimus judex qui minimum sibi" (75).

Conclusion and Supplementary Observations

The predominant traits of the Belgian line of discussion, as they emerge from the preceding critical account, can be summed up under the following heads: conception of logic as a pragmatic study, and an unclear idea of the rationality of legal argument; failure to distinguish between the materially legal and the methodological level; misrepresentation of the differences between pure fields and law as involving a corresponding distinction between formal and nonformal, "rhetorical" logic; a paradoxical disregard of the logical and methodological similarities between law and empirical science; a certain tension between emphasis on the pragmatic aspects of legal argumentation and interest in the nonrhetorical aspects of theoretical construction in law; disagreement and change in the use of the basic terms "logic" and "legal logic".

Since the Louvain Colloquy, studies in jurisprudence, and especially in legal methodology, including practical methodology of particular legal systems, have been sponsored by the Belgian Center and edited by Perelman under the comprehensive designation "studies in legal logic". The discussion of the nature of legal argument has continued at the Center and has attracted wide attention, in particular in France. Two volumes which appeared in Paris, viz. an *Introduction to Legal Logic* by Kalinowski, 1965 [42], and a collective volume *The Logic of Law*, 1966 [50], are closely related to the Belgian discussion. A selective account of a few relevant passages of these publications (chiefly of the 1966 Paris volume) will now be given, by means of quotations, with a view to a reexamination of the doctrine of nonformal legal logic with special regard to the definitely *anti*formalistic motives of its upholders.

Michel Villey (Paris), in his editorial introduction [75] to the 1966 volume, considering that "one has the right to defend oneself against actual usage", opposes the restriction of legal logic to formal logic. He appears to identify the latter with deductive logic, since he declares: "I find it disquieting to limit the field of logic to compelling arguments alone" (XIV). He suggests that it would be better "to restore to the word 'logic' its extension of old" (XV) and to replace formal logic in the field of law by "another logic", of a "dialectical" nature, "a logic no longer of demonstration but rather of invention" (X) and "of controversy" (XII)[15]. In the same volume, Perelman [62] likewise reaffirms "the existence of a nonformal logic, devoted to the study of argumentation, i. e. of the totality of arguments brought to support or to counteract a thesis and allowing one to criticize and to justify a decision" (2). He explains that "legal logic involves the study of nonformal argumentative schemata, proper to the legal context" (3), such as the classical *argumenta*, teleological arguments, or arguments by analogy (6), and he argues that "if legal logic is to study what is specific in legal reasoning, it cannot restrict itself to the study of the formal aspects of reasoning, for its essential role is to analyze argumentation as it evolves in a legal context" (6).

Kalinowski, at variance with his former denial of specific legal logic (see above, pt. II, sect. 2), now adopts an elaborate position. In his contribution [43] to the 1966 volume, he observes that "there exist *nonlogical rules* of reasoning" and grants that "this precisely constitutes one of the specificities of legal logic" (15). More explicitly, though with due qualification, he admits that "there exists a legal logic. But ... it is logic only insofar as it uses logical rules; when it has recourse to nonlogical, especially extralogical rules, it remains legal, properly speaking, but is logic by analogy only" (22). In his textbook [42], he relates that "it was meditation on the positions of Mr. Perelman and of Mr. Gregorowicz which brought him [Kalinowski] to notice the analogical character of the concept of logic and subsequently to modify his original opinion about the sense and soundness of the term 'legal logic'" (39, n. 13). Accordingly, he agrees that "in view of the analogical character of the concept of logic and hence of the name which signifies it, one can, following the example of Mr. Perelman and Mr. Gregorowicz respectively, extend the name of legal logic to the study of legal argumentation of a rhetorical character as well as to the study of 'extralogical' rules of the interpretation of law" (39). Yet, regarding his own book: "If we deal with applied logic, we try nevertheless to leave aside what can be called 'logic' by analogy only" (40). This restriction of the book's scope accounts for Perelman's view, ex-

---

15 Villey expresses similar views in [76].

pressed in the preface, that the book, in the main, offers "the elements of formal logic indispensable for the study of legal logic proper"; and it accounts for his hope that Kalinowski will yet produce "another work devoted, this time, to legal logic itself" (VI). J. Parain-Vial (Dijon, France), in her contribution [58] to the 1966 volume, observes that "formal logic is general and not proper to law" and that "if one can conceive of a legal logic proper, it is in the general sense of methodology" (47). "The specificity of legal logic results therefore solely from the specificity of the relations it elaborates, relations which are found at the point of articulation of reality and value" (55).

A. Bayart, in his account [05] of the position of the Belgian group published in the 1966 volume, remarks that "it would not be difficult to cite several works which, besides the title 'legal logic', have no common point between them" (172). He relates that "the Center became antiformalistic in the sense that one is rather sceptical there as to the interest which may attach, in the present state of affairs, to the attempts to formulate for legal argument rules of the same kind as those found in formal logic and, in particular, in mathematical logic" (175). He points out that "whoever is an antiformalist in respect to legal logic will not fail to insist on the fact that the techniques of the lawyer's reasoning vary according to circumstances" (175). In particular, "legal logic as the Center understands it" (174) involves the study of "social techniques apt to warrant the judges' wisdom" (177) and of those flexible rules which allow that "moral sentiment intervenes decisively in legal reasoning" (179). With respect to formalism, the question arises "whether one cannot hope to transform the nonexact sciences, by progressively substituting purely formal concepts for the not absolutely precise concepts which are found in these sciences. If one intends to pronounce on whatever the progress of the logicomathematical sciences will be able to realize in the future, it appears to us impossible to demonstrate rigorously that this ideal is realizable or that it is not. Personally, however, we opt for the negative" (177). Paul Foriers [22], in the 1967 volume of Logique et Analyse, relates that since the legal section of the Belgian Center became convinced that "legal argument differs from mathematical argument", it was decided "to carry on in the way of gradually deepening the analysis of legal argument in order to make an inventory of techniques. The answer to the question of formalization was postponed, and the question of whether such a formalization is possible and, in that case, desirable, was reserved for the future" (27). For the time being, "an attitude of scepticism with respect to formal logic" (40) prevails at the Center.

Two kinds of views appear to mix in the Franco-Belgian doctrine: a philosophical thesis and some ancillary theoretical views about the nature of legal argument and legal logic, on the one hand, and some practical views and requirements, on the other. At the same time the impression is given that the members of the group, as a whole, regard the latter views rather than the former as the essential core of their "antiformalism". Accordingly, though the position under reexamination is here referred to as "antiformalistic", the philosophical thesis in question, which is the primary concern of the present inquiry, is described less extremely as "nonformalistic". The following comments[16], applying the collective label "antiformalists" to the upholders of the doctrine and disregarding whatever disagreements and nuances are evident among them, are meant to refer to the basic position which seems to be common to most of them.

The fundamental philosophical thesis of nonformalism contrasts the logic of legal argument with the logic of mathematical argument in maintaining that legal argument is essentially nonformal, i.e. nonformalizable in principle. A simple consideration strongly suggests that the very idea of such an argument is a misconception. Indeed, if the rational force of a legal argument does not reside in its ideal logical form, then what is its foundation? Supposing that all the premises of such an argument are sound, how is the soundness of the conclusion warranted, if it is neither deductively entailed nor even inductively supported by the premises? It would be futile to try to answer this question by appeal to nonformal rules of inference. For such a "material" rule, warranting the acceptability of the argument's conclusion provided that all its premises are acceptable, would be expressible by the formula "if P then C", "P" representing the conjunction of the premises and "C" the conclusion. This formula is one of a statement of fact or of a rule of law, depending on whether the conclusion is descriptive or prescriptive. For the rule of inference in question to be considered rational, the foregoing formula would have to be accepted as sound, either in science or in law. Consequently, it would be usable as a premise, and its inclusion in the argument would provide this latter with formal rational force. It

---

16 These comments are a modified version of [33].

thus seems obvious that a nonformal rule of inference is never fundamental or indispensable.

The antiformalists adduce two main considerations in support of their philosophical thesis. Firstly, they point out that, in contrast to mathematical argument, legal argument is not compelling. Secondly, they claim that legal argument is essentially a human activity, argumentation, whereas mathematical demonstration is essentially impersonal.

The former consideration visibly leans on a mistaken view of formal logic. Indeed, the antiformalists conceive of formal logic as being concerned with deductive arguments alone. Consequently, they protest against the restriction of logic in general to formal logic. Since the "noncompelling" legal argument is not a deduction, they argue, it depends on nonformal logic. If the formalistic doctrine did really involve the restriction of logic in general to deductive logic, it would certainly require modification. But it does not. It is true that deductive logic constitutes the more extensively developed branch of (formal) logic at present, but there exists an ample and rapidly growing literature concerning (formal) inductive logic. It is also true that no comprehensive system of inductive logic applicable to law is available at present. Nevertheless, there seems to be no sufficient reason for considering all eventual inductive logic inapplicable to law in principle. Adequate inductive procedures, it may be surmised, would enable the judge to compare the desirability of competing decisions rationally and to make rational choices, on the basis of the available evidence, between alternatives concerning the interpretation of a law, its applicability, the gravity of the offense, and the severity of the sanction. However, the antiformalists refuse to recognize the suitability, even in principle, of inductive logic to law. In their view, induction is restricted to the empirical sciences. This view seems to be related to the traditional usage according to which induction is conceived of as the method of establishing scientific hypotheses by generalization from particular cases. At any rate, questions of terminology apart, the antiformalists make a point of discarding the very idea of formal nondeductive legal logic. As they see it, the distinction between "exact" and "nonexact" fields essentially involves a corresponding distinction between formal and nonformal logic; and inasmuch as law intrinsically involves valuation, it is irreducibly nonexact, and hence, they argue, the logic of legal argument is essentially nonformal. This account does not seem acceptable. The relevant distinction is that between pure and empirical fields; law belongs to the latter. Empirical systems require applied logic. Applied logic provides rules involving the special terms of the system's vocabulary, but the inferential apparatus remains purely formal. The valuational aspect of legal argumentation may be seen as resolvable, in principle, into a logical element — viz. the deontic character of legal logic — and a complex residual element — confirmation — which, in turn, involves legal and methodological grounds, empirical elements — viz. psychosociological laws and particular facts — and a formal element — inductive support. The antiformalists, however, tend to discard this analysis with respect to confirmation and to consider the dependence on values to be an essentially nonempirical characteristic, distinguishing law from empirical as well as from pure fields. Their insistence on valuational confirmation hardly conceals the absence in their doctrine of objective criteria for the appraisal of the allegedly nonformal arguments as rational. They might retort that, at any rate, formal legal logic of inductive support is virtually nonexistent. This cannot be denied. As a matter of fact, legal argument is, so to speak, doomed to intuition at present. But according to the formalistic doctrine such argument can nevertheless be presumed rational under the regulative assumption of a possible formalization. Mere intuition cannot serve as a criterion of rationality.

The second subsidiary antiformalistic consideration mentioned above, to the effect that legal argument is essentially a human activity whereas mathematical argument is impersonal, hinges on the typical process-and-product ambiguity of the word "argument" ("*raisonnement*" in French). Antiformalists as well as formalists conceive of logic in general as "the study of argument". However, this characterization is equivocal, inasmuch as "argument" denotes both the activity of reasoning and the linguistic product of this activity. While formalists mean "argument" in the latter sense, suitably idealized, antiformalists use the term in the latter sense with respect to mathematics and in the former with respect to law. The formal logician, in point of principle, systematically disregards the pragmatic aspects of discourse and deals only with its linguistic products qua subject to rules of syntax and semantics. Accordingly, all such "rules of reasoning" that are rhetorical, heuristic, or legal — for it is a noteworthy fact that legal reasoning as a process is subject to legal rules — are not rules of logic in the formalists' sense. But it is precisely such rules that constitute legal logic proper according to the antiformalists. Are, then, these latter not right in maintaining that legal logic, *as they conceive it,* is nonformal? This question cannot be answered by a simple yes or no. The antiformalists are certainly right insofar as they mean to say that the pragmatics of legal reasoning is not formal logic, either pure or applied. Yet, since this assertion is trivial and by no means nonformalistic, it can hardly be seen as an adequate version of the philosophical thesis, the nonformalistic character of which resides in the contrast between legal and mathematical logic. To maintain this contrast and at the same time to preserve the thesis from absurdity, the term "logic" must be construed not as "pragmatics of argument" but as "semiotics of argument". Thus construed, the thesis amounts to this: the semiotics of legal argument is essentially pragmatics, whereas the semiotics of mathematical argument is essentially syntax and semantics. This claim is philosophically unsound. The basic ambiguity of "argument" is to be found, naturally, in all fields of reasoning. On the one hand, a mathematical demonstration is always a human realization; on the other hand, legal argumentation, inasmuch as it involves explicit and implicit premises and conclusions, never lacks an actual linguistic product or a potential ideal correlate. Would it not be possible to save the plausibility of the thesis in question by construing "logic" as "pragmatics" with respect to legal argument and as "syntax and semantics" with respect to mathematical argument? This interpretation would involve the inconvenience of using the term "logic" syncategorematically. But, at any rate, the resulting affirmation, though trivially true, would again fail to be nonformalistic.

In sum, neither of the two subsidiary considerations of the antiformalists lends support to genuine philosophical nonformalism.

Several theses of a practical nature which are involved in the antiformalistic position will now be surveyed. They concern, successively, judicial interpretation, the development of the legal system, and research and teaching.

As for interpretation, the antiformalist opposes the strict, literal application of legal rules, which is often described as "formalistic". Consequently, he requires that the judge should be free to determine the meaning of the law according to circumstances, deviating, if necessary, from the ordinary senses of expressions. This requirement is surely compatible with the doctrine of philosophical formalism. Indeed, as law is not a pure theoretical system but one applied to social reality, the formalist is not at all surprised to find that the application of legal rules depends on their interpretation. He realizes that legal interpretation, to be adequate, must depend on empirical confirmation. There is nothing in his doctrine to prevent him from recognizing that social dynamism, as manifested in the variation of the confirmatory information, necessitates flexible, continuously readjusted interpretation.

As regards the development of the legal system, the antiformalist opposes formalization. In support of his opposition he advances two main reasons. *First reason:* the formalization of the legal system is not capable of dispensing with the need for interpretation. This claim is likewise not opposed to philosophical formalism. The view that it is so opposed seems to involve a misconception of the nature of formalization and, more precisely, a failure to distinguish between pure and empirical fields. Formalization, in all cases, involves reconstruction of a system. But it is only in pure fields that such reconstruction can, at least in principle, be accomplished definitively: namely, the formalization of a pure field is effectively completed as soon as all the rules and postulates of the system have been appropriately formulated. An empirical field, on the other hand, is not determined a priori by its rules and postulates, since these possess a synthetic aspect and depend on empirical confirmation. As the confirmatory process is interminable, it follows that the reconstruction of the system, too, is interminable; in particular, the special vocabulary and the meanings of its terms cannot be "congealed" without prejudice to the system's applicability and explanatory or justificatory power. *Second reason:* legal argument is in principle not formalizable. This claim, which amounts to the philosophical thesis of nonformalism, has already been commented upon. It is worth noting that no real opposition between formalism and antiformalism with respect to formalization exists on the practical level. Indeed, though he discards the very idea of argument in principle nonformalizable, the philosophical formalist may nevertheless oppose formalization, in particular if he deems the task of little avail or too difficult.

Finally, the antiformalistic position involves a few practical requirements in relation to research and teaching. These requirements concern not only the professional question of the subject matter or field of research and teaching, but also the terminological point of the field's very designation; besides, they may either be moderate and hence more properly describable as nonformalistic or be definitely antiformalistic. Thus, on the one hand, *professional nonformalism* demands the fostering of the study and teaching of legal logic in the antiformalists' sense, i. e. mainly of practical legal methodology, whereas *terminological nonformalism* insists upon the effective employment of the term "logic" and especially "legal logic" in the antiformalists' sense. On the other hand, *professional antiformalism* opposes the fostering of the study and teaching of legal logic in the formalists' sense, whereas *terminological antiformalism* protests against the unqualified employment of the terms "logic" and especially "legal logic" in the formalists' sense. Professional nonformalism is obviously compatible with philosophical formalism, provided only that the research and teaching in question do not involve the philosophical thesis of nonformalism. But are not the three remaining requirements, too, compatible with philosophical formalism? This suggestion may appear particularly paradoxical with respect to professional antiformalism. There is, however, no radical incompatibility between the recognition of the formal nature of legal argument and the opposition to the elaboration and teaching of the formal theory of such argument. From the philosophical viewpoint there is nothing to prevent a formalist from yielding on the terminological issue as well, provided of course that the uses in question do not presuppose the philosophical thesis of nonformalism. A terminological controversy may have philosophical interest as long as it involves some conceptual disagreement. But when agreement as to concepts has been reached, the question of preferring one term to another for a given concept becomes philosophically indifferent, notwithstanding all practical interest it may have, e. g. owing to the emotive and persuasive significance of a term.

In brief, when the practical theses upheld by the antiformalists are disjoined from the philosophical thesis of nonformalism, they are not found to be radically incompatible with philosophical formalism. It seems that the antiformalists mainly care for the practical aspects of their doctrine and maintain the philosophical thesis only because they tend to consider that it constitutes an inevitable presupposition or a fitting vindication of the practical theses. Inasmuch as this consideration is unwarranted, one may feel justified in concluding that the disagreement between the antiformalism of the Belgian Center and a formalistic position such as is represented in the present book is not really deep-rooted. Indeed, when the inessential philosophical prop of practical antiformalism is disregarded, the divergence between formalists and antiformalists with respect to legal argument appears to be due to a difference of perspective. Antiformalism counts many supporters among lawyers who are professionally concerned with argumentation, while formalists are very often nonlawyers whose interest in law is philosophical. The former turn naturally towards practice, while the latter aim at theoretical insight. Consequently, the former attach basic importance to the part of legal pragmatics dealing with rhetorical, heuristic, and, of course, legal rules and methods of legal argumentation, while the latter are primarily interested in systematically reconstructed legal syntax and semantics. The prominently emotive meaning of the word "logic" as a term of positive appraisal seems to account to a large extent for the insistence with which either party claims the plain epithet "logic" for the preferred field. This terminological controversy — a clash, in fact, between two "persuasive definitions" — has a historical aspect in that formalists adopt the specialized meaning of the word "logic" which has definitely emerged in recent times, while antiformalists adhere to the older, more comprehensive meaning, which appears to be still far from obsolete.

The two perspectives are easily distinguishable. On the one hand, the lawyer is keenly interested in the art of argumentation as actually practised by the prominent members of the profession. He wishes to become acquainted with the real judicial work, in particular with the techniques the judge employs in his quest for premises, his choice of texts, their interpretation, etc. He is keenly interested in becoming familiar with the advocate's practical methods of controversy and persuasion. In brief, he wants to learn all the procedures of discourse effectively employed in the courts. He therefore needs legal logic as conceived by the antiformalists. He finds formal logic doubly disappointing: firstly, because it disregards the pragmatic context, and secondly, because it is concerned with an ideal state of the legal system rather than with its actual state. On the other hand, it is precisely in the idea of formalization that the philosophical interest of the formalists' legal logic resides: rational reconstruction of the legal system both presupposes and deepens the understanding of the intrinsic structures of law. Yet, though mutually opposed, the two perspectives illuminate one another to a certain extent. To be sure, since formal legal logic in its present state is poor, its deductive part being simple and its inductive part virtually nonexistent, its practical interest for argumentation is all the more limited. However, the idea of a formalized legal system is undoubtedly capable of guiding the rational development of the existing system and of thus ameliorating the arguments formulated within its framework. Inversely, part of current legal methodology presents some interest for formal legal logic; e. g., the heuristic types of legal argument — *a pari*, *a fortiori*, etc. — might serve as starting points for the elaboration of inductive forms and procedures.

The problem of the specificity of legal logic merits recapitulation. The rejoinder to the question of whether legal logic is specific or not must, naturally, depend on what is meant by "legal logic" and by "specific". There seem to be only a few significant alternatives. Firstly, conceived as the methodology of law, legal logic can be said to be specific to law in the same nonradical sense in which the methodology of any field of empirical science can be said to be specific to it. Secondly, as the syntax and semantics of the systematic language of law, legal logic can be said to be specific to law in the same nonradical sense in which the syntax and semantics of the systematic language of any other theoretical field — scientific, ethical, administrative, or the field of a game with rules — can be said to be specific to it. Incidentally, this latter use of "logic" is akin to the use preferred by those analytical philosophers who, in referring to conceptual schemes, speak of "the logic of" such or such other field. Thirdly, as the syntax and semantics of the logical expressions of law, legal logic can be said to be specific to law in that it is deontic logic and, as such, differs from the logic of science. Moreover, certain kinds of intuitionistic logic seem suitable to law. Finally, to the extent that the specificity of legal logic is meant to connote the nonformal nature of the rational force of legal argument, legal logic cannot be said to be specific. In the Belgian discussion, the claim that legal logic is specific does not seem to have been advanced, let alone vindicated, in any other intelligible sense.

The Discussion in the English-Speaking Countries

Introduction

Part III is devoted to a selection of texts from varied sources, all in English. The authors represented are, with one exception, students of jurisprudence. They are: Julius Stone (Sydney), Edward H. Levi (Chicago), H. L. A. Hart (Oxford), O. C. Jensen (Natal); the exception is Stephen E. Toulmin, the English analytical philosopher and historian of science.

The following appraisal of Perelman's doctrine by Stone, extracted from the latter's 1964 volume [71], will serve as a suitable transition:

Even if lawyers modestly reject the tribute implied when philosophers offer the process of legal argument and judgment on a case as a model of argument based on "good grounds", which is at the heart of "the new rhetorics", they should draw one inference from the fact that it is made. This is that the ways of reasoning which the "good grounds" philosophy and "the new rhetorics" seek to describe are not essentially different from those which common-law judges have actually been using for generations. And this fact, even while it makes such developments in philosophy interesting to jurisprudence, and offers to both lawyers and philosophers mutual comfort and support from their future cooperation in tasks now recognized to be common, still leaves the immediate usefulness of "the new rhetorics" to lawyers and judges rather limited (336).

And Stone concludes:

The "new rhetorics", in short, cannot yet provide the actors in the judicial process with new techniques to remedy the lacks they mainly feel; though it may provide the students of the process with a new terminology and a new conceptual framework with which to understand and explain it.

It may, as it were, provide jurisprudents with new pastures in which to browse; but even if these pastures look greener and richer than those familiar to us, and are set in a landscape more comforting to our eyes, it is still grass that we must continue to crop. We continue to depend in the last analysis upon our own ability to ruminate, digest, and transform what we have digested into living vision and energy. When we seek to identify the *tópoi* on which rhetorical reasoning may rest, we have first to fix the points of consensus among the wise; and for this we must first be able to recognize who is "wise", and what wisdom is on particular matters. That wisdom which has always been the governing, moderating, and evaluating core of good judgment, is still as intangible and inarticulate a presupposition of "the new rhetorics", as it is of the reasoning of lawyers and judges (336—337).

Stone does not recognize any logic other than formal logic and accordingly holds that "since logic is indifferent to the subject on which it operates, juristic logic is not a special kind of logic, but only formal logic as relevant in the field of law" (303). Yet, as a compensation for this concession to formalism, he distinguishes in the domain of law between those reasonings, conclusive-deductive, which are subject to logic and those, "rhetorical" or "topical", which are not. The primary purpose of his book is "to study the processes of judicial and juristic thought, and the place therein of logic and other kinds of reasoning" (1). He opposes the extensive use of the term "logic" be remarking that "the problems of the proper boundary in decision making, between the use of formal logic and less cogent reasoning, are already difficult and confused enough" and that "there is enough substantive modern irrationalism, even invading the field of logic itself, without risking further cross-purposes by this kind of terminological venture" (303). By what seems an ironical slip of memory, he presumes that "lawyers will accordingly be indebted to Professor Perelman ... for avoiding this wider use of the term 'logic'" (303); he is here apparently unaware of the variation in the Belgian antiformalists' basic terminology since the early fifties (see pt. II, Introduction).

To illustrate how the "topical reasonings" operate, Stone remarks: "As Wisdom's and Perelman's metaphors 'legs of a chair' and 'threads of cloth' have been seen to indicate, the 'proof' springing from a single *tópos* or *locus* is likely to be very weak, and strength comes only in the accumulation of *tópoi* relied on" (331). The mention of John Wisdom is worth expanding in view of the considerable influence that seems to have been exerted by the views on legal argument set forth by this Cambridge philosopher in his essay

"Gods", in which the metaphor cited by Stone occurs. This essay, which dates from 1944—1945 [78], happens to be the oldest source quoted in the present book. The following quotations from it are exhaustive with regard to what directly concerns legal argument. "The line between a question of fact and a question or decision as to the application of a name is not so simple as this way of putting things suggests" (190). "Things are revealed to us not only by the scientists with microscopes, but also by the poets, the prophets, and the painters. What is so isn't merely a matter of 'the facts'. For sometimes when there is agreement as to the facts there is still argument as to whether defendant did or did not 'exercise resonable care', was or was not 'negligent'" (192). "*In courts of law* it sometimes happens that opposing counsel are agreed as to the facts and are not trying to settle a question of further fact, are not trying to settle whether the man who admittedly had quarrelled with the deceased did or did not murder him, but are concerned with whether Mr. *A* who admittedly handed his long-trusted clerk signed blank checks did or did not exercise reasonable care, whether a ledger is or is not a document, whether a certain body was or was not a public authority" (195). This is succeeded by the main relevant passage, as follows:

In such cases we notice that the process of argument is not a *chain* of demonstrative reasoning. It is a presenting and representing of those features of the case which *severally cooperate* in favor of the conclusion, in favor of saying what the reasoner wishes said, in favor of calling the situation by the name by which he wishes to call it. The reasons are like the legs of a chair, not the links of a chain. Consequently although the discussion is a priori and the steps are not a matter of experience, the procedure resembles scientific argument in that the reasoning is not *vertically* extensive but *horizontally* extensive — it is a matter of the cumulative effect of several independent premises, not of the repeated transformation of one or two. And because the premises are severally inconclusive the process of deciding the issue becomes a matter of weighing the cumulative effect of one group of severally inconclusive items against the cumulative effect of another group of severally inconclusive items, and thus lends itself to description in terms of conflicting "probabilities". This encourages the feeling that the issue is one of fact — that it is a matter of guessing from the premises at a further fact, at what is to come. But this is a muddle. *The dispute does not cease to be a priori because it is a matter of the cumulative effect of severally inconclusive premises.* The logic of the dispute is not that of a chain of deductive reasoning as in a mathematic calculation. But nor is it a matter of collecting from several inconclusive items of information an expectation as to something further, as when a doctor from a patient's symptoms guesses at what is wrong, or a detective from many clues guesses the criminal. It has its own sort of logic and its own sort of end — the solution of the question at issue is a decision, a ruling by the judge. But it is not an arbitrary decision though the rational connections are neither quite like those in vertical deductions nor like those in inductions in which from many signs we guess at what is to come; and though the decision manifests itself in the application of a name it is no more merely the application of a name than is the pinning on of a medal merely the pinning on of a bit of metal. Whether a lion with stripes is a tiger or a lion is, if you like, merely a matter of the application of a name. Whether Mr. So-and-So of whose conduct we have so complete a record did or did not exercise reasonable care is not merely a matter of the application of a name or, if we choose to say it is, then we must remember that with this name a game is lost and won and a game with very heavy stakes. With the judges' choice of a name for the facts goes an attitude, and the declaration, the ruling, is an exclamation evincing that attitude. But *it is an exclamation which not only has a purpose but also has a logic*, a logic surprisingly like that of "futile", "deplorable", "graceful", "grand", "divine" (195—196).

"In the legal case", "the procedures for settling these differences" of attitudes consist of "reasoning and redescription" (197), and may involve "referring to other cases" (198). Generally, not only in the domain of law,

in criticizing other conclusions and especially conclusions which are largely the expression of an attitude, we have not only to ascertain what reasons there are for them but also to decide what things are reasons and how much. This latter process of sifting reasons from causes is part of the critical process for every belief, but in some spheres it has been done pretty fully already. In these spheres we don't need to examine the actual processes to belief and distil from them a logic. But in other spheres this remains to be done. Even in science or on the stock exchange or in ordinary life we sometimes hesitate to condemn a belief or a hunch merely because those who believe it cannot offer the sort of reasons we had hoped for (201).

Wisdom does not express his opinion as to how fully the "distillation of logic" has been achieved in the legal sphere. Stone, doubtlessly, would deem it proper to apply to Wisdom's account of legal logic the following remark, which he in fact makes in his 1964 volume [71] with respect to another author: "Agreement to these formulations leaves us still at some distance from having identified 'sense and wisdom', or the ways of achieving them" (322). In a sense, it is indeed not easy to repudiate Wisdom's formulation: its vagueness leaves room for various, even mutually opposed interpretations, thus greatly contributing to its popularity, which is due primarily to its emotional appeal. The quoted passages need not be examined now, as their most influential implications will be dealt with further on in relation to other authors and will be directly commented upon in the concluding section of pt. III.

A similar vagueness characterizes some of Stone's formulations on legal reasoning, in particular those relative to "the inbuilt dualism between leeways of choice and checks on arbitrary choice, within the very materials and methods with which the judges have to work" (234). Examination of his book would bring out both some such common confusions as that of logic with pragmatics and methodology, and some such acceptable views as that underlying the emphasis on "the 'nonlegal' factors in decision making" (210). However, his 1964 volume will not be dealt with in what follows, despite the relevance of some of its parts to the present inquiry. The volume in question is, in fact, a largely expanded and rearranged version of the first part of Stone's treatise of 1946 [70], whose three parts deal with Law and Logic, Law and Justice, and Law and Society, respectively. The sixth chapter of the first part contains the gist of Stone's avowedly unchanged views on legal argument, and has, therefore, been selected to represent his conception in sect. 1 below. In view of "the dispersal of the old ch. 6" ([71], 13) in the new volume, this selection appears all the more justified.

Sect. 2 deals with Levi's general conception of legal argument as set forth in his book *An Introduction to Legal Reasoning*, 1948. My critical account will omit the specifically legal part of the book, where Levi defends and illustrates his conception of legal reasoning by means of a detailed analysis of the evolution of three concepts, drawn from American and English case law, the United States federal statutes, and the United States Constitution. With the aid of quotations from judgments given over a period of many decades, he exemplifies changes in the meaning and scope of terms as well as changes in the terminology itself and especially emphasizes the dependence of legal reasoning on economic, social, and political conditions and on social theory.

Although Hart has not studied the problem of legal logic extensively[1], three among the seven sections to follow are devoted to his writings, thus duly reflecting his impact on contemporary analyt-

---

1 However, see "Problems of Legal Reasoning", a section in Hart's encyclopedic article [28], pp. 268—272.

ical jurisprudence. The essay discussed in sect. 3 was his first philosophical publication, and the essay discussed in sect. 4 was his inaugural lecture in Oxford. In these works, to be sure, legal argument is not the central theme but is dealt with more or less casually. However, it is viewed in the perspective of the legal language and system. Consequently, discussion of these works appears particularly relevant to the subsidiary purpose of the present book, viz. that of ascertaining the general structural properties of a legal system.

Next, two further conceptions of legal argument are examined, both somewhat influenced by Hart. Sect. 5 is devoted to Jensen's book *The Nature of Legal Argument*, 1957, and sect. 6 to Toulmin's book *The Uses of Argument*, 1958. These books, like the aforementioned books by Stone and Levi and that by Hart to be mentioned, are treated selectively. Jensen's book consists of a general introduction and three parts dealing with Logic and the Law, Negligence Cases, and Attempt, respectively. In what follows, the introduction and the first part will be considered, but not be specifically legal aspects of the other two parts. Toulmin's book is a collection of essays. In his opinion, the force of nonmathematical argument resides in the fulfillment of certain procedural requirements. This is his idea of the "jurisprudential analogy", to which the discussion in sect. 6 will be largely limited.

Sect. 7, devoted to part of Hart's book *The Concept of Law*, 1961, will not be concerned with such major topics of that book as the critical account of John Austin's legal positivism, Hart's own conception of law as the union of primary and secondary rules, or his analysis of the relations between law and morals. The discussion will be limited to a single chapter of *The Concept of Law*, the seventh, which deals with the two mutually opposed views of the nature of legal rules and legal reasoning known in jurisprudence as "formalism" and "rule-scepticism".

1. Stone on "Uses and Limitations of Formal Logic in Legal Reasoning"

The present section is devoted to the sixth chapter of Julius Stone's 1946 treatise [70]. The chapter in question, entitled "Uses and Limitations of Formal Logic in Legal Reasoning", attests to Stone's adherence to a progressive philosophical attitude and suffers from only one serious shortcoming, viz. lack of clarity in the conception of

nonconclusive modes of legal argument. This shortcoming, however, due to the restriction of the scope of (formal) logic to deductive
argument alone, may be considered virtually unavoidable, at least
as long as the applicability of inductive logic to empirical fields
remains an open problem. In this situation, indeed, a student of
legal reasoning like Stone, whose primary interest in logic is avowedly practical, can hardly be blamed for disregarding induction. Criticism of this disregard, accordingly, cannot be expected to point to
any acquired solution; at most, it is capable of bringing out the
problem. References to inductive logic, in this section no less than
throughout this book, however unguarded their wording, should
therefore invariably be construed as concerning the eventual or the
ideal, not the actual or the expedient.

In the following brief comments, which are in fact limited to
the single theme of inductive logic, Stone's views are largely implied
rather than explicitly reported. The order of his exposition is preserved, section by section, and the headings of all the sections are
quoted.

"§ 1. *Logic Concerns Implications from Premises, Not the Truth
of the Premises*" (137). This characterization ignores inductive logic.
It is deductive logic which investigates "the conditions under which
a conclusion follows from certain premises" and is concerned "with
the validity of the argument, with whether the conclusion follows
from the premises". The primary concern of inductive logic, on the
other hand, is not with the validity of "implication" or entailment,
but with assessments of inductive support.

"§ 2. *Law of the Logical Analysis and Law as Operative in
Society*" (138). "Analytical jurisprudence, in short, is concerned with
the testing of law by logic. It cannot *alone* discover or even identify
actual 'law' anywhere; it can only tell us how far legal propositions
can stand together in the same logical system. It is the concentration, therefore, of the analyst on logical self-consistency in the
law which distinguishes his 'law' from the law of any actual society."
This calls for qualification: the said "concentration" need not involve a dogmatic denial of an inductive logic of legal confirmation.

"§ 3. *Logic and Competing Premises*" (138). Though it is true
that "the choice between competing starting points cannot be made
by logical deduction" (139), this is not to say that "the process of
choice is beyond the realm of logic". Stone himself points to the

necessity of "a reference to the facts and to the standards of justice (however covert) in order to decide which analogy will give a 'preferable' result in the instant case"; but he fails to clarify the rational nature of this "reference" and its influence on "the process of choice". Again, his silence on this point is quite intelligible: legal inductive logic does not so far exist. This circumstance also explains "the often proclaimed judicial aversion to deal with such considerations"[2]. Although he wishes to oppose this attitude, the result of which "is simply to leave the very ground and foundation of judgments inarticulate and often unconscious", Stone is unable to provide the slightest indication as to how "such considerations" should be rationalized. He therefore simply condemns "the very ground and foundation of judgments" to dependence on "the prelogical choice". The inductive logician, to be sure, when confronted with "competing premises", would not be able to establish any one of them conclusively; yet, by calculating the suitable degrees of inductive support, he might provide excellent reasons for preferring some of them to others.

"*§ 4. Logic and the Limits of Analogy*" (140). Also "when, in appearance, only one analogy (or major premise) seems to be available", inductive procedures might successfully assume a role in legislative and judicial arguments that "logical deductions" are absolutely incapable of playing.

"*§ 5. Limits of Logical Compulsion*" (141). Inductive logic, while not equalling deductive logic in "logical compulsion", might nevertheless considerably reduce the waste of energy involved in "the properly vaunted trial and error of the common-law judicial process" (142). This is a prospect for the future. On the other hand, Stone is of course quite right in expecting of judges even today that, in applying specific legal concepts, they should refrain from "the automatic transposition of such concepts and their logical consequences from one subject matter to another". Intuitive reasoning, provided it leans on solid background knowledge and on sufficient experience, is certainly preferable to "automatic", thoughtless decision and may be regarded as the natural precursor of an eventual kind of distinctly elaborate and systematically controllable inductive deliberation.

---

2 This quotation and the following one are Stone's, taken from Justice Holmes.

"*§ 6. Effect of Social Change and Consequent Legal Change on the Logical Relations Between Legal Concepts and Propositions*" (142). Even if it is for some deeper reasons that "the law is not a logically monistic system", whatever the exact nature of such a system may be, it does not seem to follow that one should remain satisfied with a series of consecutive legal systems arranged "into a syllogistic pattern", especially if in such a framework "legal concepts and propositions" are capable of only "a limited amount of logically consistent arrangement" (143). To the extent that appropriate inductive methods might serve to increase "the suitability of the propositions" in question and to rationalize the "impact of changes of social structure upon the law of the particular time" (143), the gap between the "law of the logical analyst" (138) and "law as it actually operates" (144) need not be considered unavoidable.

"*§ 7. Role of Syllogistic Logic in the Law: Criticism and Confirmation*" (144). Inductive methods would be able, much more than "syllogistic logic", to "display the relations between what is already known" and to serve as an effective tool in "the process of confirmation of hypotheses" (145), though it would not aim at their conclusive "verification". Indeed, Stone's view about hypotheses, to the effect that "unless they are capable of such verification one way or the other they seem for our practical purposes in the law meaningless or strictly nonsensical", can hardly be maintained. Absolutely certain synthetic utterances are no more possible in law than in science.

"*§ 8. Role of Syllogistic Logic in the Law: Persuasion and Orderly Understanding*" (145). Proper inductive logic would presumably not lag behind deductive logic in its pragmatic virtues and would likewise constitute "a most powerful means of self-persuasion and persuasion of others". It would also no doubt merit the remark that "as long as men aspire to act rationally, that is, explicably and not capriciously, they must have resort to the critical virtues of logic". The view that "no system of law would be capable of knowledge, much less of external enforcement, if it were subject to variation with all the varied and changing situations which arise in social relations", appears to involve a considerable amount of exaggeration. In any event, the inductivization of law would be quite compatible with the open texture of legal terms and with the flexibility of their interpretation.

"§ 9. Need for a Balanced View of the Uses and Limitations of Syllogistic Analysis" (145). Stone remarks that "syllogistic analysis", when it discloses a *non sequitur* in a legal rule, "does invite an inquiry whether it can be more adequately grounded", and "by exposing the premises it invites comparison of the premises with the actualities in social life to which they refer". However, he points out, "the results of logical deduction from existing premises" cannot adequately replace "the assessment of all aspects of the given situation". He does not clarify the logical nature of the said "inquiry", "comparison", and "assessment". It is clear, though, that these activities, insofar as they involve reasoning, belong in principle to the scope of inductive logic, which thus appears capable of becoming, in a way, a most useful "means of creating law, or even of deciding what the law is on a particular point", and of serving some "other purposes" for which Stone rightly considers "syllogistic analysis" quite inadequate. When the "proper sphere of logical analysis" (146) is anticipated in such a comprehensive manner, many of "the more difficult as well as the more important aspects of the legal order" no longer appear to "lie beyond it". It then becomes all the more evident that "within its proper field, indeed, even the systematic analytical approach to law serves important purposes" (145), and Stone's opposition to "any wholesale distrust of logic as such" (137) then appears all the more cogent. Admittedly, the extent to which the anticipation of inductive legal logic can itself be vindicated remains an open question.

2. Levi: Legal Argument as a Reflection of Social Change

Edward H. Levi, in his book [52] *An Introduction to Legal Reasoning*, 1948, represents legal reasoning as a reflection and expression of the dynamism of law and of its social background. He states the aim and principal ideas of the book thus:

This is an attempt to describe generally the process of legal reasoning in the field of case law and in the interpretation of statutes and of the Constitution. It is important that the mechanism of legal reasoning should not be concealed by its pretense. The pretense is that the law is a system of known rules applied by a judge: the pretense has long been under attack. In an important sense legal rules are never clear, and, if a rule had to be clear before it could be imposed, society would be impossible. The mechanism accepts the differences of view and ambiguities of words. It provides for the participation of the community in resolving the ambiguity by providing a forum for the discussion of policy in the gap of ambiguity. On serious controversial questions, it makes it possible to take the first step in the direction of what otherwise would be forbidden ends. The mechanism is indispensable to peace in a community (1).

In anticipation of the results of his detailed analyses of judgments (which will not be dealt with here), Levi outlines "the basic pattern" and the cyclical evolution ("circular motion") of legal reasoning as follows:

The basic pattern of legal reasoning is reasoning by example. It is reasoning from case to case. It is a threefold process described by the doctrine of precedent in which a proposition descriptive of the first case is made into a rule of law and then applied to a next similar situation. The steps are these: similarity is seen between cases; next the rule of law inherent in the first case is announced; then the rule of law is made applicable to the second case (1—2).

In the long run a circular motion can be seen. The first stage is the creation of the legal concept which is built up as cases are compared. The period is one in which the court fumbles for a phrase. Several phrases may be tried out; the misuse or misunderstanding of words itself may have an effect. The concept sounds like another, and the jump to the second is made. The second stage is the period when the concept is more or less fixed, although reasoning by example continues to classify items inside and out of the concept. The third stage is the breakdown of the concept, as reasoning by example has moved so far ahead as to make it clear that the suggestive influence of the word is no longer desired (8—9).

Levi may be said to have fully succeeded in exhibiting the dynamic character of law. The following criticism will be confined to his conception of legal argument and legal logic insofar as it can be shown to depend on deficient analysis or on misleading wording. The basic expression "the process of legal reasoning" and its abbreviations "the legal process" or "the process" are systematically misleading in that they are used indiscriminately to refer to three different kinds of processes — viz., to substantively legal arguments as actually framed, to methodological procedures (operations of system construction, including specifically methodological arguments), and to historical processes (the evolution of terminology, meanings, etc.). It is true that the processes of the first two kinds are in fact closely interconnected and constitute important occurrences in the processes of the third kind; it is true, moreover, that the historical evolution of the relatively short processes of the first two kinds is comprised among the processes of the third kind. However, these facts do not lessen but rather increase the need for a rigorous distinction between the three kinds of processes in any analytical discussion of legal reasoning. It will now be shown that there is a real danger of fallacy in the mistaking of one of them for another.

The analysis of legal reasoning as "a three-step process" actually concerns processes of the first two kinds, mainly the methodological procedures, whereas the analysis of legal reasoning as a three-stage process of "circular motion" actually concerns processes of the third kind. Some other key expressions are affected by a similar ambiguity. The expression "the mechanism of reasoning" masks the important differences that exist between modes of argument (deduction, induction, intuitive inference), methods of system construction, and characteristic aspects of historical evolution. The expression "pretense" — the pretense being, as already quoted, "that the law is a system of known rules applied by the judge" (1) or, at least, "that general rules, once properly determined, remain unchanged" (2) — blurs the difference between the obviously false claims that the existing system is explicit and adequate or, at least, that the methodological rules actually used for its readjustment are adequate and invariable, and the demand for rationalization of the system and of the ways in which it adapts itself to changing circumstances. "Ambiguity", on the one hand, implies the incompleteness and in-determinateness of the antecedently understood interpretation at a given stage (logical properties) and, on the other hand, it implies the variability and flexibility of that interpretation (developmental properties). As a result of this confusion, some true statements about the developmental process and some sound methodological principles also risk misinterpretation as doubtful claims about arguments and as irrational precepts regarding them. Thus, since "in an important sense legal rules are never clear" (1) — in the sense, indeed, that they contain theoretical terms with an open and variable applicability — and since, moreover, the openness and flexibility of the rules facilitate the readjustment of the system, the author regards "ambiguity" — and he uses this term as applying also to vagueness — as desirable for "legal reasoning": "The categories used in the legal process must be left ambigous in order to permit the infusion of new ideas" (4). In formulating this recommendation, Levi makes no distinction bewteen the methodological advantage of an easily changeable interpretation and the need for the terms used in legal argument at any given moment in the development of the system to be construed univocally and with sufficient precision. He may be deemed at variance with the view that, flexibility and precision of interpretation being in fact compatible with one another, ambiguity and vagueness in reasoning should be opposed rather than encouraged. Similarly, since "the rules change from case to case and are remade with each case" (2) (or rather — to avoid exaggeration — since there always remains the possibility of changing or reformulating them) and since, moreover, "this change in the rules is the indispensable dynamic quality of law" (2), the following conclusion is drawn: "Thus it cannot be said that the legal process is the application of known rules to diverse facts" (3). Insofar as Levi means to say that law is often readjusted under the pressure of urgent problems, he is of course right. But the word "known" as he uses it is far from clear. It does not even seem certain that he intends to imply, at least, that the occasional "remaking" of the rules should involve rendering them intelligible for the purpose of application.

At any rate, Levi considers his analysis of legal reasoning a vindication of "what otherwise would be forbidden ends" (1). It may seem that he regards "the movement of concepts into and out of the law" (8), i. e. the variability of the interpretation of legal terms, as justifying both careless wording of arguments and interpretation through casual associations: "The misuse or misunderstanding of words itself may have an effect. The concept sounds like another, and the jump to the second is made" (9), until a stage is reached when it becomes "clear that the suggestive influence of the word is no longer desired" (9). Words are thus used to "free thought" rather than to "enslave it" (8). This somehow baffling conception of "reasoning by example" causes Levi to hesitate momentarily: perhaps in the described "process" "reasoning is not involved at all" (3)? This can be taken to imply that the history and methodology of a system of argument possibly differs from argument itself. However, "in a sense all reasoning is of this type" (4) — which presumably means that, in the relevant respects, the development of any empirical system resembles the development of law. Consequently, Levi promptly overcomes all hesitation and adopts the vindicatory version: "It is better to say there is reasoning, but it is imperfect" (3). For this improvised fusion of history and method with logic he is even prepared to pay the price of a series of paradoxes. These include views relative to "giving meaning to ambiguity" (104) and to "treating different cases as though they were the same" (3), or the opinion that law is both "certain, unchanging, and expressed in rules" and "uncertain, changing, and only a technique for deciding specific cases" (4), or the opinion that "the compulsion of law is clear" (104), although "the area of doubt", which is "constantly set forth" "as the system works" (104), coincides with its entire domain of application. Such paradoxes are the unavoidable outcome of an analysis which attempts to represent the dynamic character of a system of argument as involving the system's independence of certain "common standards, thought of in terms of closed systems" (3).

A few remarks in the book implicitly concern the inductive nature of legal argument; it would be an exaggeration, however, to try to interpret them as countenancing the development of inductive legal logic. [For Levi himself, who respects the traditional usage, induction is reasoning "from part to whole", whereas reasoning by example, which characterizes law, is reasoning "from part to part" or "from case to case" (1).] Thus Levi points out that although legal reasoning may "appear to be simply deductive", "it is not simply deductive" (8). He refers, moreover, to "the mechanism required for a moving classification system" (4), and emphasizes that in legal reasoning "attention is directed toward the finding of similarity or difference" (3) and that "the law forum" "requires the presentation of competing examples" (5). He is right, of course, when he explains that no effectual "overall rule" which would transform reasoning from case to case into deductive reasoning can be found, as "the legal process does not work with the rule but on a much lower level" (9). However, he hardly says anything positive about the functioning of "the mechanism" referred to, i. e. about the manner in which "the process" evolves on its "low level" and the ways in which "competing examples" participate in "the finding of similarity or difference", as required. Yet, it is interesting to note that, referring to the changing extension of legal terms, he qualifies the "area of expansion or contraction" that is "foreshadowed as the system works" as "probable" (104).

In concluding the book, he declares that "the emphasis should be on the process" (104). Here again he presumably means the developmental process, which he regards as embodying or reflecting the logical and methodological aspects of legal reasoning. Indeed, he explicitly refuses to disentangle this conceptual knot, for he adds: "The contrast between logic and the actual legal method is a disservice to both" (104). In what sense and why should the process be emphasized? What is involved in the alleged disservice? Since no clear answers to these questions seem to be found in the book, the view that a distinct apprehension of the contrasts between history, methodology, and logic is a necessary prerequisite of all discussion concerning argument and reasoning in any field whatsoever appears to re-emerge unaffected by Levi's analyses. That "legal reasoning has a logic of its own" (104) seems to be his main general conclusion. As this claim does not appear to be sufficiently clear, it is difficult to take a stand with respect to it. What Levi has in view here presumably goes beyond the obvious fact that systems of law differ from other domains of argument in aim, vocabulary, and semantics, in methods of construction, in features of development, and so on. At any rate, if he is trying to say — and this seems likely — that legal argument is specific in a strong sense, in particular in the sense that its rational force is of a nonformal nature, his conclusion must be viewed as based on a deficient analysis. Then again, if his conclusion involves the claim — and this too seems likely — that the methodology and history of law differ radically, or "essentially", from the methodology and history of other empirical fields, it must be viewed as at best unproven.

3. Hart on "the Ascription of Responsibility and Rights"

In his 1949 essay [25], H. L. A. Hart writes:

> There are in our ordinary language sentences whose primary function is not to describe things, events, or persons or anything else, nor to express or kindle feelings or emotions, but to do such things as claim rights ("This is mine"), recognize rights when claimed by others ("Very well, this is yours"), ascribe rights whether claimed or not ("This is his"), transfer rights ("This is now yours"), and also to admit or ascribe or make accusations of responsibility ("I did it", "He did it", "You did it"). My main purpose in this article is to suggest that the philosophical analysis of the concept of a human action has been inadequate and confusing, at least in part, because sentences of the form "He did it" have been traditionally regarded as primarily descriptive whereas their principal function is what I venture to call *ascriptive,* being quite literally to ascribe responsibility for actions much as the principal function of sentences of the form "This is his" is to ascribe right in property (145).

Hart relates the ascriptive function of language to what he proposes to call the *defeasible* nature of legal concepts and judgments. To say that such a concept as that of a murder or of a contract is defeasible amounts to saying that the proof of the existence of all the positive factual conditions for its applicability is inadequate if the defendant is able to prove the existence of some of the conditions that constitute the legal defenses against an unreserved application of the concept; e. g., the principal defenses against an otherwise valid claim in contract include those which refer to the defendant's knowledge or will, those which refer to some general principles of legal policy, and so on. "It is plain, therefore, that no adequate characterization of the legal concept of a contract could be made without reference to these extremely heterogeneous defenses and the manner in which they respectively serve to defeat or weaken claims in contract. The concept is irreducibly defeasible in character and to ignore this is to misrepresent it" (150).

Concepts of rights and responsibilities — this seems worth noting immediately — are theoretical concepts. Accordingly, an ascriptive sentence can be said to be a sentence with a legal or quasi-legal theoretical predicate. Such predicates and sentences are essentially *open:* a theoretical predicate cannot be adequately defined by means of a finite set of observational predicates; hence, a sentence in which such a predicate occurs is not reducible without remainder to any finite combination of observational sentences.

Hart closely approaches this sense of ascriptivity and defeasibility. He mentions a property of legal concepts which seems identifiable with open texture — namely, "a vagueness of character very loosely controlled by judicial traditions of interpretation" (147). He even makes it accountable for the impossibility of adequately defining what is, say, a trespass or a contract, without the use of the word "etcetera". But he refrains from discussing this property in detail since he considers it of lesser importance for his purpose than defeasibility, "which makes the word 'unless' as indispensable as the word 'etcetera' in any explanation or definition" of a legal concept. To be sure, he numbers both properties among "the characteristics of legal concepts which make it often absurd to use in connection with them the language of necessary and sufficient conditions" (147). His own point of emphasis, however, seems to be that the "positive elements" of legal concepts do not exhaust their meanings. The "irreducibly defeasible character" of a legal concept is primarily due, Hart claims, to the indispensable "negative" components, indicated by the word "unless". This emphasis is misleading, since the negativity of a property is always relative: P (or non-Q) is negative relatively to non-P (or Q), just as non-P is negative relatively to P.

It is, of course, possible to agree that a property P is to be regarded as negative if it is in some respect less simple than non-P. But even then, the negativity of part of the components of meaning is not peculiar to theoretical concepts in general, nor to typically defeasible legal concepts in particular; for example, if a macroscopic material object which is neither white, black, grey, nor transparent is called "colored", then the predicate "colored" and the sentences in which it occurs, such as "this sheet is colored", possess negative components of meaning, though they are obviously observational.

Hart no doubt feels that the negativity of some of the components of meaning does not in itself yield defeasibility, for he supplements his analysis by pointing to the "heterogeneity" of the negative components and, further, to the pragmatic aspects of the defeating procedure. He thus emphasizes that the defenses against claims in contract are "extremely heterogeneous" (151), that the seemingly "positive" mental element in criminal liability is merely "a restatement or summary of the fact that various heterogeneous defenses or exceptions are admitted" (152), and the like. This emphasis too misses the point: the irreducible defeasibility of an ascription is not really due to the diversity of the possible defenses but rather, as already suggested, to their openness with respect to observable conditions. Hart nowhere says that a finite list of observational defenses is incapable of exhausting the meaning of a defeasible ascription. On the contrary, his insistence on the heterogeneity of the defenses creates the impression, and is anyway compatible with the assumption, that in his opinion the list of defenses, though multifarious, is finite. If it is not required that the elementary defeating predicates be observational, then their number can indeed be finite. But then the transition from a seemingly "postive" but in fact "merely summarizing" term to its negative components does not constitute a decisive advance in the term's analysis, inasmuch as among those components there must still remain some "merely summarizing" predicates. E. g., the concepts of "innocent misrepresentation", "fraud", and "undue influence" are hardly less theoretical than the concept of "true, full, and free consent" which their negatives are purported to elucidate; a similar example is provided by the attempt to analyze "*mens rea*" in terms of "no mistake", "no accident", "no provocation", and so on. It should be remarked at this point that Hart does not distinguish between observational and theoretical descriptive concepts; he clearly tends to regard the domain of "facts" as limited to observable facts alone, and to consign theoretical paralegal statements to the domain of "law".

Referring to the pragmatic aspects of legal procedure, Hart points out that the onus of proof is usually placed on the defendant and that the judge must base his decision "upon the claims and defenses actually made and pleaded before him and the facts brought to his attention, and not on those which might have been made or pleaded" (155). The role of these rules of procedure being to ensure greater efficacy in adjudication, their mention seems hardly relevant to the elucidation of the logical concept of defeasibility. It is only in a casual way, to be sure, that Hart relates defeasibility to procedure, so that it may be presumed that in his essay he is not particularly concerned with the pragmatic aspects of the question under discussion. On the other hand, it is quite clear that he is interested in their logical aspect. Referring to such ascriptive phrases as "this is his", he declares: "It is the logical character of these with which I am concerned" (159). He regards a legal ascription as "a compound or blend of facts and law" (146) and he emphasizes "the fact that the elements in the compound are of distinct logical types" (154—155).

It seems worth trying to account for the assertions that a judicial ascription is "a compound or blend of facts and law" and that the ascription of responsibility or rights in ordinary language, out of court, is "like a judgment, a blend of fact and rule if not of law" (158). What may be intended here is, firstly, that an ascription A, made either in or out of court, is generally a conclusion from a simple or compound statement of fact D and a legal rule R and, secondly, that R is generally a conditional of which D is the antecedent and A the consequent. In contrast to D, A is not a statement of fact but a theoretical-prescriptive utterance; this point will be explained in the next paragraph. As for the descriptive utterance D, it can either consist of observational statements alone or involve theoretical components. The latter case is more important in the context of Hart's essay: R has the form "if D_t then A", "D_t" representing a descriptive statement with theoretical components; e. g., if two parties signed a conventional formula of contract with true, full, and free consent, then they are bound by a valid contract; if a man kills another with *mens rea,* he is guilty of murder.

The utterances A should be regarded as theoretical-*prescriptive,* since they not only constitute the consequents in rules of the form

"if D then A" with factual antecedents, but also function as antecedents in other rules, of the form "if A then P", the consequents P of
which are plainly deontic; e. g.: if two parties are bound by a valid
contract, then, under such and such conditions, they have the obligation to ..., are permitted to ..., and are forbidden to ...; if a man
is guilty of murder, he is to be punished by life imprisonment[3]. The
ascriptive utterances A thus serve, in the framework of the theoretical system to which they belong, as mediating links between descriptions and deontic prescriptions. This mediating function can be seen
as a further aspect of their "compound" character involving elements
of "distinct logical types".

The theoretical-descriptive antecedents D_t of legal rules create
serious problems for the practice of adjudication. They also seem
to have embarrassed Hart in his analysis. In court as well as in
ordinary life, reliable factual evidence consists initially of observational statements D_o. These, though capable of either strengthen-
ing or weakening both the theoretical statement D_t and the ascription
A which it warrants, are incapable of either establishing or refuting
them conclusively. Here, indeed, lies the defeasibility of the theoretical utterances D_t and A. Hart is well aware of the logical gap between factual evidence and legal conclusions, but his treatment of
this problem is handicapped both by his aforementioned tendency
to restrict the class of statements of fact to observational descriptions
alone and by the concomitant disregard of the distinction between
the theoretical-descriptive utterances D_t and the theoretical-prescriptive utterances A which they warrant. Accordingly, his central
term "ascriptive" is in a way ambiguous: it can be construed either
comprehensively as "theoretical" ("nonobservational") or specifically as "theoretical-prescriptive". The latter interpretation suits the
legal tenor of the essay much better. (If, however, the former interpretation is preferred, there is room to distinguish between descriptive and prescriptive ascriptions; this distinction can be conveniently
rendered by replacing "D_t" by "A_d", and "A" by "A_p".)

Hart maintains that the defeasibility and vagueness of the legal
element in judgment "conspire to make the way in which facts
support or fail to support legal conclusions, or refute or fail to
refute them, unlike certain standard models of how one kind of

---

3 The deontic prescriptions can themselves be more or less theoretical
and in need of an antecedently understood interpretation.

statement supports or refutes another upon which philosophers are apt to concentrate attention" (146). It may be presumed that the standard models in question are those of conclusive syllogism. Accordingly, the quoted passage can be taken to imply that a legal ascription is not derived from the factual evidence and the appropriate legal rule in the same conclusive way in which a statement of fact is derived from another statement of fact and an appropriate general premise. This view is also expressed in a passage quoted earlier, to the effect that "there are characteristics of legal concepts which make it often absurd to use in connection with them the language of necessary and sufficient conditions" (147). In ordinary language too there are utterances, such as "this is his" or "he did it", which involve "defeasible concepts like those of the law and similarly related to supporting facts" (159); Hart, hence, does not regard them as descriptive but as ascriptive. Clearly, he holds that the precarious logical ties by which ascriptions are related to their factual evidence is due to their specifically legal or quasi-legal nature. The same precariousness, however, already marks the theoretical-descriptive statements by which the ascriptions are warranted.

Hart points to the specific nature of judicial reasoning thus: "Since the judge is literally deciding that on the facts before him a contract does or does not exist, and to do this is neither to describe the facts nor to make inductive or deductive inferences from the statement of facts, what he does may be either a *right* or a *wrong* decision or a *good* or *bad* judgment and can be either *affirmed* or *reversed* and (where he has no jurisdiction to decide the question) may be *quashed* or *discharged*. What cannot be said of it is that it is either *true* or *false,* logically necessary or absurd" (155). The main point of the consequent must certainly be granted, but not the grounds as given in its support in the antecedent: the reason why a judgment should not be said to be either true or false is simply that a judgment is not a descriptive utterance but a prescriptive one. The view that it is neither deductively nor inductively related to the supporting evidence seems inacceptable. On the contrary, a judgment cannot be said to be rationally justifiable by appeal to factual evidence unless it is seen as obtainable, in principle, by an inductive inference followed by a deductive one: psychosociological statements of a theoretical nature — regarding, e. g., the true, full, and free consent of the parties in contract — are first induced from the available evidence, whereupon the judicial conclusion is derived from suitable legal rules, the theoretical statements obtained in the first inference, and possibly some further relevant premises.

Attempting to refute the indeed mistaken view that law provides "an example of a deductive system at work" (156), Hart argues that even in the simplest cases, in which the inquiry only concerns "an issue of fact" (i. e. of observable fact), "the timeless conclusion" cannot be derived deductively from "the statements of temporal fact". The fallacy of this argument appears clearly in the assertion that follows: "Rules of law even when embodied in statutes are not linguistic or logical rules, but to a great extent rules for deciding" (156). Hart here not only ignores the inductive support lent by observational factual data to psychosociological conclusions, but blatantly disregards the essential role of legal rules as premises that bridge the logical gap between factual statements and specifically legal conclusions. In his opinion, the gap is wide open: the elements of the legal "compounds" are of different "logical types", and the transition from "facts" to "law" is neither deductive nor inductive. An ascription, in his terms, is not established by *inference from* the given facts, but is made by a *decision based on them;* e. g., in saying "this is his" in appropriate circumstances, "like the judge, the individual decides, *on* certain facts, that somebody else has certain rights" (158).

To say that an ascription involves a decision is to point to a psychological aspect, whereas to say that the decision is based on facts is no doubt to imply the existence of an "objective" relation between the factual data and the corresponding ascription. If, then, this relation is not one combining entailment with inductive support, what is its nature? Like many others, Hart tries here to make a safe passage between the formalistic Scylla and the irrationalistic Charybdis: it is a mistake, he maintains, to identify "the meaning of an expression with which we make decisions or ascriptions with the factual circumstances which, in the absence of other claims, are *good reasons* for them" (159) (the italics are mine). So the "rules for deciding" are rules for *reasoning*, and an ascription thus appears to be a conclusion of an argument. It is, however, a noninferential conclusion, Hart would insist. The idea of specific, noninferential (or nonlogical) legal argument and of special, nonformal legal logic (or theory of nonlogical reasoning) clearly is inherent in Hart's analysis. Unfortunately, he gives no indication as to the nature and criteria of the rational force of the allegedly specific legal argument and, hence, offers no adequate objection to the formalistic conception of all rational reasoning, especially to the view that legal argument too, insofar as it is rational, is subject to formal-logical rules in principle. There is no real opposition between inference and rational decision. Inductive inference, in particular, being nonconclusive, involves decision in a stronger sense. The special prominence of the aspect of decision in the actual practice of rational judgment is due, moreover, to the fact that inductive paralegal inferences cannot as yet be adequately controlled by explicit formal means and must therefore, in point of fact, rely largely on intuition.

Hart's views concerning ordinary language are not directly relevant to the discussion. I would, however, like to point out that, while his contention that the possessives "mine", "yours", and "his" are primarily used as quasi-legal terms to claim, recognize, or ascribe proprietary rights seems sound, his "similar but perhaps more controversial thesis that the concept of a human action is an ascriptive and a defeasible one" (160) certainly requires qualification. It has already been suggested that the term "ascriptive" can be construed in two ways which are not discerned in the essay, viz. either as "theoretical" in general or as "theoretical-prescriptive". In the former sense "ascriptive" is contrary to "observational"; in the latter it is also opposed to "theoretical-descriptive". It is only in the former sense that the concept of a human action can be said to be ascriptive (and, as such, defeasible). Hart, however, since he leaves no room between observable fact and law, erroneously tends to conclude that the concept of a human action is quasi-legal. He thus maintains (with some diffidence, to be sure) that "I did it", "you did it", "he did it" are "primarily utterances with which we *confess* or *admit* liability, make accusations, or *ascribe* responsibility" (160). Once, however, the theoretical-descriptive category is duly recognized, there remains little doubt that the primary use of the aforesaid sentences is to make statements about certain complex human phenomena with nonobservable psychological elements. Such statements occur, as factual components, in the antecedents of the legal rules of ascription, as analyzed above, and not in their specifically legal consequents. The concept of a human action belongs primarily to theoretical psychosociology and, though basic to law (paralegal), is not a specifically legal or quasi-legal concept.

To conclude, these comments should by no means be considered as involving the imputation of lack of methodological proficiency.

On the contrary, the problem of the theoretical terms had not yet been sufficiently elaborated by the methodologists of science in the late forties, so that in the perspective of that time Hart's essay appears as a progressive and most stimulating attempt to elucidate this problem from the very interesting but relatively little known viewpoint of the student of jurisprudence.

4. Hart on "Definition and Theory in Jurisprudence"

Hart states the aim of his 1953 Oxford inaugural lecture [26] thus: "The perplexities I propose to discuss are voiced in those questions of analytical jurisprudence which are usually characterized as requests for definitions: What is law? What is a state? What is a right? What is possession?" (3). Adopting a progressive methodological approach to the problem of the nature and function of specifically legal terms, he points out that the technical words of law "do not have the straightforward connection with counterparts in the world of fact which most ordinary words have" (5). Hence, they cannot be adequately reduced to words of the latter kind: "If definition is the provision of a synonym which will not equally puzzle us, these words cannot be defined" (14). In order to clarify their meaning and function they must be examined "not alone but in examples of typical contexts where these words are at work" (9), in "statements such as 'A has a right to be paid £ 10 by B', 'A is under a duty to fence off this machinery', 'A & Company, Ltd., have a contract with B'" (9). But such utterances are not reducible to observational factual statements. They presuppose the legal system, out of which they have no function or meaning. In brief, the "characteristic role" of the terms in question "is not played in statements of fact but in conclusions of law" (15).

However, Hart seems to adhere to the view, as he did in his former essay (see above, sect. 3), that his findings are peculiar to law. In suggesting that "the common mode of definition is ill-adapted to the law" (3), or in relegating the elucidation of legal concepts to "methods properly adapted to their special character" (3—4), he appears to ignore the fact that in the respects under consideration law is no different from any other kind of empirical system. He no doubt regards the jurisprudential "perplexities" that he discusses as essentially due to the nondescriptive nature of law, as if descriptive, scientific theories did not present similar method-

ological problems. Still apparently disregarding the dependence of
law on theoretical psychosociology, he continues to use the terms
"fact" and "factual" as referring to the observable domain alone.

The "statements of rights and duties" (9) analyzed by Hart
clearly belong to the category of the ascriptive utterances with
which he was concerned in his 1949 essay. But he no longer calls
them "ascriptive". He now emphasizes their logical "distinctive
function" (9): in the utterance "A has a right", the expression
"a right" "does not describe or stand for any expectation, or power,
or indeed anything else, but has meaning only as part of a sentence
the function of which as a whole is to draw a conclusion of law
from a specific kind of legal rule" (10). Such an utterance, Hart
says, is "the tail end of a simple legal calculation: it records a result
and may be well called a conclusion of law". He points out that
"though, given certain facts, it is correct to say 'A has a right', one
who says this does not state or describe those facts" (10). Hart
nevertheless speaks about the conditions under which "a statement
of the form 'X has a right' is true" (16), in striking contrast to his
essay of 1949, in which he explained, it will be remembered, that
the ascriptive utterances of law cannot be said to be either true or
false. He now insists that "if we take a very simple legal statement
like 'Smith has made a contract with Y', we must distinguish the
meaning of this conclusion of law, from two things: from (1) a statement of the facts required for its truth, e. g. that the parties have
signed a written agreement, and also from (2) the statement of the
legal consequences of it being true, e. g. that Y is bound to do certain things under the agreement" (21). This new way of speaking
is misleading, for it blurs the prescriptive nature of the theoretical
utterances of law. If a "legal statement" is not a statement of fact,
it is certainly preferable to call it right, good, sound, just, justified,
or effectual rather than true. Indeed, the paradoxical talk about
a "true statement" that does not state or describe any facts needlessly fosters the feeling that "there is here at first sight something
puzzling; it seems as if there is something intermediate between the
facts given which the conclusion of law is true and the legal consequences" (21).

Terminology apart, there is some obscurity and indecisiveness
in Hart's conception of the logical status of the legal utterances
under discussion. On the one hand, he says, in a passage already
quoted, that such an utterance "may be well called a conclusion of

law", and he calls it so several times in the essay. On the other hand, however, he states on a number of occasions that such an utterance "is used in drawing a conclusion from the rules in a particular case" (14) and remarks that in this respect it resembles the expression "he is out", which in cricket "is used to draw a conclusion from a specific but unstated rule under which such a consequence follows on such conditions" (22). Do, then, the utterances under consideration *constitute* legal conclusions or are they *used in drawing* legal conclusions? The former alternative squares better with the acount of those utterances as based on factual data. The latter alternative, however, is clearly indicated by the reference to their logical "function", and it also better suits the text as a whole, including the analysis of the main examples provided. Hart hesitates between the conception of the utterances in question as theoretical "statements" and their conception as representing sets of nonformal rules of inference for "particular cases" (cf. "rules for deciding" in the 1949 essay). At any rate, he still leaves both their rational force as "conclusions" and the rational grounds for their "use in drawing conclusions" unaccounted for. In his 1949 essay, it will be recalled, Hart emphasized the dependence of the legal ascription on the act of decision and refused to regard it as involving an inference, whether deductive or inductive, from factual data.

The solution of this query is now at hand and can be given a simple indication with the aid of the symbols formerly introduced. As in sect. 3, let "if D_t then A" and "if A then P" be legal rules in which "D_t" represents a simple or compound descriptive utterance with theoretical components, "A" an ascriptive utterance, and "P" a simple or compound deontic prescription; and let "D_o" stand for a statement of observational factual data. Clearly, A is "a conclusion of law"; namely, under the rule "if D_t then A" it is both a deductive conclusion from D_t and, indirectly, an inductive conclusion from D_o. No less clearly, however, A is also "used in drawing a conclusion of law", namely as a premise which, under the rule "if A then P", entails P. Only the combination of these two roles, i. e. to constitute the conclusion in arguments of legal ascription and to serve as a premise in arguments of deontic legal prescription, exhausts the logical function of legal utterances of kind A. The reason why such utterances cannot properly be said to mean "the facts alone or the consequences alone or even the combination of these two" (21) is now well apparent: their specific function is that of logical mediation between the factual data and the deontic consequences. Hart no doubt approaches this insight very closely, but he does not state it with sufficient clarity and completeness.

Yet, the question naturally arises as to why such mediation is required at all. Indeed, would the legal system not be simpler if it directly included rules of the form "if D_t then P", instead of the couples of rules "if D_t then A" and "if A then P"? Hart implicitly hints at an answer to this query when he remarks that "in any system, legal or not, rules may for excellent practical reasons attach identical consequences to any one of a set of very different facts" (11). That is to say, very different conjunctions of factual data may lead to the same ascription A and, by its mediation, to the same deontic consequences P. This finding seems to point to two advantages of the theoretical mediating links A. First, they simplify both the formulation of legal rules of a very general character and the metalogical investigation with a view to the system's rational development. Second, they greatly facilitate the readjustment of law as necessitated by social change and by the development of psychosociology: the modifications are largely absorbed by the less theoretical components of the system, i. e. by the factual data D_o and the deontic prescriptions P, whereas its internal theoretical frame, consisting of the elements D_t and A, is to a large extent preserved from the impact of external change. These advantages appear yet considerably amplified when the structural articulations of the legal system are more closely considered. One feature, which seems to account decisively for the duality of A and P, can be described somewhat metaphorically as follows. The utterances A serve not only as points of convergence of numerous and diverse premises D_o and D_t, but also, in combination with some further premises, as points of divergence towards various consequences P: sets of rules of the form "if A and D_1 then P_1", "if A and D_2 then P_2", and so on, are indeed very frequent. The theoretical and practical importance of the legal ascription appears clearly when they are thus seen as major junctions in the legal system. (That the formulae "if D_t then A" and "if A then P" are oversimplifications in yet further respects will be pointed out in the concluding section of pt. III.)

Hart uses the words "theory" and "theoretical" not in the methodological sense in which they are used in the present book, but as referring, in a derogatory way, to unwarranted speculative hypotheses. He is opposed to those jurisprudential or commonsensical "theories" wich introduce fictions and hypostases by way of alleged "definitions" of basic legal concepts. His aim to unravel the hypostases by the analysis of the use of terms, in the spirit of "the beneficial turn of philosophical attention towards language" (28), raises no objections in principle. Hart shows convincingly how such an abstract legal concept as that of a corporation is formed by analogical extension and how it involves the use of old words in new senses; and he rightly resists the temptation of hypostatic theorization:

Analogy with a living person and shift of meaning are therefore of the essence of the mode of legal statement which refers to corporate bodies. But these are just what they are. Analogy is not identity, so though we can now (as lawyers) say that a Company has intended to deceive, this has no theoretical consequences; and shift of meaning is not fiction, so the need for logical consistency with an irrelevant notion of a law-created pure Will need not have been added to the difficulties of judges who, in a case-law system, have to decide how far the analogies latent in the law permit them to extend to corporations rules worked out for individuals when justice seems to demand it (27).

A single comment seems called for: the logical nature of the said "analogies latent in the law" certainly merits some clarification.

It can be said, in conclusion, that Hart's exposure of the speculative fictions points clearly to the unqualifiedly theoretical (non-observational) character of the legal terms and utterances analyzed, but it is impaired by the disregard of their specifically prescriptive nature.

5. Jensen: Legal Argument as a Nonlogical Mode of Decision

O. C. Jensen begins his book *The Nature of Legal Argument* [38] by stating:

The aim of this book is to show that one reason for the law's delays and uncertainties is the inconclusiveness of the arguments which are given in support of legal decisions, or which are advanced by counsel on behalf of their clients, and that this inconclusiveness is due to the nature of the concepts and modes of thought used. ... An attempt is made in this work to apply to the legal difficulties an analysis similar to that which has recently been tried out with some success in the field of philosophy. The nature of legal argument is illustrated by the detailed analysis of the official reports on a number of leading cases (XIII).

Whoever adopts the general outlook of the present study will certainly agree with the characterization of typical legal argument as "inconclusive". He will also admit that "one source of difficulty is the vagueness and ambiguity of some legal concepts and rules" (XIII), inasmuch as this diagnosis can be taken to refer to the prominently theoretical character of legal concepts. He will subscribe to the therapeutic suggestion, advanced "with diffidence", "that legal decisions should be made with more explicit reference to the social and other ends to be served by our legal institutions, and that legal concepts and rules should be shaped and used with these ends kept more in the foreground" (XIII). Furthermore, he will agree that for a satisfactory solution of the problem affecting legal argument suitable legal knowledge is required, "in addition to some competence in modern logical analysis" (XIV) and, hence, that it is for the lawyers themselves to solve their difficulties and, in particular, to inquire to what extent "some of the concepts and rules that have proved troublesome will show themselves to be unnecessary" (XII). But he may feel reluctant to admit that Jensen, in his analysis of some current legal concepts and rules, has succeeded in his attempt "to show how they might be made more precise and yet left flexible enough to give a court of law the freedom it requires, if it thinks that these concepts must be used" (XIII). More generally, one may feel that, despite his appeal to recent analytical philosophy and to "modern logic and semantics" (2), the manner in which he undertakes "the main purpose of the work", which is "to point to the logical source of some legal difficulties" (XIV), is open to objection.

Jensen states that his analysis "does not deal with the reasoning used to establish factual judgments", since "this kind of reasoning is not specifically legal"; he is concerned with "the other kind of reasoning and judgment, namely, that which is the settling of a question of law" (2). However, he points out, "the distinction between question of fact and question of law which will be maintained throughout this book is not identical with the similar but rather ambiguous distinction made in law"; e. g., "whether a defendant's conduct has been negligent is, in law, a question of fact if it is left to a jury to decide; but whether his negligent conduct is the sole legal cause of the injury complained of, thus making him liable in damages, is a question of law because it is one the judge must answer. As far as this treatise is concerned, the first question is as much a question of law as the second, at any rate it is equally nonfactual; for even when all the relevant facts are known, it still has to be decided whether the defendant's conduct *was* negligent" (2—3).

The basic distinction between "question of fact" and "question of law", and Jensen's declared deviation from the current usage of these terms, can be represented in a fairly adequate manner with the help of the threefold distinction between observational statements D_o, theoretical descriptive statements D_t, and theoretical legal ascriptions A (cf. sects. 3 and 4 above). According to the lawyers' current opinion, the distinction between question of fact and question of law corresponds to the distinction between descriptive statements, either D_o or D_t, and legal utterances of kind A: the jury agrees to accept D_o or D_t, whereupon the judge decides on A, either by an appeal to precedents or by a creative judgment. Jensen, on the other hand, conceives the distinction between question of fact and question of law as differentiating between D_o and D_t: a decision based on a rule of the kind "if D_o then A" concerns a question of fact, whereas a decision based on a rule of the kind "if D_t then A" concerns a question of law. Thus, "a verdict of guilty on the strength of circumstantial evidence" (2) concerns a question of fact, whereas the question "whether a defendant's conduct has been negligent", on the decision of which his liability in damages may depend, is a question of law.

In this methodological issue Jensen can hardly be said to have made his point against the current opinion. Like Hart before him, he tends to identify the factual with the observable and to consider the theoretical character of concepts peculiar to law. In his opinion, an utterance is not a descriptive, factual statement unless it can be, at least in principle, either verified or falsified by conclusive observational evidence. The idea of the essentially nonconclusive confirmation or disconfirmation of theoretical descriptive statements by observational evidence seems to be foreign to him. He apparently regards scientific induction as a virtually conclusive mode of reasoning, for he compares legal "judgements with regard to the matters of fact which have to be inferred from actual observations" to "the same kind of scientific reasoning that has explained, say, the presence of glacial moraines, or the contorted strata of folded mountains" (2). He remains apparently unaware of the amply theoretical character of such scientific reasoning, which in this respect does not seem to differ in nature, though it may differ in complexity, from the kind of reasoning used in court to support a claim of negligence as a cause of injury. The issue is far from straightforward, however, and will be reconsidered later (in the concluding section of pt. III).

Jensen's conception of logic is basically pragmatic. He points out emphatically: "My concern as a student of logic is with the *process* leading to judicial decisions insofar as they revolve round a question of law" (1), and the context leaves no doubt that he means "process" in the pragmatic sense. He attributes essential logical importance to the question of whether "the reasoning a judge gives in support of his decisions" is also, as it is believed to be, "the reasoning by means of which he arrived at them" (1). The negative answer to this question is considered the major general result of the analysis: "The purpose of this work is to show that the nature of the reasoning involved in legal judgment has been generally misunderstood, that it is hardly ever inferential at all, though it *is* forced into a semblance of inference; and this nonlogical reasoning provides far less justification for judicial decisions and must play a much smaller part in determining them than is generally supposed. At any rate, a court case when first looked at from the standpoint of modern logic does resemble some strange conjuring performance. The case the judge has before him is the hat, and his decision is the rabbit that has to be extracted from it" (1). Jensen's emphasis on the argumentative activity leads him to disregard the logical importance of the argumentative product: the naive question whether the judge does not "flick the rabbit out of his sleeve" (1) instead of pulling it out of the hat obfuscates the cardinal question of the quality of the rabbit itself. The claim that certain judgments "are not inferential at all, although they may be set out as if they were" (130), besides involving a confusion, is opposed in aim to the properly conceived rationalization of law. From the viewpoint of its logical value, a piece of reasoning should by no means be discarded on the ground that in the context of justification "it is forced into a semblance of inference" which was not present or was not sufficiently distinct in the original context of discovery. On the contrary, the development and amelioration of the technique of justification should be fostered in all spheres of argument, for the question of the rational force of argument concerns the context of justification rather than the pragmatic circumstances of discovery.

Not only the term "logic", but also "syllogism", "deduction", and "induction" are used by Jensen in a distinctly pragmatic sense. Thus we are told that the fact that a certain argument "may be put into the same grammatical form as a deductive process — whether syllogistic or nonsyllogistic — is no evidence that it *is* deductive"

(17). Logical importance is here granted to deductive process, not to deductive form. In the case of induction, the pragmatic conception is further strengthened by the still current definition according to which "induction is a procedure for arriving at natural laws, and at other generalizations, which state how events are related" (28). Thus, attempting to show that arguments of a certain kind are not inductive, Jensen surveys what the judge actually "examines", "notes", and "formulates" (29), and he also points to some practical aspects of the advocate's and the counsel's activities. In declaring that "formal deduction occurs rarely in legal cases" (25), he uses the terms "deduction" and "formal", too, in the practical sense prevailing among lawyers: the context makes it clear that he intends these terms to refer to the rigidity of reasoning, in particular to the refusal to deviate from the explicit letter of the law. The absence of a properly drawn distinction between logic and methodology likewise affects the formulation of some otherwise judicious remarks: "There is no rule of logic against semantically contracting, or stretching, a term" (9), or: "That the logical structure which is unambiguously indicated by the logical words in a statement should be taken as the one intended by the author of the statement is not a rule of logic. On the contrary it is logical to give the statement the other logical structure if there is *factual* evidence that this is the one the author of the statement intended" (27).

It is in the context of such a pragmatic and methodological conception of logic that the main conclusion of the book must be construed, viz. that "the reasoning involved in legal judgment" on "a question of law" is "nonlogical reasoning" (1). In particular, it can be seen that this conclusion is related to the view that "deduction" and "induction", as understood by the author, exhaust the modes of "logical" reasoning. Typical legal reasoning, he holds, is neither deductive nor inductive. "Put symbolically, the legal argument is: All *S* is *P*; *this* is *S* (is not *S*); therefore, *this* is *P* (is not *P*)". However, "legal reasoning revolves mainly around the establishment of the minor premise", in which highly abstract, often mentalistic concepts are normally involved; e. g., in a specifically legal reasoning, "a court of law has to decide whether or not certain acts or their results (or other events) are to be classified as 'legal (responsible) cause'; 'remote consequences'; 'attempt' etc." (20). "The problem is one of classification rather than one of deduction" (16), Jensen points out. What is required here is "the fixing of the label", and this is completely different from deducing conclusions once the label is fixed. On the other hand, classification does not involve procedures of generalization and, therefore, is not induction.

Jensen's "account of deduction and induction to serve as a contrast to legal argument" (20) is supplemented by his insistence on the inconclusiveness of specifically legal reasoning, which normally "does not revolve round logical constants" (27), but round legal terms that "are so lacking in any definite content that no criteria by virtue of which the terms are applied can be said to be implied by these terms" (28). In the absence of adequate "tests and definitions" (129), the classificatory arguments under consideration "are not inferential at all" (130), appearances notwithstanding, especially since comparisons with precedents "do not provide a sufficient reason for the decision given" (20). It is thus an illusion to think that decisions on questions of law "are inferred from legal principles" and "are not arbitrary and unaccountable" (1). Indeed, in cases under consideration, "it is possible to argue as 'logically' one way as the other" (148). Such arguments, that is to say, are of a nonlogical nature: they "consist of circular discussion of principles, rules and definitions, and *ad hoc* application of them to the case *sub judice*" (130). In short, a judgment such as "guilty of attempt" is by no means a logical conclusion from the premises but rather is merely "the expression of a decision" (29).

Inductive support, as an eventual alternative to both conclusiveness and arbitrariness, is not mentioned. However, it is far from clear whether Jensen holds that the nonlogical character he attributes to legal reasoning is essential to it in principle or merely that, in point of fact, it affects legal reasoning as practised at present but can be coped with and eventually overcome. On the one hand, he apparently attempts the analysis of "the *nature* of legal argument". On the other hand, however, he is dissatisfied with "the present methods of reasoning" (129) and even hints at ways to improve them. His point is, in substance, that "questions of law" should be converted into "questions of fact", in his senses of these terms; e. g., he suggests "treating the question whether a particular deed is an attempt as a question of fact, and not a question of law" (163). He proposes definiteness as a cure against arbitrariness: "If decisions on the particular facts of each case are not to be quite arbitrary, there must be some rule sufficiently definite" (148) for a court to establish its decisions unambiguously, in every kind of case. This suggestion is arguable insofar as it can be construed simply as recommending the bridging of the gap between the legal system and the domain of application by rules of interpretation as detailed and precise as possible. Jensen's point, however, seems to be much more radical. It can be expressed thus: only direct and complete bridging of the gap between law and the observable social reality will enable legal argument to become logical; in other words, the rationalization of legal argument must involve the relinquishment of the use of theoretical terms. This view should be discarded as misguided and not feasible. To be sure, Jensen himself has some reservations about it: he remarks that, in principle, "it is true that a test or rule may be made too precise, so that in some unforeseen case it will not allow of a just decision" (148) and that, in practice, "it would sometimes be a difficult factual problem to decide whether the conduct of the accused had given conclusive evidence" (163) for the establishment of one or another legal decision. But he proposes no escape from such difficulties.

He rightly observes that "the purpose of criminal law is to prevent certain deeds" and that "these deeds follow from intentions, and intentions may be changed or checked by punishment" (161). This is precisely why law cannot relinquish the use of such theoretical concepts as those of intention, negligence, attempt, etc. It is interesting to note that Jensen seems to admit the legal importance of the mentalistic concepts and of their analysis when he says: "The nature, including the strength, of the intentions we are dealing with is therefore basic in a practical approach to the problem of attempts" (161). It is hard to see, however, how this claim squares with the general antitheoretical trend of his therapeutic doctrine. The problematic concepts, the irreducibly theoretical nature of which seems to escape Jensen, are unavoidable within the framework of a rational legal system and should be treated as highly theoretical, preferably quantitative concepts of psychosociology; e. g., quantitative standards of negligence are required in various fields of social activity to enable degrees of negligence to be taken into account in the ascription of responsibility and in the determination of sanctions. That such an approach to the psychosociological concepts basic to law is not altogether foreign to Jensen may be regarded as attested to by his reference to "the strength of the intentions". The inconsistencies discernible in his position seem to indicate that in his opinion legal argument is nonlogical by its very "nature", not only in actual fact; they also seem to account for the "diffidence" with which he offers some of his suggestions for the improvement of legal argument.

In sum, then, both Jensen's diagnosis of the weaknesses of legal reasoning and his proposals for remedying them can be seen to suffer from lack of clarity. Yet, the imperfections of his analysis notwithstanding, his views appear to be largely acceptable, as has already been pointed out. His specific demand that sociology be regarded as basic to law, that "the inchoate sociological knowledge that judges have unsystematically acquired" be expanded, and that "this knowledge, which probably does influence a judge's decisions" (163), be explicitly formulated, certainly merits no less approval than does the underlying general requirement for the amelioration of law through extensive rationalization of legal argument.

6. *Toulmin: Legal Argument as Archetype of Argument in General*

In the Introduction to *The Uses of Argument* [74], Stephen E. Toulmin remarks that the several essays which compose his book serve as "*ballons d'essai,* trial balloons designed to draw the fire of others. This being so, they may seem a little inconsequent." He even adds: "For literary reasons I have avoided too many expressions of hesitancy and uncertainty, but nothing in what follows pretends to be final" (1).

When speaking about arguments, Toulmin quite indistinctly employs the terms "valid" and "sound" as virtually equivalent. For the purpose of the present criticism, however, I shall keep them apart. As I have done throughout this book, I shall follow the formal logicians' use of the words "valid" and "validity". (This, of course, does not apply to their occurrences in quotations from Toulmin.) I shall go on using the word "sound" as referring to well-established premises and conclusion. I shall also need the words "correct" and "correctness", to refer to the argument's property of fulfilling certain obligatory "formalities", other than formal-logical requirements. I am thus able to say, without risk of ambiguity, that Toulmin's dissatisfaction with formal logic is due to its being concerned with the validity of arguments, whereas he considers that logic should be concerned with their soundness: according to its true task, "logic is concerned with the soundness of the claims we make — with the solidity of the grounds we produce to support them, the firmness of the backing we provide for them — or, to change the metaphor, with the sort of *case* we present in defense of our claims" (7).

Obviously, then, Toulmin conceives logic as a part, at least, of the methodology of sound reasoning. Accordingly, he proposes a new conception of logical form: "Mathematical ratios and geometrical figures carry with them a clear enough idea of form; so no wonder the doctrine that logical form could be construed in the same way has proved extremely attractive. The analogy between rational assessment and judicial practice presents us with a rival model for thinking about the idea of logical form. It now appears that arguments must not just have a particular shape, but must be set out and presented in a sequence of steps conforming to certain basic rules of procedure. In a word, rational assessment is an activity necessarily involving *formalities*" (43). Toulmin enumerates several procedural stages of argument. First, the problem is stated. Then, various possible solutions are examined and some of them eliminated. Finally, one solution is chosen. The examination of the tentative solutions also follows a certain order. First, the *warrant* is given: it is a material rule licencing the passage from the *data* to the *conclusion*. The warrant's applicability is then examined with due regard to special *conditions of rebuttal* which may either prevent the drawing of the conclusion or necessitate its *modal qualification*. (Toulmin explicitly relates the conditions of rebuttal to Hart's concept of defeasibility.) Finally, the *backing* of the warrant is examined. Warrants and backings, as well as the criteria for their assessment and the conditions of their applicability, are *field-dependent*, i. e. are specific to the particular field to which the argument belongs; on the other hand, Toulmin holds, the procedural pattern itself is *field-invariant*.

Here are three of his examples of argument set out according to the new model. To denote the various parts, the following symbols are used: *D*, data; *Q*, modal qualifier; *C*, conclusion; *R*, conditions of rebuttal; *W*, warrant; *B*, backing. *First example* (105): Harry was born in Bermuda (*D*); so, presumably (*Q*), Harry is a British subject (*C*), unless both his parents were aliens / he has become a naturalized American / ... (*R*), since a man born in Bermuda will generally be a British subject (*W*), on account of the following statutes and other legal provisions: ... (B). *Second example* (111): Petersen is a Swede (D); so, almost certainly (Q), Petersen is not a Roman Catholic (C), since a Swede can be taken to be almost certainly not a Roman Catholic (W), because the proportion of Roman Catholic Swedes in less than 2 percent (B). (In this example no conditions of rebuttal are given.) *Third example* (126): Anne is one of Jack's sisters (D); so, presumably (Q), Anne now has red hair (C), unless Anne has dyed / gone white / lost her hair / ... (R), since any sister of Jack's may be taken to have red hair (W), on account of the fact that all his sisters have previously been observed to have red hair (B). I shall return to Toulmin's model.

Meanwhile, it is worth lingering on his very conception of logic as "generalized jurisprudence" (7). To avoid a merely terminological issue, however, I shall forego criticizing his use of the terms "logic" and "validity". From the point of view of the present inquiry, the important question concerns Toulmin's opinion as to the status of formal logic with respect to logic conceived as the methodology of soundness. Insofar as he wishes to emphasize that formal logic is not methodology and that reasoning requires methodology besides formal logic, his position raises no substantial objection. But it can no more easily be assumed that he needs his "trial balloons" to test such indisputable claims than it can be maintaned that he is merely defending some terminological preferences. So there seems to be little doubt that he seriously demands the replacement of formal by "jurisprudential" logic in the very centre of the theory of nonmathematical argument. He grants, to be sure, that formal logic can still fulfill the secondary task of ensuring that good arguments are not affected by linguistic inconsistencies. But, though a "tidy" argument is certainly preferable, "to call such an argument formally valid is to say only something about the manner in which it has been phrased, and tells us nothing about the *reasons for* its validity. These reasons are to be understood only when we turn to consider the *backing* of the warrant invoked" (143). One can hardly resist the impression that Toulmin paradoxically ascribes to formal logicians the ludicrous view that formal validity involves soundness.

It is perhaps a vague desire to escape such plain paradox that makes him occasionally somewhat weaken the antiformalistic emphasis, as in this passage, already quoted: "It now appears that arguments must not just have a particular shape, but must be set out and presented in a sequence of steps conforming to certain basic rules of procedure" (43). This can be taken to mean that the rules of procedure supplement the rules of validity without impinging upon them. Elsewhere Toulmin seems to envisage the "two rival models" with some hesitation, for his preference for the "procedural" model over the "geometrical" does not prevent him from asking: "Does the notion of logical form somehow combine both these aspects, so that to lay an argument out in proper form necessarily requires the adoption of a particular geometrical layout?" (95). The anticipated negative answer well suits Toulmin's position: there is no necessary connection between the two aspects of argument outside the mathematical field. But even a casual, nonessential connection between "practical argument" and "geometrical shape" seems to puzzle him, for he goes on asking: "Supposing valid arguments can be cast in a geometrically tidy form, how does this help to make them any more cogent?" (95). The only answer to this question to be found in the book is the already cited remark that rules of formal logic are relevant to the avoidance of linguistic inconsistencies. On the whole, then, Toulmin's transitory hesitations notwithstanding, the trend of his book is strongly antiformalistic, its central view being that formal logic, inasmuch as it is not concerned with soundness, is unsuitable for the rational assessment and guidance of nonmathematical argument.

The fallacy inherent in this view is obvious. In representing the formal validity of an argument as merely regarding "the manner in which it has been phrased" (143), Toulmin forgets that a valid deductive argument functions so as to preserve soundness: the soundness of all the premises of such an argument entails the soundness of its conclusion. Valid deductive argument thus fulfills an essential function in the elaboration of applied theoretical systems and in their confirmation and permits the proper rational use of premises drawn from well-established systems. In nonconclusive arguments with sound premises the conclusion cannot be accepted as sound unless it is adequately supported by the premises. For the assessment of such support inductive logic is required. However, Toulmin's antiformalistic position can hardly be construed as involving the demand for the supplementation of contemporary deductive logic by inductive logic, for the latter, properly conceived, is no less formal than is the former.

It is worth considering the "jurisprudential analogy" more closely. Why, in his search for criteria of soundness, does Toulmin turn to jurisprudence rather than to the methodology of science? One reason seems to be that practical legal methodology belongs, at least in part, to law itself. In particular, rules of procedure are legally binding. Accordingly, "lawsuits are just a special kind of rational dispute, for which the procedures and rules of argument have hardened into institutions" (8), and this process has produced "a whole battery of distinctions" (96) concerning legal procedure and utterances. This can be granted. It should be noted, however, that the contemporary methodology of science is no less rich in conceptual apparatus, even though its terminology is perhaps less precise and less uniform than jurisprudential terminology. With regard to the present question, at any rate, the decisive difference between legal and scientific argument lies in the dependence of the former on "formalities": the disregard of these at any stage of the judicial process may render the court's conclusion legally void, even if there is no doubt as to its soundness. Scientific argument is not subject to such rigid conditions of correctness: the conclusion of a sound scientific argument is by no means disqualified as scientifically void by the mere fact that the investigation upon which the argument is based disregards some methodological precepts.

Toulmin, surprisingly enough, when proposing legal argument as the archetype of argument in general, does not at all point to the institutionalized character of legal argument, nor to the strictness of its rules of correctness, nor even to the applicability of those rules in various stages of the argumentative process in the context of discovery. He ascribes logical importance to correctness only insofar as it is reflected in the final formulation of the properly framed argument and, moreover, only insofar as he deems it capable of providing evidence of the argument's soundness. This double limitation is essential to Toulmin's position. He states explicitly: "Logic is concerned not with the *manner* of our inferring, or with questions of *technique:* its primary business is a retrospective, justificatory one — with the arguments we can put forward afterwards to make good our claim that the conclusions arrived at are acceptable, because justifiable, conclusions" (6). For logic to be "generalized jurisprudence", the basic pattern of good argument must be thought of as "field-invariant": "Insofar as the form of the argument we present reflects these similarities of procedure, the form of argument in different fields will be similar also" (22). The procedural correctness of argument in general is thus ultimately limited to the context of justification: the new model is put forward as the correct pattern of the argumentative *product*. The "jurisprudential analogy" thus appears to be very tenuous indeed. It paradoxically fails to apply to legal argument itself, for a correctly laid-out legal argument may surely be unsound. Toulmin would perhaps try to meet this objection by distinguishing between the specifically legal correctness of legal argument and its general argumentative or "logical" correctness, by which alone its soundness could be tested. However, even so qualified, his "analogy" remains untenable.

His basic mistake lies in the assumption that the soundness of an argument can be somehow secured and reflected by the "proper form" of its pattern, with no regard to its formal-logical characteristics. He may have been misled by the formal paradigm itself: formal validity, indeed, is reflected in and is even constituted by the form of the formalized argument. In this sense, validity or invalidity can be said to be an inherent property of the formalized argument. The concept of soundness, on the other hand, is not purely logical: the soundness of an argument's conclusion depends on some logical and pragmatic properties of its premises as well as on the formal-logical relation between the premises and the conclusion. Mere correctness of the pattern provides no evidence for the soundness of the argument even if the rules of correctness concern its formal-logical structure, let alone if they do not. The following quotation seems significant in the present context: "A clearly analyzed argument is as much one in which the formalities of rational assessment are clearly set out and which is couched 'in proper form', as one which has been presented in a tidy geometrical shape" (143). Toulmin speaks here, in a rather artificial way, about "a clearly analyzed argument" and not, as would seem appropriate, about a sound argument. He may, therefore, be taken to be affected by the previously mentioned "hesitancy and uncertainty" not only regarding the exact relationship between correctness and validity, but with respect to the very substance of his "jurisprudential" conception of logic and of argumentative soundness.

There can obviously be no model, "procedural" or other, of soundness, as there are formal patterns of validity and of inductive support. The demand can be made, to be sure, that the formulation of an argument should include information about the sources of the premises and their firmness (relative to the best available knowledge). Such information can be used, in a separate methodological argument, in support of the claim about the first argument's soundness. There is, however, nothing new in the request to supplement arguments with such information: this is the current practice in those basic operations of confirmation which have always constituted a major rational activity in all spheres of argument. Though it is true that the formulation of the methodological information in nonlegal spheres is rarely subject to as rigid conditions of "proper form" as in law, it is always, clearly enough, the information itself that is relevant to confirmation; the pattern according to which it is included in the argument's formulation has merely practical importance. It is by no means possible to regard such subsidiary patterns as "rival" to the formal-logical ones, since the latter in fact determine the very relevance of the methodological information to the question of the soundness of the argument's conclusion.

A closer examination of the "jurisprudential" model and of its illustrations reinforces the impression that, despite its unnecessary entanglement, it is interpretable and analyzable in terms of the usual methodological and formal-logical categories and hence is not as new as Toulmin seems to believe. The main complication of the model arises from his view of the nature and function of the theoretical utterances upon which arguments rest: he does not regard them in the usual way, as premises, but as "backings for warrants". He conceives of the warrants as qualified material rules of inference. He is obviously wrong in thinking that the use of a warrant frees the argument from dependence on formal rules. For instance, in the second of the three examples cited above, the transition from the datum, "Petersen is a Swede", to the qualified conclusion, "almost certainly, Petersen is not a Roman Catholic", is based in fact on the consideration of a simple formal relation of inductive support. The warrant, "a Swede can be taken to be almost certainly not a Roman Catholic", actually combines the functions of a statistical premise (which is stated in the backing, "the proportion of Roman Catholic Swedes is less than 2 percent") and a formal derived rule of inductive support (viz.: the conjunction of "the proportion of Ss among Ps is less than p percent" and "x is S" supports "x is not P" with a degree of inductive support greater than $100 - p$ percent). The assumption that the soundness of a conclusion, though dependent on the soundness of the premises, does not essentially depend on formal relations between the premises and the conclusion can always be shown to be due to some sort of mistake or illusion.

Aside from the theoretical utterance itself, the indication of its source is also normally included in the backing in Toulmin's model. When the theoretical utterance is duly transferred from the backing to the main body of the argument as a premise, the residual backing becomes a methodological comment relevant to the question of the argument's soundness. It is interesting to note that Toulmin disregards the need to provide the data premise with backing. As for the conditions of rebuttal, they should be adjoined to the theoretical premise they qualify. The modal qualifier requires clarification as a formal-logical element, related to the nature of nonconclusive arguments with a theoretical premise. However, such clarification belongs to the general context of research on inductive logic and does not especially concern Toulmin's model. The conclusion is the only element in Toulmin's model that leaves no room for reservations.

The deceptive belief that the "rival model" frees argument from its essential dependence on formal conditions naturally involves the depreciation of the category of premise as an essential component of argument. "Can we properly classify all the elements in our arguments under the three headings, 'major premise', 'minor premise', and 'conclusion', or are these categories misleadingly few in number? Is there even enough similarity between major and minor premises for them usefully to be yoked together by the single name of 'premise'?" (96). The negative answer to these questions is clearly implied. The exposure of Toulmin's basic mistake brings out the propriety, simplicity, and fruitfulness of the conception of argument as composed, in the context of justification, of premises and a conclusion formally interrelated. The recognition of the premise as an essential element in argument must be accompanied by understanding the need for logical and methodological differentiation between sentences serving as premises, according to their structure, source, and functions outside the argument. Logic and methodology have long since been dealing with such distinctions. The fruitfulness of the formalistic conception of logic cannot be doubted: concern for the formal propriety of argument in any field promotes the continuous process of rationalization, in particular the progressive development and adequate readjustment of the theoretical system as the framework for the elaboration of missing premises, for the elimination of ambiguities, etc. Yet, the decisive superiority of the formalistic over the "jurisprudential" conception is, of course, that the former does not depend, as does the latter, on mistaken views.

The three arguments cited above as illustrations of Toulmin's model can be reinterpreted as inductive arguments with strong inductive support. In the first example, the conjunction of the statement that Harry was born in Bermuda, the appropriate legal provision, and the statistical statement about the relative rarity of cases fulfilling the conditions of rebuttal, strongly supports the claim that Harry is a British subject. The high degree of inductive support represented by the second example (concerning the Swede Petersen) has already been pointed out. The argument in the third example is properly construed as an enthymeme lacking both the indication of the time or times at which Jack's sisters were observed to have red hair and the relevant statistical data regarding the persistence of the color of hair under determined circumstances: the conjunction of the observational finding, the aforesaid additional data, and the statement that Anne is one of Jack's sisters, lends sufficiently strong inductive support to the claim that Anne has red hair at an appropriate time. Such arguments are not conclusive. But insofar as they are rational, they are nevertheless based, at least in principle, on formal relations. All alleged jurisprudential affinity, on the other hand, is entirely irrelevant to the analysis or assessment of their rational force.

In conclusion, it seems that the comments in this section amply justify the unqualified rejection of Toulmin's antiformalistic conception of argument, including the "jurisprudential analogy", in which he attempts to represent legal argument as the archetype of argument in general. It cannot be denied that the study of legal argument is most likely to be of much interest to general methodology and to the methodology of some special nonlegal fields. But what seems no less worth emphasizing is that, conversely, general methodology, which has developed so far in much closer contact with science than with law, is certainly capable of enriching and considerably advancing the methodology of law. Mutual rapprochement and systematic cooperation between students of jurisprudence and students of the philosophy and methodology of science should not be delayed any longer.

7. Hart on "Formalism and Rule-Scepticism"

The seventh chapter of Hart's book *The Concept of Law* [27] is entitled "Formalism and Rule-Scepticism". Though that chapter is largely independent of the remaining nine, the following preliminary comment is needed. It concerns a basic notion introduced by Hart earlier in the book, the notion, namely, of what he calls the "internal aspect" of legal rules. As explained and illustrated on several occasions, the internal aspect of a rule consists in the citizens' conscious acceptance of the rule through the recognition of its "binding force". The latter is meant as soundness rather than as prima facie legitimacy. At any rate, Hart seems to imply that the binding force of a rule is *established* by its internal aspect. It may be objected that the acceptance of a rule, though certainly relevant to its actual effectiveness, cannot be considered a determinant factor of the very binding force which it presupposes. The notion of the internal aspect can thus be seen to involve the evasion of the problem of rational legal confirmation. The corresponding conception of legal soundness will be referred to as "mentalistic" in what follows.

In the chapter under consideration Hart represents judicial reasoning as importantly involving choice. On the basis of this conception, he discusses and assesses the rival jurisprudential doctrines of formalism and rule-scepticism, in turn, and concludes by setting forth a compromise between them. In what follows, both his own views on legal reasoning and his comments on the two doctrines will be examined; the reappraisal of these latter will depend, moreover, on their thorough reinterpretation. Consequently, when they are finally found largely compatible with one another, this conclusion will be seen to differ considerably in significance from the aforementioned compromise.

Like many other authors, including some of those whose views have been discussed above, Hart too, while attempting to unravel what is peculiar to legal reasoning qua legal, emphasizes some of its features that are due in fact to the theoretical and empirical nature of law. He thus points to the vagueness and the open texture of legal rules and observes, rightly of course: "Particular fact situations do not await us already marked off from each other, and labelled as instances of the general rule, the application of which is in question; nor can the rule itself step forward to claim its own instances" (123). The point here is, in methodological terms, that the rules of interpretation of the theoretical system of law cannot be derived from the system alone, but must be based both on legalistic and on empirical grounds. From this Hart concludes, no less rightly, that "subsumption and the drawing of a syllogistic conclusion no longer characterize the nerve of the reasoning" (124) in interpretation. But, in a positive way, what is the nature of such reasoning? The gist of Hart's answer to this question seems to be that specific judicial reasoning involves acts of free and yet rational choice. In the introductory first chapter, anticipating the main results of the book, he says: "In most important cases there is always a choice. The judge has to choose between alternative meanings to be given to the words of a statute or between rival interpretations of what a precedent 'amounts to'. It is only the tradition that judges 'find' and do not 'make' law that conceals this, and presents their decisions as if they were deductions smoothly made from clear pre-existing rules without intrusion of the judge's choice" (12). It is thus free, creative choice and not induction that Hart opposes to "smooth deduction". As, however, judicial choice, insofar as it is based on reasoning, can hardly be deemed irrational, he assumes that creativeness in legal reasoning can be reconciled with rationality: "The conclusion, even though it may not be arbitrary or irrational is in effect a choice" (124).

The diffidence apparent in the wording of this assumption is comprehensible. Indeed, it is very hard to see how interpretative choice can combine the two qualities of freedom and rationality. Let us consider Hart's own example. It concerns a rule to the effect that no vehicle may be taken into the park. The question arises whether or not a toy motorcar electrically propelled may be taken into the park. To decide this, the judge must determine whether or not such a toy car should be considered a vehicle in the sense of the general rule. Let us now suppose that effective criteria for the assessment of the alternative semantic interpretations are available and that the judge finds which of the two has a higher degree of rational force. His choice now obviously cannot be both free and rational: unless he chooses, so to speak, to choose irrationally, he is bound to choose the interpretation that has a higher degree of rational force, just as anyone wishing to remain rational is bound to accept the conclusion of a deductive argument that he recognizes as valid and sound.

Hart is rather vague regarding the nature and criteria of the rationality of judicial reasoning: he points out that the judge "chooses to add to a line of cases a new case because of resemblances which can reasonably be defended as both legally relevant and sufficiently close". As the notion of relevant or essential resemblance has already been discussed on several occasions above, there is no need now to deal with it again. To be sure, Hart does not commit the fallacy of considering the said "resemblances" a datum; on the contrary, he admits that "in the case of legal rules, the criteria of relevance and closeness of resemblance depend on many complex factors running through the legal system and on the aims or purpose which may be attributed to the rule. To characterize these would be to characterize whatever is specific or peculiar in legal reasoning" (124). The difficulty of the task resides in "our relative ignorance of fact" and in "our relative indeterminacy of aim" (125). Hart can thus be seen to leave out what may be considered the main purpose of the analysis of legal reasoning, viz. the elucidation of the relation between the "many complex factors", whatever their particular nature, and the final conclusion. For example, when, in order to settle the question of whether toy electric cars may be taken or must not be taken into the park, the judge considers the aims of the general rule that prohibits the taking of vehicles into the park, on the one hand, and the children's need for play, on the other, in what does the rational force of his "consideration" consist? By what method and according to what rules do different, often mutually opposed factors guide the judge's decision? What is the rational element in the judge's choice? What is the logic of his nonarbitrary decision, or the nature of his criteria for the appraisal of the non-syllogistic legal reasoning? Hart's primarily pragmatic conception of legal argument, reinforced as it is by his mentalistic conception of the soundness or "binding force" of legal rules (see above, at the beginning of this section), prevents him from envisaging the right kind of answer to these questions.

And yet, on more than one occasion he comes quite near to conceiving the logical aspect of legal argument in a proper way. Thus, the mention of "complex factors" points to the possibility of supplementing intuitive reasoning by the addition of explicit relevant premises, whereas the allusion to the relative "ignorance of fact" and "indeterminacy of aim" strongly suggests that the conclusion, to be rational, must be accountable for, to the largest possible extent, in terms of the relevant facts and aims as actually known or determined. Not much is needed to pass from this insight to the recognition of the inductive nature of legal argument qua rational. Indeed, the view that the effective rationalization of legal argument depends on the elaboration and use of appropriate inductive methods in various sections of the legal system seems almost implied by Hart. Referring to the actual indeterminacy of judicial decision, he observes: "We need to remind ourselves that human inability to anticipate the future, which is at the root of this indeterminacy, varies in degree in different fields of conduct, and that legal systems cater for this inability by a corresponding variety of techniques" (127). In particular, "the legislature sets up very general standards and then delegates to an administrative, rule-making body acquainted with the varying types of case, the task of fashioning rules adapted to their special needs" (127—128). Similarly, "at the margin of rules and in the fields left open by the theory of precedents, the courts perform a rule-producing function which administrative bodies perform centrally in the elaboration of variable standards" (132). The problem of the logical nature of legal argument can be felt here close to the surface; it remains submerged, however, by the overall context of the discussion, in which the rational force of reasoning is conceived as analyzable in terms of mental attitudes and of "techniques" rather than in terms of logical relations.

On the background of his own emphasis on choice in judicial reasoning, Hart presents "the vice known to legal theory as formalism or conceptualism" as consisting "in an attitude to verbally formulated rules which both seeks to disguise and to minimize the need for such choice, once the general rule has been laid down" (126). This characterization can be seen to be ambiguous in several respects. Its meaning depends, in the first place, on how "the need for choice" is construed. One possibility is to take this expression to refer simply to the need for judicial interpretation. That this need really exists cannot be denied, of course. Thus — to use Hart's example once more — the judge must decide, through semantic interpretation of the general rule, whether or not a toy electric car should be considered a vehicle. The need for interpretation is due to the nature of law as a theoretical system applied to an empirical domain. Insofar as it involves the denial or disregard of this need, legal formalism should certainly be discarded. Such a position can be designated as "naive formalism". Whether it has any serious adherents today is very doubtful. Intentional disguise or misrepresentation of the need in question does not seem justifiable either; but this is a matter of legal policy which need not be discussed here.

"To minimize" not only means to disregard or underestimate but to reduce as well, and this latter meaning also suits the formalistic doctrine as usually understood. A certain reduction of the need for judicial interpretation can be achieved through the enactment of well-articulated rules with detailed interpretation. If excessive, this tendency would encounter serious difficulties, due to the diversity and indeterminateness of the possible cases of application; besides, the anticipation of an excessively precise interpretation would not be worthwhile because of social dynamism. On the level of adjudication the restrictive tendency appears as rigorism, i. e. the demand for rigid application of the rules without sensible deviation from the letter of the law — that is to say, from the ordinary meanings of the terms it contains. Legal formalism, in fact, is usually construed as rigorism. Hart too seems to construe it thus; this is borne out by the fact that he relates formalism to the attempt to secure certainty and predictability in adjudication through the fixation of meanings, notwithstanding the reduced adaptability of law to varying conditions. To the extent that the doctrine in question depends on the disregard of the theoretical nature and the dynamism of law, it should be discarded as a kind of naive formalism. It can, however, be defended perhaps as a principle of legal policy, regarding the division of tasks between the legislature and the courts.

Obsolete or obsolescent in its naive version, formalism is yet susceptible of reinterpretation and reappraisal. Indeed, once the discordance between freedom and rationality in legal reasoning is duly recognized, the formalistic opposition to judicial choice can be significantly construed as concerning free, subjective interpretation alone rather than interpretation in general. Such a doctrine can be designated as "progressive" or "up-to-date formalism". It represents the theoretical-regulative view that adequate standards of rationality for legal reasoning exist in principle, though judicial free choice may often be necessary in practice. This view naturally involves the philosophical conception of arguments of legal interpretation as inductive arguments resting on a vast body of paralegal and methodological knowledge. It may also be taken as a practical position countenancing systematic measures for reducing judicial choice not subject to rational control. Such reduction can be achieved through the development of canons of confirmation and of estimation, even if only partial and crude, for various sections of the legal system. Admittedly, the enormous difficulties which the project of rationalizing legal reasoning beyond a certain limit would have to encounter must not be ignored; however, in the present context there can be no question of even beginning to enquire how far the rationalization of law could proceed without itself ceasing to be rationally justifiable. As for the tendency to disguise the judges' dependence on modes of reasoning that in actual fact escape the full and distinct control of logic, it cannot be seen as characterizing progressive formalism. Indeed, since no effective amelioration of legal reasoning is possible without the investigation of its nonrational links, these latter should be exposed rather than disguised. Nor does the connection between the tendency in question and progressive formalism seem to be any closer if what is aimed at is the concealment of the non-rational elements of adjudication from the general public, whatever the justification of this aim from the viewpoint of general legal policy may be. It should be noted, however, that the imputation of artfulness to formalism, whether naive or progressive, seems largely due to the misconception of the formalistic insight that the pragmatic aspects of argument are irrelevant to the assessment of its rational force. Insofar, therefore, as the tendency to "disguise" judicial reasoning can be construed as the attempt to reconstruct the context of justification of the conclusion in relative independence of its context of discovery, such a tendency is essential to formalism. But whereas naive formalism tended to regard typical judicial argument as smoothly deductive and syllogistic, up-to-date formalism recognizes its involved inductive nature.

I now turn to rule-scepticism. Hart distinguishes between an extreme and a moderate version of this doctrine: according to the former, "talk of rules is a myth, cloaking the truth that law consists simply of the decisions of courts and the prediction of them", while according to the latter, "statutes are not law until applied by courts, but only sources of law" (133). Both these apparently paradoxical views can be conveniently reinterpreted in the light of up-to-date methodology so as to yield a defensible doctrine. Namely, it seems most appropriate to construe the words "rules" and "law" in the quoted formulations as meaning *observational* rules and law. Thus understood, the two versions tend to coincide in the view that the so-called rules of law have *no observational meaning* until they are effectively applied to particular cases. This conception, basically characterized by emphasis on the theoretical nature of law, squares well with the rule-sceptics' insistence, pointed out by Hart, on the vagueness and open texture of legal terms. The essentially theoretical legal rules, lacking a permanent interpretation, must be reinterpreted anew in every case. This is the basic methodological principle of up-to-date rule-scepticism: it clearly involves systematic disregard of the ordinary meanings of the words that occur in legal texts. The underlying view is consistently supplemented by emphasis on the dependence of law on social dynamism and by some reservations regarding the possibilities of improving the logical quality of legal argument.

With a view to reappraising rule-septicism, I turn to Hart's comments on it. It is interesting to note that some of his objections seem to beg the question when applied to the up-to-date version of the doctrine. Thus, to begin with, his remark that "a rule that ends with the word 'unless . . .' is still a rule" (136) clearly misses the up-to-date rule-sceptic's point, inasmuch as such rules generally contain highly theoretical terms. The more fundamental objection that "though every rule may be doubtful at some points, it is indeed a necessary condition of a legal system existing, that not every rule is open to doubt on all points" (148—149) can be met by retorting that the existence of a legal system presupposes only that some of its rules are effectively applied, but this condition does not exclude the possibility of considering every rule plainly theoretical before it is applied. Every rule may thus be "open to doubt on all points" in the sense of having no preestablished application to any observable state of affairs whatsoever. To say that a legal system exists certainly means to imply that some unambiguously identifiable rules belong to it, but the prima facie legitimacy of these rules need not involve their observational determinacy prior to application. Hart also argues that the extreme version of rule-scepticism is inconsistent, for the reference to "the decisions of courts" presupposes some rules of adjudication. But rules of adjudication are no exception to the sceptical principle: they too fail to materialize as genuine, observationally determinate law until they are actually applied in adjudication.

Hart's sole major concession to rule-scepticism is "the contention that, so far as the courts are concerned, there is nothing to circumscribe the area of open texture: so that it is false, if not senseless, to regard judges as themselves 'bound' to decide as they do" (135). The second part of the contention (after "so that") requires qualification. Though admittedly the judges, while engaged in their interpretative task, are not bound by the rules they interpret, nor indeed by the entire theoretical system in isolation, they are nevertheless logically determined in principle and considerably restricted in fact by all the legalistic and paralegal grounds relevant to alternative interpretations. To be sure, Hart points out that despite vagueness and open texture there is in every rule "a core of settled meaning" (140). But now the question arises as to how this observation squares with his foregoing admission that "there is nothing to circumscribe the area of open texture". The answer seems to be that, in his view, it is merely a matter of fact that rules "exist", in the sense that their "cores of settled meaning" are, on the whole, respected by the judges, whereas rule-scepticism is nevertheless right in principle, "as a theory of the function of rules in judicial decisions" (135). Judges, that is to say, have no fundamental obligation to respect "settled meanings": "The existence of rules at any given time does not require that there should be these impossible guarantees against destruction" (142). Hart thus apparently perseveres in his attempt to accomodate the free creativeness of judicial choice with its rationality. He tries to resolve this dilemma by conceiving judicial decision as, so to speak, free in principle and yet rational in practice. However, the idea of merely de facto rationality of argument is a misconception. Standards of rationality are always ideal. Within an empirical system, moreover, rationality of argument must at present be conceived as a regulative principle for guiding the development of the existing system. It is only in this sense, it would seem, that legal argument today can be considered rational in nature, though judicial decision is often "free", and hence possibly irrational, in actual practice.

The strongly intuited "cores of settled meaning" appear prima facie accountable for in terms of especially high degrees of inductive support by the available information. Hart relates them to the "internal point of view". He thus emphasizes that "individuals do exhibit the whole range of conduct and attitudes which we have called the internal point of view" (134) and that legal rules "are *used* as rules, not as descriptions of habits or predictions" (134—135). Curiously enough, he regards the sceptics' insistence on the intuitive character of interpretative reasoning as involving the psychologistic fallacy;

he holds, namely, that they confuse the acceptance of the rule with the concomitant mental phenomena. It seems, however, that the sceptics' reference to intuition can be significantly construed as a pseudopsychological way of pointing out that the conclusion in judicial reasoning does not appear to be logically grounded on the premises. Moreover, it appears that it is Hart himself who yields to genuine psychologism. For indeed — to amplify a point made earlier — the acceptance of a rule is a psychosociological phenomenon with no intrinsic logical aspect.

Similarly, when the rule-sceptics impute "pretense or 'window dressing'" (137) to certain judges, they chiefly intend to emphasize the nonlogical character of those judges' decisions, and it is only in a subsidiary way that they point to some pragmatic aspects of adjudication. Hart tries to defend the judges by objecting that "for the most part" judicial decisions "are reached either by genuine effort to conform to rules consciously taken as guiding standards of decision or, if intuitively reached, are justified by rules which the judge was antecedently disposed to observe and whose relevance to the case in hand would generally be acknowledged" (137). This remark seems doubly irrelevant. Firstly, it clearly refers to the context of discovery, while the main weight of the sceptical view bears upon the context of justification. Appeal to the most "genuine effort" of a judge to conform to the general rule which prohibits taking a vehicle into the park is not apt to serve the purpose of the justification of the special rule, whether prohibitive or permissive, regarding toy electric cars, as is reference to appropriate grounds. Secondly, the rules the judge knows in advance are precisely those which require interpretation and hence are the very object of rule-scepticism, whereas the concrete results of interpretation, which alone are genuine law in the sceptics' sense, are not known to the judge in advance. At any rate, Hart's objection misses the point of the up-to-date rule-sceptic, who refuses to endow rules with any settled observational meaning whatsoever prior to application.

This last remark applies likewise to Hart's comment, partly sound, concerning the finality of judgment. Appeal to the fact that judicial decision is final, he observes rightly, lends no support to rule-scepticism. Indeed, the rule of finality has merely practical justification. As judicial decisions can surely be good or bad, their legal finality does not in principle exclude the existence of logical criteria for the assessment of their rational force. But in Hart's opinion a judgment is bad if it does not properly reflect "the non-predictive aspect of rules" and "the internal point of view of the rules as standards accepted" (143) by the judges. As he frames it, therefore, his objection appears to disregard the up-to-date rule-sceptical tenet, according to which legal "rules" do not have any "nonpredictive aspect" at all and there can be no question of accepting them as standards to guide their own interpretation. Hart makes an analogy here with a game where the scorer's decision, though final, is not infallible. This comparison is misleading, inasmuch as the rules of scoring, unlike legal rules, have sharp observational meanings that hardly require interpretation. Even more open to objection is the comparison of judicial decision with playing chess: "In many cases, predictions of what a court will do are like the prediction we might make that chess players will move the bishop diagonally" (143). This comparison disregards an essential difference: the rules of chess are formal, whereas legal rules require empirical support. To be sure, Hart does not limit the distinction between good and bad judgments to cases in which the judge's decision concerns the "core of settled meaning" of a rule; but he fails to throw any light upon the nature or criteria of the rationality of judgment in the margin of vagueness of legal rules.

Hart's final appraisal of formalism and rule-scepticism appears to depend closely on his underlying conception of judicial reasoning as involving two essential elements, viz. the acceptance of rules from the "internal point of view", on the one hand, and free, creative decision, on the other. He accepts either doctrine insofar as he considers that it emphasizes the former or the latter of these elements, respectively. He holds that rule-scepticism, right in principle, corrects formalism "at the fringe" of law, while formalism, in point of fact, happily keeps rule-scepticism away from "the vast, central areas of the law" (150). He thus regards the opposition between the two doctrines as involving a false dilemma: "Formalism and rule-scepticism are the Scylla and Charybdis of juristic theory; they are great exaggerations, salutary where they correct each other, and the truth lies between them" (144). From the standpoint of the foregoing comments, this conclusion leaves room for reservations, regarding both the conception of reasoning on which it leans and the interpretation of the two doctrines to which it refers.

Reinterpreted in the light of the principles of up-to-date methodology, formalism and rule-scepticism appear as mutually compatible and complementary to a large extent, and even, in their moderate versions, as converging on several basic points. Progressive rule-scepticism, like progressive formalism, opposes the naive-formalistic denial of the need for the continuous reinterpretation of law. They both plainly recognize that actual legal reasoning depends on intuition. The rule-sceptical tendency to identify the law with "the decision of courts and the prediction of them" squares well with the neo-formalistic view about the empirical and inductive character of judicial conclusions. There is, finally, no incompatibility between the acceptance of the formalistic regulative principle of rationality and the sceptical recognition of the practical difficulties of rationalization. However, the two doctrines present some differences in emphasis which, accentuated in the doctrines' extreme versions, may appear as real divergencies. Thus, while rule-scepticism emphasizes the intuitive character of legal argument in practice, formalism insists on its rational character in principle. While the former points to the uncertainty of judicial conclusions, the latter lays stress on their logical nature. But chiefly, as mutually opposed trends of policy, formalism aims at an extensive rationalization of law with the help of proper inductive methods, whereas rule-scepticism tends to restrain such projects. There is, of course, room for intermediate positions between extreme formalism, which would seriously demand the indefinitely protracted and ever more thorough formalization of the legal system, and extreme rule-scepticism, which would categorically oppose even a partial amelioration of the formal-logical aspects of law. It is in this sense that, no doubt, "the truth lies between them".

In *The Concept of Law* Hart's views on legal argument and legal logic are implied or adumbrated rather than explicitly and fully stated. They are, however, sufficiently clear to impair his conception of legal reasoning by his pragmatic approach to questions of logic. The concepts of "a social rule" and of "the internal aspect of rules manifested in their use as guiding and critical standards of conduct" (151), though certainly suitable to the analysis of the pragmatic aspects of law, cannot be deemed directly relevant to the unravelling and establishing of the rational force of legal decisions. The investigation of "the distinctive operations of the law" and of "the ideas which constitute the framework of legal thought" (151) undoubtedly requires an adequately distinct separation of the logical context from the psychological, sociological, and historical.

Conclusion and Supplementary Observations

A comprehensive view of the positions dealt with in pt. III reveals both similarities and differences, as follows. The authors discussed — Stone, Levi, Hart, Jensen, and Toulmin — emphasize the dynamic character of legal rules and their flexibility, which are particularly apparent in the case-law method. This emphasis involves a tension between the conception of legal argument as a mode of decision depending on choice and the conception of it as sociologically determined. These authors grasp the nonobservational character of legal terms, but they tend to regard the theoretical postulates of law as material rules of inference or as nonlogical rules of decision. They tend, moreover, to identify the specifically legal with the theoretical in general and thus to confound the prescriptive legal ascriptions with their descriptive antecedents. They often treat argument and logic pragmatically, without a clear distinction between the contexts of discovery and of justification. Yet, they differ in opinion on the nature and scope of legal argument and logic. Stone sees legal logic as formal-deductive, but he also recognizes modes of legal reasoning that do not conform to such logic. Toulmin, who sees procedural jurisprudence as more or less constituting legal logic and as the archetype of nonmathematical logic in general, rejects the formalistic conception of all argument outside of mathematics proper. Levi extends the scope of legal logic even further by indistinguishably including in it the study of the development of legal systems. Hart sees authentic legal argument as involving choice. Jensen explicitly characterizes such argument as nonlogical. Finally, the authors dealt with in pt. III fail to explain the rational nature which they attribute to legal reasoning and, in particular, they fail to see the relevance of the idea of inductive support to the clarification of the claimed rationality.

The following supplementary observations will be concerned, successively, with the general structure of a legal system, the relations between law and sociology, the methodological similarity between law and science in general, and some topics previously reserved for reconsideration.

The theoretical-prescriptive nature of legal ascriptions and their role at the heart of a legal system, as mediators between descriptions (factual statements) of a theoretical nature and deontic pre-

scriptions, were pointed out above (pt. III, sects. 3 and 4). The schematic formulae "if D_t then A" and "if A then P" were used there
to represent rules of ascription and rules of deontic prescription,
respectively. Both formulae, however, are oversimplifications. It has
already been remarked, in the spirit of Hart's analyses of legal concepts, that deontic prescriptions P are often warranted by an ascription A conjoined with appropriate descriptions D, by virtue of a set
of rules of the form "if A and D_1 then P_1", "if A and D_2 then P_2",
and so on. Similarly, it is now worth noting, ascriptions are often
warranted by conjunctions of descriptions and ascriptions and also
by ascriptions alone. Accordingly, the general form of the rules of
ascription is more adequately rendered by the formula "if B then A",
in which "B" stands for a description *or* an ascription *or* a conjunction of descriptions and ascriptions. The corresponding general
form of the rules of deontic prescription can be rendered by the
formula "if A and C then P", in which "C" is either of the kind
of "B" or void. More precisely still, given an ascription A, prescriptions P are often entailed through the mediation of series of suitable
rules belonging to the system, of this form:

If A and C_1 then A_1; if A_1 and C_2 then A_2; ...; if A_{n-1} and C_n
then P.

Here "A_1", ..., "A_{n-1}" stand for ascriptions, and "C_1", ..., "C_n"
are of the kind of "C". The internal part of a legal system can thus
be seeen to consist of implicational postulates involving three kinds
of variously combined theoretical components. What is well reflected in the oversimplified schematic formulae "if D_t then A" and "if
A then P" is that descriptions occur only in the antecedents of the
postulates, deontic prescriptions only in their consequents, and
ascriptions in either. The empirical import of the system depends
on rules of interpretation for the nonlogical, descriptive terms of
the theoretical descriptions, on the one hand, and of the deontic
prescriptions, on the other. This analysis of the general structure
of a legal system represents the function of law as involving the
transition from observational data to observational consequences
through the succesive mediation of theoretical-descriptive findings,
ascriptive rulings, deontic judgments, and observational executive
instructions. The purely legal (nondescriptive) attributes ascribable
to legal subjects (individuals or corporations) are given no direct
observational interpretation whatsoever and can thus be seen as

constituting the innermost theoretical core of the conceptual scheme of law. They determine the legal status of the subjects to which they are ascribed and can be variously classified as involving kinds of duties, liabilites, responsibilites, guilt, rights, powers, capacities, etc., according to the syntactic and semantic properties of the deontic prescriptions they warrant by virtue of postulates belonging to the system. Significant distinctions between kinds of postulates, such as Hart's well-known distinction between primary and secondary rules, can be set out in a similar way. A line of fruitful investigation in analytical jurisprudence seems to be well in view.

The proper domain of the application of law is society qua subject to direction and coordination in accordance with the general will. The relevant aspects of society can be investigated scientifically in a specialized sociological framework. The intimate relations between law and sociology are reflected in the systematic articulation of the two fields. Law can be said to be rooted or grafted in sociology rather than linked with it in a bridge-like way. Indeed, the descriptive terms occurring in legal rules proper, whether rules of ascription or of deontic prescription, are not relevant to the specific function of law unless they are effectively construed as sociological terms. The correspondence between law and sociology can thus be seen as installed *within* the framework of law: in this case bridge postulates are internal postulates. Consequently, all the rules of interpretation for law belong, in principle, to the domain of sociology. In actual fact, however, judicial interpretation is not based on solid science, and the methodological requirement of the antecedent intelligibility of domains of application can hardly be said to be fulfilled in the case of law. Several circumstances contribute to this situation. Sociological theory, in general, is neither well developed nor strongly established. In particular, the progress of legal psycho-sociology, or paralegal science — the branch of sociology basic to law — is hindered by its highly theoretical nature. This concerns not only the underlying concepts of public utility, coordination, and effective general will, but the descriptive concepts of law as a whole, ranging from such patently abstruse concepts as those of *mens rea* or of negligence to such seemingly observational ones as those of a vehicle (in the park) or of a dog (in the grocery shop). The scientific foundation of law must involve the elaboration of specialized conceptual schemes, including detailed typologies, suitable to the treatment of piecemeal tasks of legislation and adjudication. To a large extent, indeed, legal psychosociology must be able to provide solutions made to order, so to speak. As the rule-sceptics point out, the most effectual interpretation of a legal rule varies with the circumstances of application. The descriptive concepts of law are, in this respect, not unlike such parametrical concepts as that of the bank rate, the optimum value of which is subject to variation. Moreover, the legal system itself, as actually functioning, is a most important social factor among the circumstances relevant to the scientific treatment of legal problems, both general and particular. Legalistic grounds thus appear as intrinsically involved in the empirical confirmation of law. This aspect of legal reasoning is fittingly referred to as "dialectical".

In view of the intimate relations between law and sociology, the frequently voiced allegation that legal argument differs radically from scientific argument in methodological respects is not well taken. In fact, those methodological aspects of legal reasoning which are often singled out as specific to the legal sphere are, on the whole, not even limited to reasoning in social science alone, but are found in natural science as well. Though experimental techniques and mathematical tools differ from field to field according to the subject matter, the methodology of reasoning remains substantially field-invariant. In all branches of empirical science, just as in law, theoretical postulates are "open" and "defeasible", and their observational interpretation is selective in that it involves both a proper elaboration of the supporting material and a "dialectical" interrelation with the system. Like law, empirical science changes continuously by progressive extension and readjustment and occasionally by real revolution. And just as in the case-law method the evolution of the system is promoted by the adaptation of old laws to new sets of circumstances, so the explanation of new phenomena by an accepted scientific theory often occasions a beneficial readjustment of the latter. To be sure, there are differences in the evolutionary "style": a system of law, especially of common law, is subject to methodological operations to a much wider extent than are, on the whole, systems of science. While a well-established scientific theory can be compared to a town in which only a few buildings at a time are under reconstruction though active new construction may be undertaken at the outskirts, a legal system in operation appears as a town in which reconstruction is a pervasive and permanent phenomenon in all quarters. The prescriptive character of law, being its distinguishing feature with respect to science, naturally gives rise to a "reflexive" peculiarity: practical legal methodology can be legally enforced; in particular, the process of legal reasoning can be subjected to rules of procedure. The corresponding characteristic of science, as a whole, is that its pragmatic aspects can be scientifically investigated. But there seems to be no deeper difference between legal and scientific reasoning from the methodological point of view[4].

Some questions left open can now be conveniently reconsidered. One moot point, it may be recalled, concerned the predicate "more" involved in *argumentum a maiori ad minus* (see above, pt. II, sect. 7). The question was wether "more" should be considered a specifically legal or a sociological predicate and whether, accordingly, particular postulates to the effect that action *a* is "more" than action *b* should be regarded as rules of law or as statements of fact. The former alternative may seem supported by the consideration that the predicate in question, as actually applied, often relates such plainly legal elements as rights and duties. However, it is the latter alternative which appears preferable once it is realized that purely legal concepts have a sociological aspect directly relevant to the application of law, in view of their role as mediators between observational social data and observational social consequences. "More" is of course a "legal" predicate in the sense that it is referred to in a legal postulate, viz. in the general principle *a maiori ad minus*. But, though relevant to the application of law, the comparative relation in question is not established by virtue of legal postulates, being primarily a theoretical-descriptive concept of legal psychosociology. The unravelling of the corresponding typological parameters, or compara-

---

4 A thorough defense of the contrary contention has been undertaken by Gidon Gottlieb in his book [23]. This author, apparently at variance with Stone's view that "the process of choice is beyond the realm of logic", purports to lay the foundation of "the logic of choice", which he conceives, in the main, as practical methodology of "rule-guided reasoning", i. e. reasoning in prescriptive and normative fields. He does not, however, seem to have been more successful than his predecessors in the attempt to establish the logical and methodological distinctness of legal reasoning with respect to scientific reasoning. In fact, his considerations eclectically combine and partly amplify most of the relevant features which were criticized above in the discussion of other positions, especially in pt. III. Among these features, the "procedural" conception of the rationality of argument is prominent in Gottlieb's analysis.

tive scales, of social desirability is a scientific task, no less so because purely legal attributes too can, in certain respects, be related as "more" or "less". In brief, "more" clearly appears to be a paralegal predicate, not a purely legal (ascriptive) one.

Another undecided issue concerned the distinction between questions of fact and questions of law (see above, pt. III, sect. 5). Jensen, it will be remembered, holds that the question "whether a defendant's conduct has been negligent" is a question of law, "for even when all the relevant facts are known it still has to be decided whether the defendant's conduct *was* negligent". This view of Jensen's seems open to objection. Admittedly, the question at issue is not one of observable fact as is the question of the defendant's overt conduct. Nor it is a question of such disconnected fact as could be ascertained with no regard to the relevant parts of the existing legal system. But it is a question of paralegal fact, i. e. fact statable in terms of theoretical legal psychosociology. Thus construed, the allegation that the defendant was (or was not) negligent can be paraphrased as a statement to the effect that in the given circumstances the application of the rule under interpretation is more conformable to the general will than is its nonapplication (or vice versa). Again, "the given circumstances" are meant to comprise all the relevant aspects of the existing society, including those of its legal system. Jensen, while recognizing the importance of sociology for adjudication, seems to ignore the comprehensive context of the question: in referring to "all the relevant facts", he presumably means the defendant's observable conduct alone. The judicial question of the optimum interpretation is scientific in nature. To be sure, the open texture of law would frustrate all attempts to state the optimum interpretation exhaustively. But it need not prevent the judge from attempting to determine whether the facts of the case do or do not fall within the scope of the unstatable optimum interpretation. Theoretical paralegal statements cannot be conclusively established. They can, however, be more or less strongly supported by the available information. As long as legal confirmation, lacking a suitably elaborated and sound scientific basis and adequate logical canons, remains amply intuitive, what are really empirical questions of interpretation have the appearance of mere matters of choice. Such questions can, of course, be described as "questions of law" provided that the classes of questions of law and questions of fact are not considered mutually exclusive. However, it seems preferable to preserve the dichotomy and to restrict the designation "question of law" to questions concerning the legal system considered in abstraction from all observational interpretation. At any rate, the effectual application of law involves questions of observable fact and of paralegal fact, so that the framework of judicial argument comprises, besides the legal system proper, its entire domain of application.

The view that questions of interpretation are not questions of fact seems directly inspired by passages from John Wisdom's essay "Gods" [78] which have been quoted above (pt. III, Introduction) but which have not yet been commented upon directly. Wisdom pointed out, in particular, that "sometimes when there is agreement as to the facts there is still argument as to whether defendant did or did not 'exercise reasonable care', was or was not 'negligent'" (192). To be sure, Wisdom does not confront a question of fact with a question of law, but with "a question or decision as to the application of a name" (190). Nor does he claim that a question of this latter kind is not a question of fact, but rather maintains that it is neither "merely a matter of 'the facts'" (192) nor "merely a matter of the application of a name", inasmuch as "with the judges' choice of a name for the facts goes an attitude" (196). By "the facts", like Jensen later, he undoubtedly means observable facts alone; he explicitly refers to "so complete a record" of the defendant's "conduct" (196). As for the judges' "attitude", he clearly takes it to depend on reasons, and of the reasons he says that they cooperate severally "like the legs of a chair" (195). It seems therefore most unlikely that, having admitted not only the defendant's recorded conduct but also references to "other cases" (198) as providing kinds of relevant reasons, he would wish to discard such further kinds of reasons as information concerning the consequences of, and expressed attitudes to, recorded instances of similar conduct. Nor is there any indication in his essay that he would wish to oppose even less obviously "factual" inquiries aiming at the determination of the corresponding "general attitude" of society.

Two further influential implications readily attributed to Wisdom are worth examining in the context of his essay, as they carry the suggestion of a nonformal legal logic. They are, first, that legal logic is neither deductive nor inductive and, second, that legal argument is essentially a matter of choice and decision. The former implication, not to be distorted, must be construed as relating to a narrow conception of induction. Indeed, in maintaining that legal argument is not inductive, Wisdom refers to "inductions in which from many signs we guess at what is to come", "as when a doctor from a patient's symptoms guesses at what is wrong, or a detective from many clues guesses the criminal" (196). His point is, no doubt, that judicial reasoning is not the kind of primitive induction based on commonsensical generalizations from observable phenomena. In pointing out that "the discussion is a priori and the steps are not a matter of experience" (195), he undoubtedly uses "experience" in the sense of "observation", and "a priori" in the sense of "theoretical" rather than "nonempirical". Accordingly, granted that in arguments of legal interpretation both the conclusion and part of the premises are indeed of a theoretical nature, there seems to be nothing in Wisdom's text to discard the suggestion that his idea of legal logic is, to say the least, not incompatible with the idea of an inductive logic of confirmation, adequately elaborated to suit the theoretical paralegal domain. That this suggestion is an understatement is borne out by the very metaphor "the legs of a chair" as well as by the admission that in interpretative discussion "the process of deciding the issue becomes a matter of weighing the cumulative effect of one group of severally inconclusive items against the cumulative effect of another group of severally inconclusive items, and thus lends itself to description in terms of conflicting 'probabilities'" (195). In brief, it is very misleading to describe Wisdom without reservation as a noninductivist with respect to legal logic.

To attribute to him a mentalistic conception of legal argument is just as unwarranted. Surely, it cannot be denied that "the solution of the question at issue is a decision, a ruling by the judge". "But it is not an arbitrary decision", since it leans on "rational connections" (196). That Wisdom does not conceive of logic in general as concerned with the pragmatic aspects of reasoning is well indicated by his remark that in some spheres "we need to examine the actual processes to belief and distil from them a logic" (201). As he sees it, such a task involves "sifting reasons from causes" and ascertaining, in particular, "what things are reasons and how much" (201). Logic, that is to say, is not directly concerned with the discovery of conclusions, but with their rational justification by relevant premises, it being admitted that in legal argument "the premises are severally inconclusive" (195).

It thus appears in more than one way that no nonformalistic conception of legal argument and legal logic is unambiguously implied by Wisdom's remarks. The impression to the contrary, chiefly due to crude views about theory and induction, is fostered by his style, which combines vagueness with emotional appeal. Particularly influential in this respect has been, it would seem, his remark that the logic of judicial choice is "surprisingly like that of 'futile', 'deplorable', 'graceful', 'grand', 'divine'" (196). To avoid the imputation of inconsistency with its context, this remark must be construed as involving the assumption that ethical, aesthetical, and religious attitudes too, like judicial attitudes, depend on "rational connections" and supporting grounds. Since this assumption alone may be seen to lend sufficient significance to the remark my making it anticipate the wide scope and the unifying power of an eventual inductive logic, the remark in question need not be taken to evince any further insight into the logical nature of legal argument.

General Conclusion

The thesis that legal argument and legal logic are nonformal in nature appears inherently ambiguous. Its several versions referring to nonformal "arguments" or "reasoning" should in fact be construed as applying to arguments and linguistic processes of various kinds, viz.: nonformalized arguments, inconclusive arguments, and arguments accompanied by methodological information; activities of convincing and persuading; heuristic processes involving choice and decision, often accompanied by an intuition of evidence or acceptability; interpretation that disregards ordinary meanings; operations of theoretical construction; operations carried out according to rules of procedure; processes by which systems develop; and complex processes in which arguments may be included. Similarly, the formulations referring or alluding to "nonformal logic" should in fact be construed as applying to various fields, in particular to the following: applied logic, pragmatics of reasoning, heuristics, methodology, the study of the evolution of systems, and complex fields of inquiry, possibly comprising (formal) logic as a component.

Interpreted accordingly, the nonformalistic thesis does not contradict the formalistic conception of legal argument and legal logic. It is unquestionably true that law is a special field requiring applied logic and that social change requires the continuous readjustment of the legal system on a pragmatic basis. Nor can it be denied that adjudication involves mental processes and acts. But to suppose that such facts refute or weaken the formalistic position is to misconceive it. To be sure, misconception has been fostered by the errors of some formalists who disregarded recent advances in analytical methodology. The disagreement between the two sides depends largely on different uses of basic terms; besides, terminological differences appear within the camp of the nonformalists themselves. But the nonformalistic thesis also depends on substantively erroneous views, such as the views that legal rules can be nonempirically established, that there exists an adequate "model" of sound argument, or that the modes of argument framed within a given legal system are identical with the modes of the system's development.

The claim that legal argument is rational, as it appears in non-formalistic writings, is evidently unclear. Its intrinsic weakness is chiefly due to disregard of a clear-cut distinction between the syntactic and semantic context, on the one hand, and the pragmatic context, on the other. The formalists take inductive support, albeit only as an explicandum or a regulative idea for the time being, to be the criterion of the rational force of nonconclusive argument. Their opponents, on the contrary, say nothing that is clear about the nature of the criteria by which intuitive legal argument, taken by them to be rational, is to be assessed. What nonformalists do say concerning the "internal", mentalistic aspects of legal rules, or concerning their "teleological" or "axiological" confirmation, only conceals the absence of such criteria. Their reluctance to accept intuition itself as the warrant of rationality is of course justified; but consistent nonformalism cannot avoid recognizing intuition as warrant and thus abandoning the view that legal argument is rational. These difficulties point to the theoretical and practical advantages of the rival conception, according to which the idea of a formalized legal system directs the rational development of the existing system, as well as the improvement of the arguments framed within it.

Examination of the nonformalistic thesis has naturally involved accentuating the most general properties of legal systems as rationally applied systems. The prescriptive nature of law requires deontic logic, while its dependence on empirical confirmation calls for inductive logic. More guardedly, typical legal argument, insofar as it is rational, in principle involves inductive support, and its special varieties can be characterized semantically. Because of its socially directive and coordinative function, law depends on theoretical psychosociology and, in particular, on the concepts of individual and public will. The social dynamism that directs the evolution of the legal system continually subjects legal argument to methodological operations, especially to changes in interpretation.

Those components of a legal system by means of which duties, rights, liabilities, powers, etc. are ascribed to legal subjects are essential. Their nature is theoretical-prescriptive, since they mediate systematically between theoretical psychosociological descriptions and deontic prescriptions. The concepts of duties, rights, and the like, can be clarified as syntactic and semantic concepts in a deontic context. A similar clarification can be made of significant distinctions between kinds of rules.

The old jurisprudential conflict between formalism and rule-scepticism can be considerably attenuated. It can be substantially resolved on the basis of the conceptions of the legal system as consisting of theoretical postulates, and of legal argument as essentially interpretative and confirmatory in function. The extent to which the systematic reconstruction of law would be worth undertaking may be subject to dispute. What is feasible and desirable in this respect can be decided only by close collaboration between jurists, psychosociologists, and logicians.

Be that as it may, recent analytical methodology, including its formalistic conception of argument and logic, is undoubtedly relevant to the study of the legal system as the framework of rational legal argument.

Appendix

Concerning the Third Edition of Klug's "Juristische Logik"

Ulrich Klug's *Juristische Logik* was first published in 1951; the second edition appeared in 1958, and the third in 1966. The first two editions stimulated the discussion of legal logic as represented above in pt. I and, also, in pt. II, sect. 7. My account of Klug's book refers to the second edition [45], which differs very little from the first.

The third edition [46] involves a few important changes, based to a large extent, as Klug avows in his new Preface, on H. Fiedler's "Ulrich Klugs Juristische Logik" [20]. When submitting my own "Ulrich Klug's Legal Logic" [31] for publication, I was unaware both of Fiedler's review and of the third edition of Klug's book. In point of fact, my criticism, though independent of Fiedler's criticism and differing from it considerably in scope and detail, agrees with it as regards the most prominent shortcomings of Klug's analyses, viz.: restrictive conception of legal logic; confusion between technical and nontechnical senses of logical terms and of the designations of legal *argumenta: e contrario, a maiori ad minus,* etc.; disregard of inductive logic and of modal logic; analysis of analogical inference in terms of the problematic notion of the "circle of similarity"; erroneous extension of analogical inference to cases where legal assumptions are a necessary but not a sufficient condition for legal consequences; and misconception regarding the axiomatization and "calculization" of law.

However, the definitive impact of Fiedler's criticism was rather limited. As Klug indicates in his Preface to the third edition, his

treatment of the following topics was affected: the relationship between mathematics and modern logic; causality and implication;
the importance of axiomatization for law and for the science of
law; the conception of "legal analogical inference"; and the formalization of *argumenta a fortiori, a maiori ad minus,* and *a minori
ad maius.* Two new sections were added, viz.: "The Violation of
Laws of Thought in Law" and "Electronic Data-Processing Ma-
chines in Law".

Only part of these changes have a direct bearing on the present
inquiry. Some of them are seemingly insignificant. Thus, whereas
in the second edition legal logic was described as "that part of logic
which finds application in the science of law" ([45], 5; quoted above,
p. 19), it is described in the third edition as "logic especially insofar
as it finds application in the science of law" ([46], 5); moreover,
in the sentence where the "part of logic" in question was formerly
said to be "very essentially more elementary than, for example, the
part of logic required for the construction of mathematics" ([45],
5; quoted above, p. 21), the word "very" has been omitted ([46], 5).
Another example: the claim that "according to the state of contemporary science, logically unobjectionable foundations are conceivable only as axiomatic" ([45], 150; quoted above, p. 49) has
been replaced by the claim that "according to the state of contemporary science, logically unobjectionable foundations ought to
be axiomatic" ([56], 175—176).

The main relevant change concerns analogical inference. As Klug
points out, "the designation 'legal analogical inference' is not applied now any longer to one single deductive inference but remains
reserved for the legal analogical procedure as a whole" ([46], VII).
The text has been modified accordingly. Thus, in the second edition
we read: "On the basis of the formal-logical structure of analogy
developed above, one can show the possibilities available in its
practical application for deciding when a certain analogical inference is admissible and when inadmissible. But the criterion for
this question, so essential in practice, is not provided by the figure
of inference as such, but rather by the definition of the suitable
circle of similarity" ([45], 128; quoted above, p. 34). In the third
edition, the first quoted sentence reoccurs virtually unchanged; the
second, however, has been thus altered: "The criterion for this
question, so essential in practice, is not provided by the foregoing

inferential formula which terminates the analogical procedure, but rather by the definition of the suitable circle of similarity"; and the following comment has been added: "Herein reside the substantively decisive questions of analogy, whose formal specification, though perhaps possible, cannot be pursued here any further" ([46], 123). Also Klug's analysis of *argumentum a maiori ad minus* (discussed above, pp. 111—112) has been modified; he points out: "The formalization of *argumenta a fortiori, a maiori ad minus,* and *a minori ad maius* has been changed; these appear now as instances of a uniform mode of inference, which in final analysis is determined teleologically" ([46], VII).

With the qualifications implied by the foregoing remarks, the account given in the present book of the second edition of Klug's *Juristische Logik* applies, on the whole, to the third edition as well.

List of References

[01] ACHINSTEIN, PETER, Concepts of Science, Baltimore: The Johns Hopkins Press, 1968.

[02] ALCHOURRÓN, CARLOS E., Logic of Norms and Logic of Normative Propositions, Logique et Analyse 47, 1969, pp. 242—267.

[03] ALCHOURRÓN, C. E., and E. BULYGIN, Normative Systems, Wien—New York: Springer-Verlag, 1971.

[04] ARSP (Archiv für Rechts- und Sozialphilosophie), edited by authorization of the International Association for Philosophy of Law and Social Philosophy, published by Franz Steiner Verlag GmbH, Wiesbaden, from 1907 on.

[05] BAYART, A., Le Centre National Belge de Recherches de Logique, [50], pp. 171—180.

[06] BOBBIO, NORBERTO, Considérations introductives sur le raisonnement des juristes, [73], pp. 67—83.

[07] BUNGE, MARIO, Scientific Research, Vol. I: The Search for System, Vol. II: The Search for Truth, Berlin—Heidelberg—New York: Springer-Verlag, 1967.

[08] COHEN, L. JONATHAN, The Implications of Induction, London: Methuen & Co. Ltd., 1970.

[09] CONTE, A. G., Bibiliography of Normative Logic 1936—1960, M. U. L. L., 1962, pp. 89—100 and 162—177.

[10] DEKKERS, R., Communication de M. Dekkers: Réflexions sur un outil, [15], pp. 271—272.

[11] ENGISCH, KARL, Logische Studien zur Gesetzanwendung, 3rd ed., Heidelberg, 1963 (1st ed. 1942).

[12] ENGISCH, KARL, Einführung in das juristische Denken, 3rd ed., Stuttgart, 1964 (1st ed. 1956).

[13] ENGISCH, KARL, Sinn und Tragweite juristischer Systematik, Studium Generale 10, 1957, pp. 173—190.

[14] ENGISCH, KARL, Aufgaben einer Logik und Methodik des juristischen Denkens, Studium Generale *12*, 1959, pp. 76—87.

[15] Essais de logique juridique. A propos de l'usufruit d'une créance, Journal des Tribunaux, no. 4104, Bruxelles, 22 avril 1956, pp. 261—274.

[16] Ethics: An International Journal of Social, Political, and Legal Philosophy, published by the University of Chicago Press, Chicago, from 1890 on.

[17] Etudes de logique juridique (Travaux du Centre National de Recherches de Logique), edited by CH. PERELMAN, Bruxelles: Etablissements Emile Bruylant, from 1966 on.

[18] FEYS, ROBERT, Avant-propos, [15], p. 261.

[19] FEYS, ROBERT, et MARIE-THERESE MOTTE, Logique juridique, systèmes juridiques, Logique et Analyse *6*, 1959, pp. 143—147.

[20] FIEDLER, HERBERT, Ulrich Klugs Juristische Logik, Archiv für Rechts- und Sozialphilosophie *45*, 1959, pp. 439—449.

[21] FORIERS, PAUL, Communication de M. Foriers, [15], pp. 266—271.

[22] FORIERS, PAUL, L'état des recherches de logique juridique en Belgique, Logique et Analyse *37*, 1967, pp. 23—42.

[23] GOTTLIEB, GIDON, The Logic of Choice: An Investigation of the Concepts of Rule and Rationality, London: George Allen & Unwin, 1968.

[24] GREGOROWICZ, JAN, L'argument *a maiori ad minus* et le problème de la logique juridique, Logique et Analyse *17-18*, 1962, pp. 66—75.

[25] HART, H. L. A., The Ascription of Responsibility and Rights, reprinted in A. G. N. FLEW (editor), Logic and Language: First Series, Oxford: Basil Blackwell, 1951, pp. 145—166. (Originally appeared in the Proceedings of the Aristotelian Society for 1948—1949.)

[26] HART, H. L. A., Definition and Theory in Jurisprudence: an inaugural lecture delivered before the University of Oxford on 30 May 1953, Oxford: Clarendon Press, 1953.

[27] HART, H. L. A., The Concept of Law, Oxford: Clarendon Press, 1961.

[28] HART, H. L. A., Philosophy of Law, Problems of, The Encyclopedia of Philosophy, edited by PAUL EDWARDS, Vol. VI, New York: Macmillan Co., Free Press, London: Collier-Macmillan, 1967, pp. 264—276.

[29] HELLER, THEODOR, Logik and Axiologie der analogen Rechtsanwendung, Berlin: Walter de Gruyter, 1961.

[30] HEMPEL, CARL G., Philosophy of Natural Science, Englewood Cliffs, N. J.: Prentice-Hall, 1966.

[31] HOROVITZ, JOSEPH, Ulrich Klug's Legal Logic: A Critical Account, Logique et Analyse 33, 1966, pp. 78—144.

[32] HOROVITZ, JOSEPH, Exposé et critique d'une illustration du caractère prétendu non-formel de la logique juridique, [50], pp. 181—204.

[33] HOROVITZ, JOSEPH, La logique et le droit, Logique et Analyse 37, 1967, pp. 43—56.

[34] Index to Foreign Legal Periodicals, published by the Institute of Advanced Legal Studies, University of London, in cooperation with the American Association of Law Libraries, London, from 1961 on.

[35] Index to Legal Periodicals, published by the H. W. Wilson Company in cooperation with the American Association of Law Libraries, New York, from 1926 on.

[36] Index to Periodical Articles Related to Law, selected from journals not included in the Index to Legal Periodicals, published by F. B. Rothman, South Hackensack, N. J., from 1958 on.

[37] ISSMAN, S., et J. LOREAU, Résumé des discussions du Colloque de Logique (Louvain, septembre 1958), Logique et Analyse 5, 1959, pp. 30—47.

[38] JENSEN, O. C., The Nature of Legal Argument, Oxford: Basil Blackwell, 1957.

[39] Jurimetrics Journal, published by the American Bar Center, Chicago, Ill., from 1966 on. (Formerly M. U. L. L.; see [57].)

[40] KALINOWSKI, GEORGES, Y a-t-il une logique juridique? Logique et Analyse 5, 1959, pp. 48—53.

[41] KALINOWSKI, GEORGES, Interprétation juridique et logique des propositions normatives, Logique et Analyse 6, 1959, pp. 128—142.

[42] KALINOWSKI, GEORGES, Introduction à la logique juridique, Paris: Pichon et Durand-Auzias, 1965.

[43] KALINOWSKI, GEORGES, De la spécificité de la logique juridique, [50], pp. 7—23.

[44] KAZEMIER, B. H., as related in [37], p. 40.

[45] KLUG, ULRICH, Juristische Logik, 2nd ed., Berlin—Göttingen—Heidelberg: Springer-Verlag, 1958 (1st ed. 1951). (See [46].)

[46] KLUG, ULRICH, Juristische Logik, 3rd ed., Berlin—Heidelberg—New York: Springer-Verlag, 1966. (See [45].)

[47] KOTARBINSKI, TADEUSZ, Kurs logiki dla prawników, 5th ed., Warsaw, 1961, p. 164.

[48] KRAUTH, LOTHAR, Die Philosophie Carnaps, Wien—New York: Springer-Verlag, 1970.

[49] KYBURG, KENRY E., JR., Philosophy of Science: A Formal Approach, New York: Macmillan Co., London: Collier-Macmillan, 1968.

[50] La logique du droit, Archives de Philosophie du Droit *11*, Paris: Sirey, 1966.

[51] Law and Computer Technology, published by the World Peace through Law Center, Washington, D. C., from 1968 on.

[52] LEVI, EDWARD H., An Introduction to Legal Reasoning, 7th impr., Chicago: University of Chicago Press, 1961 (c 1948).

[53] Le raisonnement juridique et la logique déontique: Actes du Colloque de Bruxelles (22—23 décembre 1969), Logique et Analyse *49-50*, 1970.

[54] Logique et Analyse: nouvelle série, Centre National Belge de Recherches de Logique, Editions Nauwelaerts, Louvain, Béatrice-Nauwelaerts, Paris, from 1958 on.

[55] MOTTE, MARIE-THÉRÈSE, La rigueur du raisonnement dans les débats juridiques, [73], pp. 84—91.

[56] MOTTE, MARIE-THÉRÈSE, Communication de Mlle Marie-Thérèse Motte, [15], pp. 261—266.

[57] M. U. L. L. (Modern Uses of Logic in Law), Quarterly Newsletter of the American Bar Association Special Committee on Electronic Data Retrieval in collaboration with Yale Law School, 1958—1966. (It now appears as [39].)

[58] PARAIN-VIAL, J., La nature du concept juridique et la logique, [50], pp. 45—57.

[59] PERELMAN, CH., Communication de M. Perelman: Problèmes de logique juridique, [15], pp. 272—274.

[60] PERELMAN, CH., as related in [37], p. 39.

[61] PERELMAN, CH., Logique formelle, logique juridique, Logique et Analyse *11-12*, 1960, pp. 226—230.

[62] PERELMAN, CH., Raisonnement juridique et logique juridique, [50], pp. 1—6.

[63] PERELMAN, CH., et L. OLBRECHTS-TYTECA, La nouvelle rhétorique: Traité de l'argumentation, 2 vols., Paris: Presses Universitaires de France, 1958. (See [64].)

[64] PERELMAN, CH., et L. OLBRECHTS-TYTECA, The New Rhetoric: A Treatise on Argumentation, translated by JOHN WILKINSON and PURCELL WEAVER, Notre Dame, Ind.: University of Notre Dame Press, 1969. (This is an English translation of [63].)

[65] RUDNER, RICHARD S., Philosophy of Social Science, Englewood Cliffs, N. J.: Prentice-Hall, 1966.

[66] SALMON, WESLEY C., Logic, Englewood Cliffs, N. J.: Prentice-Hall, 1963.

[67] Schilpp, P. A. (editor), The Philosophy of Rudolf Carnap, La Salle, Ill.: Open Curt, 1963.

[68] Simitis, Spiros, Zum Problem einer juristischen Logik, Ratio (Frankfurt a. M.) 3, 1960—1961, pp. 52—82. (See [69].)

[69] Simitis, Spiros, The Problem of Legal Logic, Ratio (Oxford) 3, 1960—1961, pp. 60—94. (This is an English translation of [68].)

[70] Stone, Julius, The Province and Function of Law: A Study in Jurisprudence, Cambridge, Mass., 1950. (First Australian edition: Sydney, 1946.)

[71] Stone, Julius, Legal Systems and Lawyers' Reasonings, London: Stevens & Sons, 1964.

[72] Tammelo, Ilmar, Outlines of Modern Legal Logic, Wiesbaden: Franz Steiner Verlag GmbH, 1969.

[73] Textes des exposés et des discussions sur la Théorie de la Preuve qui a fait l'objet de la deuxième partie du Colloque International de Logique organisé les 28 et 29 août 1953 à la Maison Ernest Solvay à Bruxelles par le Centre National (Belge) de Recherches de Logique, Revue Internationale de Philosophie 8, 1954.

[74] Toulmin, Stephen E., The Uses of Argument, Cambridge: Cambridge University Press, 1958.

[75] Villey, Michel, Liminaire: Données historiques, [50], pp. VII—XVI.

[76] Villey, Michel, Questions de logique juridique dans l'histoire de la philosophie du droit, Logique et Analyse 37, 1967, pp. 3—22.

[77] Waismann, F., Verifiability, reprinted in A. G. N. Flew (editor), Logic and Language: First Series, Oxford: Basil Blackwell, 1951, pp. 117—144. (Originally appeared in the Proceedings of the Aristotelian Society, Supplementary Volume XIX.)

[78] Wisdom, John, Gods, reprinted in A. G. N. Flew (editor), Logic and Language: First Series, Oxford: Basil Blackwell, 1951, pp. 187—206. (Originally appeared in the Proceedings of the Aristotelian Society for 1944—1945.)

[79] Wróblewski, J., Zagadnienia teorii wykładni prawa ludowego, Warsaw, 1959, p. 304.

[80] Ziemba, Z., Logika formalna w myśleniu prawniczym, Państwo i Prawo 2, 1957, pp. 272 ff.

Index of Names

Subject Index